Thurrock and Basildon College

To Russ Campbell
teacher, scholar, mentor, and friend
from Kathi

To the Sookdeo family
for teaching me Life's Most Important Lesson
from Andy

To Joan Morley
for a lifetime of dedication to our field
from David

Thank You

The series editor, authors, and publisher would like to thank the following individuals who offered many helpful insights throughout the development of the **TeacherSource** series.

Linda Lonon Blanton	University of New Orleans
Tommie Brasel	New Mexico School for the Deaf
Jill Burton	University of South Australia
Margaret B. Cassidy	Brattleboro Union High School, Vermont
Florence Decker	University of Texas at El Paso
Silvia G. Diaz	Dade County Public Schools, Florida
Margo Downey	Boston University
Alvino Fantini	School for International Training
Sandra Fradd	University of Miami
Jerry Gebhard	Indiana University of Pennsylvania
Fred Genesee	McGill University
Stacy Gildenston	Colorado State University
Jeannette Gordon	Illinois Resource Center
Else Hamayan	Illinois Resource Center
Sarah Hudelson	Arizona State University
Joan Jamieson	Northern Arizona University
Elliot L. Judd	University of Illinois at Chicago
Donald N. Larson	Bethel College, Minnesota (Emeritus)
Numa Markee	University of Illinois at Urbana Champaign
Denise E. Murray	NCELTR Macquarie University
Meredith Pike-Baky	University of California at Berkeley
Sara L. Sanders	Coastal Carolina University
Lilia Savova	Indiana University of Pennsylvania
Donna Sievers	Garden Grove Unified School District, California
Ruth Spack	Tufts University
Leo van Lier	Monterey Institute of International Studies

TABLE OF CONTENTS

ACKNOWLEDGMENTS

This book is, of course, the product of input from many people, to whom we are extremely grateful.

First and foremost, we wish to thank Donald Freeman, the series editor of TeacherSource, who was kind enough to entertain the possibility of adding another title to the series. Discovering you have another book to produce when you thought the series was done is a little like having a late and unexpected baby—but we hope that the result, like a late baby, will bring him much joy.

Second, we wish to thank first Erik Gundersen and later Thomas Healy at Heinle & Heinle, who both were supportive throughout the process of producing this volume.

We want to thank our helpers at the Monterey Institute of International Studies, Deanna Kelley, Anne Delaney, Karen Vanderveen, Angela Dadak, and Mark Manasse, who word-processed huge chunks of scrawley, multi-colored texts written in various forms of international e-mail cuneiform and three sets of awkward handwriting that did little to make our third-grade teachers proud. Anne and Angela worked miracles with the figures on a computer that should have been retired years ago. Deanna, Karen, and Angela proofread the manuscript, checked library references, and pointed out a fair amount of unclarity and silliness in the drafts. Mark, who wanted to be a writer when he began working on this project, read the entire manuscript, gave us feedback from the viewpoint of a novice teacher, and then word-processed reams of revisions. If these talented young people are half as good at language teaching as they are as editorial assistants, they will be brilliant language teachers indeed.

We are also grateful to Sanny Kwok at the University of Hong Kong and to Bea Williams at the Monterey Institute of International Studies for helping us manage the production and transportation of the manuscript across two continents and the three universities' e-mail systems.

We are most appreciative of the constructive criticism provided by Neil Anderson, Donald Freeman, and three anonymous readers, whose clear comments helped us substantially revise the manuscript.

Tab Hamlin, our brilliant copy editor, offered many helpful suggestions. He gently but consistently reminded us to attend to details for the reader's benefit.

Finally, the TeacherSource series is based upon the concept that teachers' knowledge is important and should be broadcast, examined, discussed, and acknowledged. We are deeply grateful to those teachers whose voices are included in this book next to ours. Whether their ideas are things we collected from public accounts or were generated specifically for this volume, we are very happy to have been able to use them—as illustrations, as cases, as sources of puzzles, and as inspiration.

How We Came to Write This Book Together

KATHLEEN M. BAILEY

My regular job is as a teacher educator in California, where I am a professor of applied linguistics at the Monterey Institute of International Studies. My professional interests include teacher education, language assessment, second language acquisition, sociolinguistics, and language classroom research.

However, during the 1996–97 academic year I was very fortunate to be able to teach EFL in the English Language Teaching Unit at the Chinese University of Hong Kong. While I was there I met Andy Curtis—first as the coordinator of a program I was teaching in and second as a colleague. I had already known David Nunan for many years through our work in the TESOL association.

While I was at the Chinese University I kept a diary of my teaching for the year. I was really lucky to be able to teach EFL and have the time to reflect on that teaching by keeping a journal. I was also very fortunate to have colleagues who supported me in my efforts to improve my teaching.

ANDY CURTIS

Until recently, I was an assistant professor in Hong Kong. However, while working on this book, I came to realize that I am concerned enough about teaching and learning, my own in particular, to leave universities for a while. I have also realized, again as result of this book, the importance of focused and sustained periods of personal-professional development. Most of us become teachers because of our interest in learning, but doing both at the same time and doing both well is not easy. Consequently, I am now enjoying a break from institutionalized teaching to focus on my own learning. I am already missing teaching, and look forward to returning to it after this period of reflection and evaluation.

DAVID NUNAN

I am a professor of applied linguistics at the University of Hong Kong. My professional and research interests include teacher education, classroom research, learning styles and strategies, task-based teaching and learning, inductive approaches to the teaching of grammar, and communication in the multilingual, multiethnic workplace.

As we wrote this book, I was able to draw on my own experiences as a classroom teacher. During the time it took to produce a final first draft of the manuscript I taught a speaking class to EFL students as well as a range of ESP courses in the areas of academic writing, English for nursing students, and English for law. I also did teacher training courses in our graduate program at the University of Hong Kong as well as working in teacher training programs in Latin America and Asia.

SERIES EDITOR'S PREFACE

As I was driving just south of White River Junction, the snow had started falling in earnest. The light was flat, although it was mid-morning, making it almost impossible to distinguish the highway in the gray-white swirling snow. I turned on the radio, partly as a distraction and partly to help me concentrate on the road ahead; the announcer was talking about the snow. "The state highway department advises motorists to use extreme caution and to drive with their headlights on to ensure maximum visibility." He went on, his tone shifting slightly, "Ray Burke, the state highway supervisor, just called to say that one of the plows almost hit a car just south of Exit 6 because the person driving hadn't turned on his lights. He really wants people to put their headlights on because it is very tough to see in this stuff." I checked, almost reflexively, to be sure that my headlights were on, as I drove into the churning snow.

How can information serve those who hear or read it in making sense of their own worlds? How can it enable them to reason about what they do and to take appropriate actions based on that reasoning? My experience with the radio in the snowstorm illustrates two different ways of providing the same message: the need to use your headlights when you drive in heavy snow. The first offers dispassionate information; the second tells the same content in a personal, compelling story. The first disguises its point of view; the second explicitly grounds the general information in a particular time and place. Each means of giving information has its role, but I believe the second is ultimately more useful in helping people make sense of what they are doing. When I heard Ray Burke's story about the plow, I made sure my headlights were on.

In what is written about teaching, it is rare to find accounts in which the author's experience and point of view are central. A point of view is not simply an opinion; neither is it a whimsical or impressionistic claim. Rather, a point of view lays out what the author thinks and why; to borrow the phrase from writing teacher Natalie Goldberg, "it sets down the bones." The problem is that much of what is available in professional development in language-teacher education concentrates on telling rather than on point of view. The telling is prescriptive, like the radio announcer's first statement. It emphasizes what is important to know and do, what is current in theory and research, and therefore what you—as a practicing teacher—should do. But this telling disguises the teller; it hides the point of view that can enable you to make sense of what is told.

The TeacherSource series offers you a point of view on second/foreign language teaching. Each author in this series has had to lay out what she or he believes is central to the topic, and how she or he has come to this understanding. So as a reader, you will find this book has a personality; it is not anonymous. It comes as a story, not as a directive, and it is meant to create a relationship with you rather than assume your attention. As a practitioner, its point of view can help you in your own work by providing a sounding board for your ideas and a metric for your own thinking. It can suggest courses of action and explain why these make sense to the author. You in turn can take from it what you will, and do with it what you can. This book will not tell you what to think; it is meant to help you make sense of what you do.

The point of view in **TeacherSource** is built out of three strands: **Teachers' Voices**, **Frameworks**, and **Investigations**. Each author draws together these strands uniquely, as suits his or her topic and—more crucially—his or her point of view. All materials in **TeacherSource** have these three strands. The **Teachers' Voices** are practicing language teachers from various settings who tell about their experience of the topic. The **Frameworks** lay out what the author believes is important to know about his or her topic and its key concepts and issues. These fundamentals define the area of language teaching and learning about which she or he is writing. The **Investigations** are meant to engage you, the reader, in relating the topic to your own teaching, students, and classroom. They are activities which you can do alone or with colleagues, to reflect on teaching and learning and/or try out ideas in practice.

Each strand offers a point of view on the book's topic. The **Teachers' Voices** relate the points of view of various practitioners; the **Frameworks** establish the point of view of the professional community; and the **Investigations** invite you to develop your own point of view, through experience with reference to your setting. Together these strands should serve in making sense of the topic.

We generally think of teaching as what we do in classrooms with students. Unfortunately, this view leaves unseen—and even ignores—the important private thinking, analysis, and reflection that can underlie the public face of teaching. In this book, *Pursuing Professional Development: The Self as Source*, Kathi Bailey, Andy Curtis, and David Nunan reconnect the public and private to illuminate the inner work of teaching. They present concrete ways in which teachers can make sense of their daily work with students and, more crucially, they examine why it is so important to do so.

Theirs is no abstract, armchair discussion. These authors do what they write about and they write about what they do. This book has grown out of a unique configuration of relationships. The authors are all classroom teachers. They all present, write about, and indeed are internationally known for their work in second language teacher education. When they conceived of *The Self as Source*, as the book came to be called, they were all three in Hong Kong, which provided them a unique opportunity to collaborate as teachers and peers in pursuing their professional development. Thus the book came into being through a year of work together as they taught in different institutions while pursuing a common aim. The work that results is firmly anchored in the daily practicalities of classrooms while examining larger issues of sensemaking in teaching.

The Self as Source warrants an added comment, however. It is Kathi Bailey's second book in the **TeacherSource** series and an excellent further contribution. When Bailey and her colleagues first suggested the project, the series was officially closed to further titles. There is something validating however, when an author who knows intimately the unique demands of the series, both in design and in writing, turns again to its principles as the vehicle for her ideas and experiences. And, like revisiting a familiar haunt, she brings along two outstanding colleagues to visit, convinced that they too will find it useful and intriguing. I am very pleased that she did, for this book shows the excellent result of that collaboration, and the series is richer for it.

—*Donald Freeman, Series Editor*

1

WHY BOTHER WITH PROFESSIONAL DEVELOPMENT?

Because teaching can take up a lot of our lives in one way or another, an increasing number of us want to find out more about ourselves, our teaching and the relationship between the two. Then we ask ourselves, how can we use what we discover to guide our future development? In individual terms, how can I become the best teacher I can be for my students? (Edge, 1992,1)

DAVID RECALLS A CONVERSATION

One day in the autumn of 1996, Kathi Bailey and I were sitting in a pub on the eleventh floor of the K.K. Leung Building at the University of Hong Kong. Kathi had come across town from the Chinese University of Hong Kong (CUHK), where she was spending her sabbatical year, to do a workshop for some of my students, who were inservice and preservice teachers of English as a Foreign Language (EFL). We got to talking about how teachers learn—partly because we'd just been working with a group of teacher-learners and partly because the *TESOL Quarterly* had put out a call for papers for a special theme issue about teacher education, to which we wanted to submit an abstract.

David Nunan

"Well, how do you learn? You, yourself, as a teacher?" I asked Kathi. "How do you improve *your* teaching?"

"Me? Well," (Kathi paused), "I think I make progress in my teaching when I have a chance or a need to try something new."

"Like what? Give me an example."

"Like right now, for instance. For the past 20 years I've been teaching English as a Second Language (ESL) in the States to university students and working with graduate students—both preservice and inservice teachers—who want to teach English or some other modern language. Now here I am at CUHK, teaching EFL to college freshmen. It's a totally different world—and it's stretching my skills, my thinking, my abilities, almost everything—because I'm facing new challenges."

"Like what? Give me an example," I asked again.

"Well, like the last two weeks, I had to teach a new class to an audience I've never worked with before, and I had to team teach it with the coordinator of the program, who's someone totally new to me. And I knew next to nothing about the topic!"

"Wait a minute. What's this? What course? Who's the team teacher?" (I was laughing because the situation seemed bizarre to me.)

"The course was called 'Running Effective Meetings,' and it was being offered to the MBA [Masters of Business Administration] students at Chinese University. It's something I promised that I'd do, in an unguarded moment, so I got stuck working on this team, teaching a topic I'd never taught before, with a totally new person as my teaching partner, to students I didn't know and would probably have no further contact with. And this was on top of my regular teaching load!"

"It sounds horrible!" I exclaimed.

"No, actually, it was a great experience," Kathi replied with a surprised look on her face, as if she were startled by her revelation.

"Why?" I asked, incredulously.

"Well, because I learned a lot of new stuff about the topic—running effective meetings—that I think will be useful to me personally, since I have to attend and run a lot of meetings. And the students were a lot more proficient in English than my regular CUHK students are, so it was a nice change of pace. But mostly because my team-teaching partner is somebody I can really work with and learn from."

"Who is it?" I asked.

"Oh, he's this funny guy named Andy Curtis. He was the coordinator for the business students' course, so in that context he was my boss. The rest of the time, he's one of my new colleagues in the department. He's an amazing teacher and a good team manager. I think we might become friends...."

1.1 *LEARNING SOMETHING NEW*

Think about a time when you were in a situation that led you (or forced you) to learn something new about teaching. (This task may seem to be easier if you have teaching experience, but even if your teaching experience is limited, it may be useful.) Answer the following questions:

1. What did you learn?

2. How did you learn it?

Make some notes about the factors that influenced your learning about teaching. (Save these notes, please, for a later Investigation.)

Now broaden your thinking a bit from the specific instance documented above. How would you answer the questions David put to Kathi: "How do you learn? You, yourself as a teacher? How do you improve *your* teaching?"

As the afternoon wore on, Kathi and I talked more about the things that had actually worked for us as teachers trying to improve our teaching. In my case, the things that had worked well all had a direct connection to my own practice and helped me deal with challenges and solve problems—conducting action research, for instance. We found in this discussion that every successful professional development experience entailed our ownership of the focus: That is, we, as teachers, had chosen those elements of our teaching that we were trying to improve.

The conversation turned to things that *hadn't* worked for us, in terms of helping us grow as teachers. For Kathi, a particular teacher training device that hadn't seemed effective was micro-teaching, which had been featured in both her undergraduate training and her certification as a secondary school English teacher. She remembered it as constraining, circumscribed, and flat—not multidimensional like real teaching.

Kathi asked me, "What didn't work for you?"

My immediate response: "Supervision."

Kathi asked me why.

"I think the times that I was being supervised, the person who was supervising me was focusing on one issue and I was concerned with other issues or problems. So on one occasion, the supervisor gave me feedback about the way that I introduced a new grammar point, but my concern with that particular class was how to set up and manage group work activities."

David Nunan

That's how the story began. This book was written by three friends—David Nunan, Andy Curtis, and Kathi Bailey—who engaged in some professional development activities together. Indeed, we decided to write this book because we were all working individually to improve ourselves as language teachers, and we were all practicing reflective teaching, to varying degrees at various times, privately. But when we three found ourselves teaching EFL in Hong Kong, and when we began to share our ideas, our concerns, our frustrations, and our triumphs, we discovered we could learn a great deal from one another. We decided we were having so much fun and learning so much about teaching that we wanted to write an article about what and how we were learning. In the process of writing the article, we found we had enough ideas and experiences to fill a book! And here it is.

1.2 *WHAT DO YOU THINK?*

What were your first impressions of the title of this book? Why do you think we chose this title? Look at the title and the subtitle separately for a moment and jot down a few reactions to each in the blank spaces on the next page or on a piece of paper:

Pursuing Professional Development: _____

_____

The Self as Source: _____

_____

If you are working with a group of people as you read this book, we suggest you compare your ideas about the two parts of the title with your classmates (if you are in a preservice training program) or your colleagues (if you are in an inservice training program or in a teachers' discussion group). Finally, please write your own definition of *professional development* before reading any further.

A DEFINITION
Having read the title of this book, you might be asking yourself two questions:

1. *"What is professional development anyway?"* and
2. *"Why should I bother with it?"*

We hope that by providing our answers to these questions, we will construct a shared definition of professional development, which can be used and exemplified throughout this text. Second, we hope to convince you (if you are not already sure) that professional development is indeed worth pursuing. We believe that reading this book will give you numerous ways to start, if you would like to begin, or to continue with your own professional development initiatives.

First, what is meant by professional development for teachers? We'll take as our starting point a definition from Dale Lange, who has worked for many years in preservice foreign language teacher education in the United States. He writes, "Teacher development is a term used in the literature to describe a process of continual intellectual, experiential, and attitudinal growth of teachers" (1990, 250). While some professional development certainly occurs in preservice and inservice training programs, Lange's use of the term allows for "continued growth both before and throughout a career" (ibid.). He adds that "the intent here is to suggest that teachers continue to evolve in the use, adaptation, and application of their art and craft" (ibid.).

1.3 *INGREDIENTS IN PROFESSIONAL DEVELOPMENT*

What factors promote professional development as a lifelong process? What elements are necessary for it to occur? Make a list of the factors you think must be present for professional development to take place. If you are working with a group of colleagues or classmates, please compare your lists. In the following Teachers' Voices section, Andy talks about what he considers to be five key ingredients for professional development.

ANDY'S IDEAS

Andy Curtis

To write what I've already learned from working on this book would be a chapter in itself. I've been so involved with my own professional development lately that I've been thinking a lot about what teacher development means to me.

Choice is a big deal. People can be subjected to assessment, appraisal, and evaluation against their will. But no one can be made to develop. Even if you have to compile a portfolio, you can't be made to develop by doing it. Teachers are too good at faking it. We have to be. We can fake development, and should do so, if someone tries to force it on us. But we develop as professionals if, and only if, we choose to. The motives may differ from teacher to teacher, but this we have in common: no choice, no way.

Trust is another important issue for me, which goes hand-in-hand with openness and honesty. I don't want some senior managers telling me that they want a warts-and-all picture, showing all my flaws as well as all my strengths, that they want it to be develop-mental, and then reminding me about 10 percent cutbacks to be made in the near future. How many of their flaws and weaknesses, how many of their "areas for development" would they show if their jobs were hanging in the balance, I wonder? So, if I don't trust the motives of the Powers That Be, then no development is likely.

More personally, I need to trust the other teachers who will be helping me to develop, otherwise why take the risk and expose myself? To my mind, there is no professional development without exposure, and exposing weaknesses is tricky unless there is com-plete trust. Same as with most other relationships, I guess.

Some sense of mutuality or reciprocity is also important for me. No matter how much older, wiser, more published, or more securely tenured the teachers may be who are helping me, I think they should be able to identify what they have learned from me too. As we have been collaborating on this book, David and Kathi haven't considered my rank or seniority. Instead they see what I can con-tribute. Making those contributions, and responding to theirs, has been a major part of my own professional development.

One point that is often overlooked is that teacher development must result in better teaching and learning. If I put together this great portfolio, *The Andy Curtis Show*, in no way does that guar-antee that my teaching—my abilities to help bring about learning—or my own ability to learn will necessarily improve unless I choose to make the changes needed.

Knowing that changes need to be made in order to bring about "better" and "more" learning (my own as well as my students') is not the same as making those changes. I may not be able to change things for many reasons (for example, the constraints within which I might be working, or because of suffering from burnout, and so on). Also, knowing that changes should be made does not necessarily mean that I will know *how* to make those changes. For example, I might realize that I need to increase my students' motivation, but not know how to do this. Not being able to bring about these changes does not mean that no teacher development has occurred. But up to this point it's not the kind of teacher development that results in more and better learning by the students and the teacher, and for me, in that sense, it's incomplete.

Finally, I am getting heart-wearily tired of the blind ignorance of (or deliberate refusal to accept) the distinction between judgmental and developmental assessment. If one more senior wise-person tells me that there's no conflict, I'm going to say something I'll regret! Yes, it is possible for the two things to be going on at the same time, and for one to be a part of the other, but they are NOT the same. Going back to the issue of choice, if the institution decides I have to have my teaching videotaped, that my classes have to be observed, that I have to compile a portfolio, then that is, for me, evaluation-driven activity, no matter how much they tell me it's about development. **I** decide if, when, why and how I develop, contract renewal or no contract renewal!

There are more things I could go on about, but these five factors—(1) choice, (2) trust and honesty, (3) mutuality and reciprocity, (4) better teaching and learning, and (5) the judgmental/developmental distinction—these are at the heart of professional development for me.

1.4 *Why Do It?*

Before reading any further, please think of as many reasons as possible for pursuing professional development. Make a written list of your ideas. If you are working with a group, you could either brainstorm such a list with your classmates or colleagues, or you could compare the list you have written to theirs.

REASONS FOR PURSUING PROFESSIONAL DEVELOPMENT

Having been collectively involved in language teaching and teacher education for over 50 years, the three of us can think of a number of reasons why we teachers should want to participate in professional development opportunities. Some of these opportunities are formal and externally organized (such as attending a course, going to a conference, or working toward higher certification), while others are smaller in scope, more private, and more informal. These include participating in teacher chat-groups, keeping a teaching journal, or studying a language, to name just a few possibilities.

Perhaps the most obvious reason to participate in opportunities for professional development is to acquire new knowledge and skills. Perhaps you want to learn some new techniques to use in your classes, either to solve a problem or just for the sake of variety and novelty. Perhaps your teaching assignment has changed, and you need to upgrade your skills to work with a new group of students with different needs for language learning. Maybe your school or program has invested in new materials or equipment, and you would like to learn to utilize them better. All sorts of professional development opportunities can help you achieve these kinds of goals.

Change is another reason to engage in professional development activities. Although your teaching situation may not have changed, the world around us changes quickly. If you completed your preparation for teaching even only a few years ago, you will probably find that keeping up with change is an important reason to continue to learn about teaching. In addition, new teachers entering the job market may have skills and knowledge that you lack (e.g., about computer assisted instruction), so staying abreast of our rapidly evolving field is another reason to participate in professional development. Sometimes changes in governmental regulations or policies (for instance, the introduction of a new national English examination in an EFL context) will have a profound impact on our classes, and we must be prepared to cope with such changes.

Another reason is that participating in professional development opportunities can sometimes lead to an increase in income and/or prestige within the context of our current jobs. In many school districts in the United States, for example, teachers can move up on the pay scale by taking additional courses to amass units of credit beyond their earlier certification. Furthermore, completing a significant training program or a research project can add an impressive line to your curriculum vitae, which may make you more competitive in your next job search.

Yet another reason to engage in professional development activities is summarized in the old maxim that knowledge is power. By increasing our knowledge base, we increase our power over our own lives. This is why the term "empowerment" is used so often in conjunction with teacher development opportunities. *Empowerment* is "working out our own way forward, based on our own understanding" (Edge, 1992, 1). Indeed, it has been our experience that participating in appropriate professional development opportunities can lead to both empowerment and inspiration. Being in charge of our own professional growth as teachers can help to keep us excited about our work by avoiding what Diane Larsen-Freeman (1998, 220) has called the "deskilling of teaching." (See also Apple, 1985.)

Continued professional growth and excitement can also help us to combat negativity in our teaching contexts. The following diary entry, called "Community of Moaners," was written by Joachim Appel, an EFL teacher in Germany. It describes an all-too-familiar situation (1995, 7):

> Staffroom talk part two. It is brimming over with anger and aggression. It is a release of tension, it is irrational and it accentuates the negative (red ink mentality). Come and join the community of moaners. I do, too. I need it. But the unity is deceptive because its sense of shared suffering is easily mistaken for the set of shared values, which, of course, does not exist. In a staff of about 100 there is, in fact, very little consensus on anything.

Kathi vividly recalls her surprise, as a young teacher of 12-year-old ESL and remedial reading students in the desert of southeastern California, at the hostility rampant in the staff room. "I show a movie every Friday," said the social studies teacher. "It cuts down on my work and keeps the little bastards quiet for an hour." Over time, such negative influences, combined with frustration and feeling unsuccessful or powerless in our work, can contribute to the conditions that lead to "burnout."

1.5 BURNOUT

What is "burnout"? Perhaps you have heard a colleague say something like, "I am totally burned out. I can't stand the thought of teaching for one more day!" Before reading further, please write your own definition of burnout.

Think of a situation in which you were (or someone you know was) experiencing burnout. What would you say are the characteristics or the behavior of a person experiencing burnout? List three such characteristics before reading further. Share your ideas on this topic with your peers.

The following Teachers' Voices section provides us with comments from and about teachers who have experienced burnout. Some have developed coping strategies for dealing with the problem. As you read, make a note of which, if any, of these situations sound familiar to you.

TALKING ABOUT FRUSTRATION

Jim Y., Dick L.,
Roger E.,
Long and Newman

A teacher can be compared to a battery. At the beginning of the school year, all the students are plugged in and drawing learning current. At the end of the school year, the battery is worn down and it must be recharged. And each time the battery is recharged it is more difficult to get it to hold its charge, and eventually it must be replaced. That is when complete burnout has taken place (Jim Y., a teacher, quoted in Maslach, 1982, 2).

Dick L., an elementary school teacher, is finding it increasingly uncomfortable to have a drink in the local bar after work. Once some other customers discover he is a teacher, they let him know the contempt they have for his profession—"You guys are doing a lousy job of teaching, and yet you have the nerve to demand bigger salaries. And you already get three months of vacation!" And so on, and so on (Maslach, 1982, 52).

After school, I work as a gymnastics coach. This gives me contact with students that is different from teaching, so it helps me see them in a different light and can offset some of the daily frustrations. Plus it gives me a chance to exercise, work off tension, and keep in good physical condition. During the summer I get as far away from teaching as possible. I look forward to that summer job: lifeguard, house painter, salesman, or whatever. Sometimes, that job becomes a year-round vocation. Moonlighting is often a financial necessity because teachers' salaries are pretty inadequate. But, more important, it is an emotional survival technique (Roger E., a teacher, ibid., 88–89).

A teacher cannot function adequately for long without an informed shoulder to lean on, without an on-the-spot human wailing wall at which to gripe, to rage, to express fears and confess mistakes, to ask questions and wonder aloud....Where the human wailing wall is carefully conceived and consistently offered, where the people provided are...informed, sensitive, sympathetic, and understanding, the turnover among teachers, even under the most incredibly difficult conditions, is remarkably lowered (Long and Newman, 1961, 5–26, as cited in Maslach, 1982, 111).

BURNOUT

Christina Maslach, who has conducted research on burnout, describes the phenomenon in this way:

Burnout. The word evokes images of a final flickering flame, of a charred and empty shell, of dying embers and cold, gray ashes.... Burnout is a syndrome of emotional exhaustion, depersonalization, and reduced personal accomplishment that can occur among individuals who do "people work" of some kind. It is a response to the chronic emotional strain of dealing exclusively with other human beings, particularly when they are troubled or having problems. Thus, it can be considered one type of job stress. Although it has some of the same deleterious effects as other stress responses, what is unique about burnout is that the stress arises from the *social* interaction between helper and recipient (Maslach, 1982, 3).

People in helping professions are particularly susceptible to burnout. Maslach's work includes data from teachers, doctors, nurses, psychiatrists, police, psychologists, social workers, and prison guards.

Maslach's research has revealed that three factors underpin the burnout syndrome: emotional exhaustion, depersonalization, and a lack of personal accomplishment. Using these constructs, Maslach devised a measurement instrument called the Maslach Burnout Inventory (Maslach and Jackson, 1986). With that instrument, Martha Pennington and Belinda Ho (1995) surveyed 95 ESL teachers and found that, compared to the 11,000 employees surveyed by Maslach and Jackson (1986):

the ESL group is slightly lower on the Emotional Exhaustion subscale, considerably lower on the Depersonalization subscale, and considerably higher on the Personal Accomplishment subscale. The surveyed ESL group therefore seems to suffer less from the stress-related effects associated with burnout than does the general population of human services workers (Pennington and Ho, 1995, 48–49).

These authors are quick to point out, however, that the vast majority of their respondents were holders of M.A. degrees living in the United States. The results are likely to differ for language teachers working in other contexts.

1.6 *INTERVIEWS*

Think of someone you know who has been teaching for at least five years longer than you have. Either interview that teacher or have an e-mail conversation with him or her. Try to find out (1) whether this person has ever experienced burnout, or is even concerned about it, and (2) what strategies, if any, he or she has for preventing burnout or coping with it. If you are interviewing the person, it will be helpful to take notes.

If you are working with a group, please compare your notes or your e-mail records with those of your peers. If several people talk to experienced teachers, it should be possible to compile a list of helpful strategies for combating burnout.

MORE REASONS

Dan Lortie has called teaching "the egg carton profession" (1975, 223), because once we close the doors to our classrooms, we are relatively isolated from our peers. Taking part in professional development opportunities can help us overcome this sense of isolation. If you participate in socially based professional development opportunities, such as conferences, workshops, teacher research teams, etc., you will have the opportunity to meet like-minded people, who are themselves actively seeking professional development experiences. There is often great reassurance at such gatherings when we teachers discover we are not alone in the problems we face in our classrooms, programs, and schools. This experience is not only uplifting for the moment; it can also help you get in touch with positive people in the long run. (We have known many enthusiastic teachers who were eventually worn down by the lack of excitement among their colleagues, so it's important to be in contact with people who can help you sustain your motivation, instead of those who deplete it.) Building a network of other professionally active teachers could be useful to you in many ways (e.g., in finding colleagues for co-developing materials, providing contacts for your next job search, offering you new teaching ideas, conducting action research with you, and so on).

Finally, even participating in private professional development opportunities (such as regularly reading new books or journal articles) can help expand our conceptual understanding of teaching and our vocabulary for discussing that knowledge. This is important because, as Donald Freeman has said, "The process of articulation—making the tacit explicit—brings into play new discourse and with it, different ways of conceptualizing teaching" (1992, 7). Being able to talk confidently with administrators, parents, students and other teachers about what we do and why we do it is an extraordinarily important part of being competent teachers and gaining respect as professionals. By participating in professional development opportunities we not only gain new vocabulary, ideas, and skills; we also gain confirmation or reaffirmation that what we do is worthwhile.

We can pursue professional development as individuals or as members of a group. Before reading further, please list the advantages and disadvantages of individual professional development and collaborative professional development.

INDIVIDUAL VERSUS COLLABORATIVE DEVELOPMENT

Some of the approaches to professional development that we will describe here are inherently personal in nature—or at least they typically start out as private or solitary endeavors. These include our focus on self-awareness and self-observation, the practice of reflective teaching, the processes of keeping a teaching journal and writing an autobiography, and the experience of compiling a teaching portfolio. However, the results of these experiences could certainly be shared with colleagues. For example, we three authors have benefited from reading one another's journals and teaching portfolios, and from watching videotapes of us team teaching. In fact, we will argue that these processes become more powerful tools for professional development when their results are shared or when they are practiced collaboratively with trusted colleagues.

Other approaches to professional development can be done either individually or as a joint effort. These include conducting action research, reading or writing case studies, learning a language, and being videotaped while teaching.

Still other procedures are inherently collaborative in nature from the outset. These include peer observation, mentoring, coaching, and team teaching. By definition, you need one or more colleagues to work with you when you are engaged in these professional development activities.

Julian Edge, who was quoted at the beginning of this chapter, has developed an approach to teacher learning that he calls *Cooperative Development*. He says,

> I need someone to work with, but I don't need someone who wants
> to change me and make me more like the way they think I ought to
> be. I need someone who will help me see myself clearly. To make
> this possible, we need a distinct style of working together so that
> each person's development remains in that person's own hands. This
> type of interaction will involve some new rules for speaking, for
> listening, and for responding in order to cooperate in a disciplined
> way. This mixture of awareness-raising and disciplined cooperation
> is what I have called *Cooperative Development* (1992, 4).

This approach, which is a "way of working together with someone in order to become a better teacher in your own terms" (ibid.), is based on the principles of respect, empathy, and honesty. We will return to the concept of Cooperative Development in future chapters. In the following Teachers' Voices section we hear Julian Edge's ideas about individual development and working with others.

Julian Edge

JULIAN'S IDEAS ON LEARNING FROM OTHERS

Firstly, as an individual, my development is in my own hands. With or without official training and education as a teacher, only I can really understand what I am trying to do in class, how it works out for me, and what I learn from it. If I follow this up, I can find a sense of personal satisfaction in my work that goes beyond that great feeling of "having a really good lesson". Every lesson can be a part of finding out more about teaching, about learning and about myself.

Secondly, as members of different schools, or societies, or cultures, only we have the insights of insiders into what is happening with our learners in our classrooms. If we follow this up, it can take us away from the frustration of seeing our teaching future defined by the latest method, the latest guru, or the latest coursebook.

At both levels, of course, we can go on learning from others: from in-service training courses, from visiting speakers, and from new (and old) publications. But the idea that we should go on taking ideas from others and applying them to our own situations meets only a part of our potential. To serve our own development we need a way of working that encourages us to look more closely at ourselves and to work on what we find.

At the same time this emphasis on self doesn't mean that we should work in isolation. The isolation of the teacher is exactly what holds us back. We all too regularly limit teaching to an individual, subjective experience shared with no one. As a direct result of this, we restrict our ability to develop as teachers, and we hand over to outsiders important questions about what good teaching is and how it might be assessed.

I want to investigate and assess my own teaching. I can't do that without understanding it better, and I can't understand it on my own. Here we are close to the heart of the paradox. When I use the word *development*, I always mean *self-development*. But that can't be done in isolation. Self-development needs other people: colleagues and students. By cooperating with others, we can come to understand better our own experiences and opinions. We can also enrich them with the understandings and experiences of others. Through cooperation, we have a chance to escape from simple, egocentric subjectivity, without chasing after a non-existent objectivity (1992, 3–4).

IS LANGUAGE TEACHING A PROFESSION?

In a local sense, we can practice Cooperative Development with our peers—the classmates or colleagues who make up our immediate professional community. In a broader sense, however, people engaged in language teaching as an occupation make up a wider community—the community of language teaching professionals.

Do you consider language teaching to be a profession? At regional, national, or international teachers' meetings you will frequently hear the words *profession*, *professional*, and *professionalism*. Participants make constant references to the teaching profession, there are many professional development sessions, and the events themselves are imbued with the spirit of professionalism (Nunan, 1999a, 1999b). What is a *profession*, and what is meant by *professionalism*? According to the *Collins Cobuild Dictionary* (1995, 1,313), "a profession is a type of job that requires advanced education and training." *The Newbury House Dictionary* defines *professionalism* as "the qualities of competence and integrity demonstrated by the best people in the field" (1996, 685). But sometimes as teachers, both in general education and in language teaching in particular, we feel we are not accorded the respect given to other professionals. In the next Teachers' Voices section, David considers what it means to say a certain occupation is a profession, and whether language teaching is a profession.

DAVID ANSWERS THE QUESTION

By looking at other occupations that call themselves professions, we can begin to identify criteria for determining whether or not our field can legitimately be considered a profession. At least four criteria must be taken into account: (1) the existence of advanced education and training, (2) the establishment of standards of practice and certification, (3) an agreed upon theoretical and empirical base, and (4) the work of people within the field who act as advocates for the profession.

The most tangible characteristic of occupations that are traditionally thought of as professions, from medicine to law, from engineering to architecture, is that they require advanced education and training. In addition, this education and training does not end on graduation but is career long. Few of us would willingly put ourselves in the hands of an unqualified airline pilot, and only desperation would drive us to seek a tooth extraction from someone who has had no dental training.

What about language teaching? In the past 20 years, there has been an explosion in the availability of formal programs of study offering both undergraduate and graduate-level education and training to potential and practicing language teachers. Thousands of individuals have completed these courses. Sadly, despite this availability of training, thousands of other individuals around the world do teach languages with no formal preparation. In fact, at some language schools in different parts of the world, the only employment criterion is fluency in the target language.

Are education and training necessary? Many people who teach English around the world have no training whatsoever. Does this matter? At some time or other, you've probably heard comments such as the following: "Some of my best teachers had no formal qualifications," or "I once had a teacher with a Ph.D. in education. He was hopeless as a teacher." The fact that some individuals without formal training happen to be "natural" teachers and the fact that some highly trained people aren't particularly good in the classroom are not good enough reasons to argue that education and training aren't necessary. Requiring people with natural gifts

David Nunan

or talent to undergo training is not going to turn them into "bad" teachers. Such training can actually promote professionalism.

But if the profession requires education and training, what types of knowledge and skill are relevant for language educators? To answer this question, we should make a distinction between *declarative knowledge* and *procedural knowledge.*

For us as language teachers, *declarative knowledge* includes all of the things we know and can articulate about language. The following statements are examples of declarative knowledge. "The passive voice is used when we want to emphasize a process rather than the performer of an action" or "When making third-person singular declarative statements in the simple present in English, we put an 's' on the end of regular verbs."

Procedural knowledge can be subdivided into discipline-specific and general knowledge. Discipline-specific procedural knowledge refers to skills that are unique to language teaching (e.g., how to introduce new grammatical items such as gerunds and infinitives). General procedural knowledge refers to skills that all teachers should possess regardless of the subject they teach. Such skills include how to manage group work, how to deal with discipline problems, and how to improve the motivation of students. (The procedural/declarative distinction also holds for students. In one EFL class, I had a student who performed flawlessly in a lesson on adjectives ending in '-ing' to describe persons, actions and things, and adjectives ending in '-ed' to describe feelings and attitudes. At the end of the lesson, I asked him how he liked the class. "Oh," he replied, "I am boring when we practice this -ing stuff!")

The second defining characteristic of a profession is a set of standards of practice developed and promulgated by that profession. Such standards are usually tied to some form of certification or license to practice. In some cases, this licensing is under the direct control of the profession. In other cases, where governments determine who should have a license to practice, the profession has a significant influence over the process, usually through professional associations. For example, in the United States, the American Medical Association has an important say in who should be allowed to work as medical practitioners. In Hong Kong, the Hong Kong Society of Accountants creates and administers the examination that determines who will work as accountants. But in language teaching, standards of practice and certification vary widely. In many countries where some form of teaching certification is required, this process is often controlled by governments and educational bureaucracies, not by professional teaching associations.

In terms of institutional accreditation, the situation also varies widely. In numerous countries, there is no professional or governmental control over language schools. In such contexts, nothing can stop individuals who see language as a marketable commodity from opening their own schools, hiring and underpaying unqualified teachers, and using illegally copied materials. We know of one such school that doesn't even pay its teachers. Native speakers of English are hired and sent out to recruit their own students. Their "salary" takes the form of a percentage of the students' fees.

A third characteristic of a profession is the existence of a disciplinary base. This theoretical and empirical basis separates professions from trades and crafts. Educator Lee Shulman (1988, 5) says that what distinguishes disciplines from one another is how "they formulate their questions, how they define the content of their domains and organize that content conceptually, and the principles of discovery and verification that constitute the ground rules for creating and testing knowledge in their fields."

A challenge for education in general, and language teaching in particular, is to define, refine, and articulate its disciplinary basis. Education is a hybrid, drawing on a range of disciplines such as psychology and sociology. In addition to these fields, language teaching is influenced by linguistics (both theoretical and applied), psycholinguistics, literature, sociolinguistics, cognitive science, and numerous other disciplines. Partly because of these varied sources of background knowledge, language teaching may seem to lack a unified disciplinary base.

The fourth and final criterion that makes an occupation a profession is that of advocacy. Most professions have professional associations, and a key function of such associations is to act as advocates for the profession. They do this by attempting to influence not only the public but also legislators, either to create legislation that is seen to be advantageous to the profession or to oppose legislation viewed as inimical to the profession. Of course, as individual teachers, we can also advocate for our programs' growth, or for our students' rights and well-being. But large-scale advocacy is usually best accomplished by groups of people banding together in professional associations.

Is language teaching a profession? The answer to this question is, it depends where you look. It is possible to find language teaching institutions around the world that fit none of the criteria set out above. However, it is also possible to find institutions and associations that are actively committed to advancing education and training, to developing standards and certification, to supporting the development of theory and research so that a disciplinary base can be established, and to working as advocates to influence broader communities in ways that are positive for language learners. It is up to those of us who are committed to language teaching as a profession to identify and promote practices that are consistent with this goal (adapted from Nunan 1999a and 1999b).

1.8 *Are You a Professional?*

Are you a member of any professional organization? If so, what stance has your organization taken toward: (1) advanced education and training, (2) standards of practice, (3) an agreed upon theoretical and empirical basis, and (4) advocacy for the language teaching profession?

If you were to rank these four criteria, what would be their order of importance for you in defining a profession? Are there other characteristics that we've omitted but that you feel are critical in defining a profession?

Given this apparent confusion about what constitutes a profession, why do any of us become language teachers? Why did you?

ANDY'S DECISION

Andy Curtis

Why did I leave a career as a hospital technician to become a teacher? Good question! I'd like to say it was a well-thought-out and much-considered move, but it was really much more a leap of faith than a carefully planned career change.

Ironically, some of the key things that made me leave the National Health Service (NHS) all those years ago are some of the same things that I think now are adversely affecting education. The NHS was health care provided by the British Labour government, paid for out of tax revenues, and premised on the belief that ability to pay should not determine the quality of health care received. But one of the first things that the right-wing Conservative party did, as soon as it got into power, was to start dismantling that service, replacing it with a private health care system. That meant that, after a very short while, it felt as if everything we did was reduced to dollars and *non*sense.

We eventually found out that the endless stream of memos about cost cutting was being sent by people who'd been recruited from industry (because they had track records of financial success) and given large, plush offices and cash bonuses based on their ability to cut costs! The man from the cookie factory was in charge of making decisions that directly affected the chances of survival of the premature newborns in the special care baby unit. The day I woke up with that thought was the day I knew I had to leave medicine. Once we've realized such personal truths, there is no turning back.

The other main reason for leaving medicine (ironically in relation to teaching) was the "de-skilling" of the paramedic profession. When I started, carrying out a biochemical assay took skill, manual dexterity, an eye for detail, and was more a craft than a science. We were required and happy to spend quite a bit of time on the wards, with patients, their families, and other medical staff, sometimes even seeing life itself begin and end. But with the coming of automated analyses, in all the excitement about the advantages of faster, cheaper, and (it has to be said) more accurate and reliable measurements, was lost the fact that we now did little more than feed small glass vials of bodily fluids into large machines. The craft side, the people-intense nature of the profession, was disappearing.

After all that negative but cathartic venting, and on a more positive note, that's where teaching came in. I believed then, as I still do now, that no amount of automation, from language labs to web-based teaching, will ever fully replace the personal nature of teaching and learning. Yes, teaching is sometimes too intense, and yes, we do take it too personally sometimes. But give me the joys and pains of this work any day of the week over any other job I've ever done.

About the money and prestige. With de-skilling also comes a loss of prestige. Indeed, at the time I left hospital work, some of the social-political commentators even said that it was part of the government's plan (i.e., as a way of making the public less sympathetic about our demands and complaints) to portray medical technicians as little more than over-qualified lab rats with inflated egos. And as for the money, I was lucky. At a fairly young age, I was able to see things that just force you, at times to the point where you want to scream, to consider what you really value.

For me this strong reaction, after more than 10 years, is proof, beyond even the most unreasonable of doubts, of the value of going inside ourselves, and thinking, writing, and talking about who we are and what we do, as professionals and as people.

CLOSING COMMENTS

In this chapter, we have explained why we feel it is important to pursue professional development, and summarized some of the variables that influence the success of that pursuit. The structure of this book overtly supports the idea of teachers managing their own professional development. We add to our theoretical basis in Chapter 2, where we examine self-awareness and self-observation, followed by a discussion of reflective teaching in Chapter 3. Then we consider five professional development procedures that can be practiced by individual teachers (though some can be collaboratively conducted too): keeping teaching journals (Chapter 4), using case studies (Chapter 5), language learning (Chapter 6), videotaping (Chapter 7), and action research (Chapter 8). Next we investigate procedures that require collaboration with colleagues: peer observation (Chapter 9), team teaching (Chapter 10), and mentoring and coaching (Chapter 11). Teaching portfolios (described in Chapter 12) involve a compilation of many such procedures. Finally, in Chapter 13, we return to "the heart of the paradox" (Edge, 1992, 3) and take a retrospective look at what we've covered.

Each chapter contains Frameworks sections that describe the particular approach, its underlying principles, related research and theory, and caveats or pitfalls to avoid when using the approach. In the Teachers' Voices sections we hear from teachers who have used the various procedures we are discussing. Sometimes these voices will be our own, either collectively or individually, and in both the Frameworks and the Teachers' Voices sections, we will use our first names or first-person pronouns to refer to us three authors. There are also places in the text where *we* and *our* will be used to refer to all of us, as members of a wider community of professionals. Most of these references are signaled by explicit phrases, such as "We, as teachers, can all benefit from…." The individual reader, or group of readers, is consistently addressed as "you" throughout the book. We hope this casual style will help to make the book user-friendly and the ideas accessible. We also hope you will not be troubled by the presence of both British and American spellings. We have maintained the original spelling of the authors we have quoted.

In the final Investigations section of each chapter, we offer suggestions for further reading, as well as additional tasks you can do to deepen your understanding of the approaches to professional development described in that chapter. The tasks involve a number of familiar formats: compare and contrast, write a definition, observe a class, list the pros and cons, analyze a transcript, and so on. Other task types may be less commonly used in teacher development (write a script, draw a timeline, interview a teacher, have an e-mail conversation, tell a story, react to a memo, etc.), but we hope they will be engaging. Also we have tried to design tasks that can be done either by individuals or by groups (e.g., of classmates or colleagues), but our strong recommendation is that you share the results of these tasks, whenever you can, with professionally oriented others. Indeed, we hope these ideas will be useful to you, whether you teach English or another modern language, whether you are a native or a nonnative speaker of the language you teach, and whether you are an experienced teacher or new to the field. We also hope that you will enjoy reading this book, as we have enjoyed writing it.

1.9 *Tasks for Development*

The following tasks are designed to provide opportunities for engagement with the concepts introduced in this chapter. We also hope you will be able to make connections between these concepts and your own personal experience.

1. Review the reasons given in this chapter for pursuing professional development. Are there other reasons you can suggest that we haven't discussed? If so, please list them.

   Now choose the three reasons (from your list and ours) that are the most important or compelling to you at this time. Please rank them in order of their importance to you. If you are working with a group, it will be helpful to share your rank-ordered list with your classmates or colleagues. You could also tally how often each reason was selected as first, second, or third most important by members of the group.

   Now imagine yourself working as a language teacher 10 or 20 years from now. Would your top three reasons for pursuing professional development change in that future time frame? If so, how? Why? If not, why not?

2. Skim the Table of Contents of this book and predict how the topics are intended to help you develop self-awareness and your skills in self-observation. Some may be obvious. (For example, by watching video-tapes of our teaching, we may become aware of behaviors we didn't know we were exhibiting.) Others may be more subtle.

3. Think about the sources of ideas about teaching (*what* teachers change) and the motivation for adopting new procedures, ideas, theories, etc. (*why* teachers change). Each of these can be either internal or external, as depicted in the grid below (adapted from Bailey, 1992, 262):

	Internal Motivation	**External Motivation**
Internal Sources of Ideas	1	2
External Sources of Ideas	3	4

So, for example, a change in quadrant 1 would represent a change we ourselves thought of, as teachers, and that we undertook for our own reasons. A change in quadrant 4 might be one suggested by a supervisor and motivated by advice to implement the suggested procedure before the supervisor's next visit.

Think of an example from your experience that illustrates each of the four quadrants above. Bailey (ibid.) has hypothesized that the numbers in the grid represent the likelihood that a true and lasting change will take place. That is, self-generated ideas that are sustained by internal motivation are the most likely to occur, and so on, while other-suggested, externally motivated changes are the least likely to occur. Does your experience support this hypothesis? Why or why not?

4. Throughout this book we will introduce many procedures that you could use to promote your own professional development. One that we would like to suggest you begin now, as you finish Chapter 1, is to keep a log of your own professional development activities. This record can be a very simple exercise, using a notebook or a computer file, in which you list the date, what professional development activity you tried, and what the

apparent results were. Or it can be a more elaborate record of your goals and efforts to develop your professional abilities.

As you read this book, we would like to encourage you to write at least your reactions to the ideas presented in each chapter, and to develop your reflective skills as you do so. This process could entail keeping a professional development journal in which you describe your initiatives in some detail and introspect about the outcomes. If your entries are based on activities in this book, we suggest you record the book title and page number as well as the date, so that you can easily come back to this book and reread the relevant sections as your ideas develop.

5. Talk to an experienced teacher who has not read this chapter, and ask him or her the questions David and Kathi were addressing in the first Teacher's Voice section above:

    A. How do you learn, as a teacher?

    B. What doesn't help you to grow as a teacher? Why?

If you are working with a group it may be informative to compare the answers to these questions from several different teachers, to see if any patterns emerge.

6. Do you remember the definitions of *metaphors* and *similes* from your high school or other English classes? Think about these definitions for a moment and try to recall any metaphors or similes used in this chapter. Throughout this book you will encounter many figurative uses of language. Please be aware of the metaphors, similes, and analogies that appear, since we will return to this issue in the Tasks following the last chapter.

Suggested Readings

David Nunan and Clarice Lamb (1996) wrote *The Self-Directed Teacher* because, "In the final analysis, all teachers have to develop and refine their own teaching style" (xiii). The book contains practical ideas for managing the learning process. It also has numerous projects that investigate various aspects of teaching such as teacher-talk, managing group work, and using resources in the classroom.

The article that started the collaboration among the three of us discusses three procedures that each receive chapter-length treatment in this book: teachers' journals, teaching portfolios, and videotaping (Bailey, Curtis, and Nunan, 1998).

Donald Freeman and Jack Richards (1996) have edited a book entitled *Teacher Learning in Language Teaching*. We cite some of the articles in later chapters of this book, but we recommend the entire volume.

Christine Pearson Casanave and Sandra Schechter (1997) have edited a collection of essays by some of the leaders in our field. Each chapter addresses the author's emergence as a professional, and each is written in an entertaining, personal style.

Dale Lange (1990) has written an article called "A Blueprint for a Teacher Development Program." It provides a general model of teacher development and is the source of the definition of professional development we use here.

In *Language Teaching Awareness: A Guide to Exploring Beliefs and Practices*, Jerry Gebhard and Bob Oprandy (1999) define an exploratory approach to professional awareness. Their book explains and illustrates processes teachers can use to open up "avenues of awareness" about what they and their students do in classes, what they believe about teaching and learning, and who they are (becoming) as teachers. Jerry Gebhard (1996) has also discussed the central factors in teacher self-development.

If you would like to learn about some of the research on burnout, we suggest you read *Burnout—The Cost of Caring*, by Christina Maslach (1982). It contains many quotes from practitioners—akin to the Teachers' Voices in this book—which illustrate the problem. Maslach also provides several helpful research-based suggestions about preventing and combating burnout.

As mentioned above, Martha Pennington and Belinda Ho conducted a survey (1995) to determine the extent to which ESL educators suffer from burnout. We have only cited a little of their article here, and it is well worth reading.

Julian Edge (1992) has written a short, readable book entitled *Cooperative Development: Professional Development through Cooperation with Colleagues*. This book has influenced our thinking here and in several of the chapters that follow.

Bailey (1992) reported on research in which she asked language teachers in the United States and Japan to think of a positive, lasting change they had made in their teaching, and then to explain what, why, and how they had accomplished that change. The paper starts with a review of several concepts derived from the research on innovation.

Two other books in the TeacherSource series explore, in different ways, some of the topics raised in this volume. Donald Freeman's book, *Doing Teacher Research: From Inquiry to Understanding* (1998a), and Karen Johnson's volume, *Understanding Language Teaching: Reasoning in Action* (1999), are both good sources of ideas for professional development.

2

SELF-AWARENESS AND SELF-OBSERVATION: CORNERSTONES

The classroom practices of language teachers are of interest to many different people. Program administrators and supervisors are interested in knowing whether the teacher's instructional practices are relevant to the program's goals and objectives. Students are interested in knowing whether the activities and experiences the teacher provides are helping them develop their language skills. And researchers are interested in studying the nature of the discourse teachers use in classrooms and the interactional structure of lessons. But those with the greatest interest in knowing what teachers do in classrooms are teachers themselves. All teachers want to know what kind of teachers they are and how well they are doing. A supervisor's evaluations and students' grades are ways of assessing this, but a more direct source of information for teachers is regular observation of their own teaching. Although few language teachers avail themselves of this resource on a regular basis, self-monitoring has much to recommend it as a component of the teacher's ongoing professional development (Richards, 1990, 118).

This chapter and the next, on reflective teaching, provide the springboard for all the concepts in this book. We will use the frameworks introduced here in subsequent chapters as we examine how teachers develop professionally.

Self-awareness and self-observation are the cornerstones of all professional development. They are essential ingredients, even prerequisites, to practicing reflective teaching. This chapter examines the construct of awareness, how we promote it, and how it functions in professional development.

2.1 WHERE, WHAT, WHEN, WHO, HOW, AND WHY?

This task is an expanded version of an investigation in Chapter 1. Think about a situation in which you felt you really learned something about being a teacher. Try to remember the context clearly. If you were teaching at the time, where were you teaching and what was the subject? Who were your students? What did you learn? How did your learning experience happen? Why did it happen at that particular time?

If you are a new teacher, how have you learned about teaching? Think about a specific instance and answer the questions above. If you are working on this task by yourself, write a page or so about this learning experience and save it. If you are working with a group, share your stories. (It will be helpful later, when we examine case studies, if you tape-record these conversations.) Are there any patterns in these stories? If so, what general statements can you make about how teachers learn?

AWARENESS, ATTITUDE, KNOWLEDGE, AND SKILLS

Diane Larsen-Freeman (1983, 266) has written that teachers need the following in order to "make informed choices" about their teaching: (1) heightened awareness; (2) a positive attitude that allows one to be open to change; (3) various types of knowledge needed to change; and (4) the development of skills. Since this chapter is about being self-aware, Larsen-Freeman's comments about the awareness component of this framework are particularly apt (ibid.):

> I cannot make an informed choice unless I am aware that one exists. Awareness requires that I give attention to some aspect of my behavior or the situation I find myself in. Once I give that aspect my attention, I must also view it with detachment, with objectivity, for only then will I become aware of alternative ways of behaving, or alternative ways of viewing the situation, and only then will I have a choice to make.

We agree. In fact, we feel that awareness is a necessary (but not a sufficient) condition for professional development to occur. Donald Freeman (no relation, but a colleague of Diane) used these same concepts in developing a descriptive model of the constituents of teaching (1989a, 36), which is reprinted here as Figure 2.1.

Figure 2.1: Descriptive Model of Teaching: The Constituents

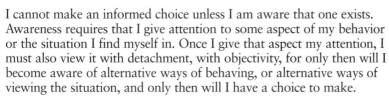

AWARENESS triggers and monitors attention to:

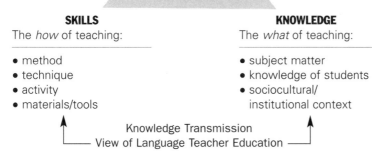

ATTITUDE
A stance toward self, activity, and others that links intrapersonal dynamics with external performance and behaviors

SKILLS
The *how* of teaching:

- method
- technique
- activity
- materials/tools

KNOWLEDGE
The *what* of teaching:

- subject matter
- knowledge of students
- sociocultural/ institutional context

Knowledge Transmission
View of Language Teacher Education

Freeman's model portrays the relationship among these four key constituents:

1. *Awareness* serves the function of triggering our attention to attitude, skills, and knowledge.
2. *Attitude* is described as a "stance toward self, activity, and others" (ibid.).
3. *Skills*, which constitute the "*how* of teaching," include our methods, techniques, activities, materials, and other tools (ibid.).
4. *Knowledge* embodies "the what of teaching," which includes our subject matter and our knowledge of the students, as well as the sociocultural and institutional context (ibid.).

According to Freeman, the traditional knowledge transmission model of teacher education only addresses the last two components—skills and knowledge. Yet long-lasting change and development must start with our awareness and our attitudes.

2.2 *YOUR ATTITUDES, AWARENESS, SKILLS, KNOWLEDGE*

Using the framework in Figure 2.1, think of a situation in which you feel you learned something in terms of your attitude, your awareness, your skills, and/or your knowledge. What did you learn and how did the learning occur? Make notes in a grid like the following:

	What I Learned	How I Learned
Awareness		
Attitude		
Skills		
Knowledge		

SELF-AWARENESS

What is awareness? According to Freeman (1989a, 33) "*awareness* is the capacity to recognize and monitor the attention one is giving or has given to something. Thus, one acts on or responds to the aspects of a situation of which one is aware."

The use of another framework will help us better understand the concept. The box diagram below is known as the "Johari Window" (Luft and Ingram, 1969). The unlikely title derives from the fact that it was designed by two men named Joseph Luft and Harry Ingram.

Figure 2.2: The Johari Window

	Known to Self	Unknown to Self
Known to Others	Open Self	Blind Self
Unknown to Others	Secret Self	Hidden Self

The Johari Window depicts the idea that things are either known or not known to us, ourselves, as individuals, and also known or not known to others. So, for instance, a teacher may feel quite nervous while being observed by a peer or a supervisor, but not reveal that anxiety to the observer. This situation falls in the "secret self" quadrant of the Johari Window. In contrast, a teacher may not realize that he or she is calling on the students on one side of the room but not the other, although a classroom visitor may quickly notice the uneven turn distribution pattern. This case would be an example of the "blind self."

Awareness consists initially of realizing something, of becoming cognizant. When we refer to *self-awareness*, we mean being (or becoming) cognizant of something about ourselves. In terms of the Johari Window, something previously unknown to oneself becomes known. In this sense, awareness involves both a moment (the act of becoming aware) and a state (being aware).

Leo van Lier (1998, 131), building on the work of cognitive scientists, has described four levels of consciousness, of which *awareness* is one:

Level 1: *Global ("intransitive") consciousness* is "just being alive and awake."

Level 2: *Awareness* is what van Lier calls "transitive" consciousness, that is, consciousness *of* something. It involves "perceptual activity of objects and events in the environment, including attention, focusing, and vigilance."

Level 3: *Metaconsciousness* is one's "awareness of the activity of the mind...."

Level 4: *Voluntary action, reflective processes,* and *mindfulness* are "deliberate and purposeful engagement in actions."

While van Lier was originally discussing consciousness in language learning, these four levels of consciousness can be related to teaching as well.

Presumably all of us are at least conscious when we teach (Level 1). What van Lier calls Level 2 (awareness) entails attention and focusing. Level 3, metaconsciousness, is divided into two sublevels: practical awareness (in our case, doing teaching) and discursive awareness (talking about doing teaching). Finally, Level 4 consists of critical awareness. In discussing consciousness and language, van Lier says that "as consciousness develops and becomes more richly layered, it becomes more intertwined with language" (ibid., 10). The fourth level in this model entails both mindfulness and intentionality—at this level, according to van Lier, "awareness and self come together to produce a sense of identity" (ibid.). We would argue that successful professional development necessarily entails repeatedly moving from Level 2, awareness, into Level 3, metaconsciousness, and on to Level 4, critical awareness.

The importance of metaconsciousness is discussed by Harri-Augstein and Thomas (1981, 25). They state that "freedom exists in the acquisition of a meta-language in which to reflect upon and therefore negotiate how one represents and uses meaning in language." Through metaconsciousness human beings create new meaning systems, and with "these new meaning systems we have greater freedom to explore the nature of the universe and so change our minds" (ibid.). In other words, by becoming aware, and by developing language with which to discuss that awareness, we find opportunities for professional development—even professional emancipation.

2.3 *A Three-Part Task*

You can use the frameworks introduced in this chapter as a way of stimulating your thinking about change. Here is a three-part task based on the Johari Window, printed above as Figure 2.2.

Try to recall an instance in which you were working as your "secret self"—for example, where you knew something about your teaching that others (your students, your colleagues, a supervisor) did not know. Now imagine what might have been gained (or risked) by moving to the "open self" quadrant by revealing your private knowledge to others.

Think of a time when someone showed or taught you something about your own teaching. In other words, try to recall an instance when you were functioning in the "blind self" quadrant and someone else helped you to move to the "open self" zone.

What were the similarities and differences between these two experiences? Which, if either, had the more profound or long-lasting effect on your development as a teacher? (If you don't have teaching experience, try to complete these tasks and answer these questions based on some other aspect of your life.)

Self-Observation

This book is fundamentally about self-awareness, and how we ourselves can bring about positive changes in our teaching. One way to increase our self-awareness is to monitor or observe our own behavior as teachers. Jack Richards (1990, 118) explains that self-observation is "a systematic approach to the observation, evaluation, and management of one's own behavior... for the purposes of achieving a better understanding and control over one's behavior." How is such self-monitoring done? Usually it begins with a simple process of data collection. Richards continues:

> In language teaching, self-monitoring refers to the teacher making a record of a lesson, either in the form of a written account or an audio or video recording of a lesson, and using the information obtained as a source of feedback on his or her teaching (ibid.).

He adds that such self-monitoring "complements, rather than replaces, other forms of assessment, such as feedback from students, peers, or supervisors" (ibid.).

Richards states that self-monitoring can help teachers in at least four ways (ibid., 119). First, for most of us, the amount of time available for professional development is quite short when compared to the length of our teaching careers, even though professional development should ideally continue throughout our teaching lives. Richards feels (and we agree) that self-monitoring can provide us with feedback for our ongoing professional growth, even within the constraints of our busy schedules. Second, self-monitoring can lead to critical reflection about our work, which is an important component of being able to improve. In addition, it can help us "better understand [our] own instructional process," (ibid.), thereby bridging the gap between what we actually do and what we think we do. Finally, self-monitoring relocates the responsibility for improving teaching squarely with us as individual teachers (rather than with external agents, such as supervisors).

In this chapter, we are intentionally using the term *self-observation* instead of *self-monitoring* because *to monitor* implies checking on something relative to an existing standard or expectation. To promote development, and even risk-taking, we are taking a more neutral stance toward thinking about our teaching. *Self-observation* implies a professional curiosity—watching, listening, and thinking without necessarily judging.

Richards (ibid., 129–130) suggests the following steps for teachers who are interested in beginning to change their teaching: (1) Decide what aspect of your teaching you are interested in learning more about or you wish to improve; (2) narrow your choices to those that seem most important to you; (3) develop an action plan to address the specific area you have identified; and (4) decide on a time frame for carrying out your goals.

Steps 1 and 2 above are largely internal cognitive steps. Step 3, developing a plan of action, however, is greatly aided by collecting data because the very act of recording events often leads to new awarenesses. For example, while teaching EFL at the Chinese University of Hong Kong, Kathi kept a journal about her lower-intermediate speaking and listening classes. For two semesters, she wrote in her journal each day she taught. In the process she summarized the lessons, evaluated her own work, thought about future lessons, and so on. The ongoing practice of making diary entries led her to some surprising insights, including a growing awareness of what she called "the vocabulary explanation trap." By rereading her journal, she found that her classes felt sluggish for the first month of the term. In spite of her teaching experience, her intellectual understanding of learner-centered classrooms, and her familiarity with the research on Asian learners' classroom participation patterns, she still had trouble getting the students to speak in class. By writing in her teaching journal she realized that she was unwittingly running a teacher-fronted classroom by over-explaining idioms and vocabulary items.

When Kathi realized, by writing in her journal, what she was doing, she made a conscientious effort *not* to explain vocabulary items unasked—and if asked, she got the students to explain to their peers instead of doing the talking herself. This example illustrates the fact that "much of what happens in teaching is unknown to the teacher" (Richards and Lockhart, 1994, 3–4). The solution to Kathi's problem came directly out of an awareness triggered by keeping a journal. (The use of teachers' journals as vehicles for professional development is covered in Chapter 4.)

The act of making systematic journal entries over time illustrates what Donald Schön (1983) has called "reflection-on-action"—that is, carefully thinking about our teaching before and/or after the teaching event. However, teachers can also critically analyze their teaching while they are in the midst of it. This latter process he called "reflection-in-action" (ibid.). Both concepts are discussed in more detail in Chapter 3. Here, we will use the following Teachers' Voices section to provide an illustration of how these ideas relate to self-awareness.

This vignette (reprinted from Bailey, 1998a, 43–45) illustrates how "puzzles of practice" (Russell and Munby, 1991, 165) led Kathi to a new awareness about someone she had considered to be a problem student. This story is reprinted here in part because it illustrates van Lier's (1998) four levels of consciousness, as well as Schön's (1983) concepts of reflection-in-action and reflection-on-action.

Kathi Bailey

KATHI LEARNS FROM PA'A

I once team taught a content course on learning styles and strategies to a group of mixed-level ESL students in California. One of the students in the class was a young Asian woman whom we will call "Pa'a." She had been orphaned as a child and her schooling had been interrupted at a very early age when she was forced into a life of selling flowers on street corners to earn her keep. Pa'a had enrolled in our Intensive ESL Program, where she hoped to learn enough English to attend a junior college. Her progress in academic English was very slow, however, and her teachers sometimes got frustrated because she seemed to be inattentive in class, to need constant extra help in doing activities, and even to disrupt lessons by not following the instructions.

One day in the learning styles and strategies class, the students were to complete a grid activity individually and then compare their results in pairs. I explained the activity carefully and everyone got to work except Pa'a, who looked at her neighbors' papers but didn't start doing the task. She called me to her desk and asked me to explain what she was supposed to do. I was very puzzled at her request because I had tried to explain the task clearly and several students whose listening proficiency was lower than Pa'a's had gotten right to work. Fortunately, my team teacher was able to work with the other students as needed. So I sat down next to Pa'a's desk and explained the task again, carefully monitoring my speech to pitch it precisely to her level. She gave me positive back-channeling (nodding, smiling, and saying "yes") throughout this brief explanation and looked as though she understood completely. When I finished, I asked her if she understood what I had said. Pa'a answered, "Yes. But what should I do?"

At that point I was more puzzled than ever. I was sure she had been attending to our one-on-one instructions session, and I was reasonably sure that the vocabulary and structures I had used were well within her grasp. To sort out where the confusion lay, I asked Pa'a to tell me what she *did* understand, step-by-step. To my surprise she was able to repeat my verbal instructions very clearly—almost word for word. I congratulated her, praised her for listening so closely, and encouraged her to get started on the task. Pa'a smiled and thanked me and asked, "But what should I do?"

I was dumbfounded. No wonder her teachers were getting frustrated. But clearly Pa'a was trying. She had understood and recalled everything I'd said. What was the problem? I looked around the room and saw that my team-teaching partner had the class well in hand. Most of the other students had finished their individual tasks and were comparing their grids with others. But Pa'a's paper remained blank, the apparently understood task as yet not started. I decided to work part of the task with Pa'a, to shift modalities and see if another approach would work. The result, of course, was that I learned a profound lesson.

As every language teacher knows, the framework of a grid is a powerful stimulus for thought and conversation, because the cells in the grid represent the conceptual intersection of whatever variable is represented by the horizontal axis with the variable represented by the vertical axis. The grid format can be used to practice many academic concepts. To practice math, for instance, variables 1 and 2 can represent numbers and the students' task can be to multiply the number on the horizontal axis by the number on the vertical axis and write the product in the cell. Or in a world geography "fact hunt" (like a treasure hunt), the horizontal axis of the grid can display a list of countries and the vertical axis can stipulate facts to be determined about each country (capital, population, main exports, etc.). The students then fill in the cells in the grid by looking up the information about the various countries in an encyclopedia or by interviewing their classmates about their home countries, if they are in a multilingual ESL class. These are tasks that every fourth-grader can do.

Just then I realized that Pa'a is not every fourth-grader. In fact, it's doubtful that she ever attended fourth grade. Suddenly the light dawned on *my* misunderstanding. I turned the paper over and on the upper half of the page I drew only the vertical lines of the grid. Together Pa'a and I labeled the columns. Then I folded the page in half and hid what we had just done. We then drew only the horizontal lines of the grid, and Pa'a labeled the rows. I then unfolded the page so that Pa'a could see the disassembled grid teased apart into its two components as we had drawn them—the vertical axis separated from the horizontal axis.

Then I had Pa'a put one hand on the vertically oriented picture (with her fingers pointing to the top of the page) and the other hand on the horizontally oriented sketch (with her fingers pointing to the side). Then, demonstrating with my own hands, I asked her to keep her hands pointed in the same directions but to lay one on top of the other.

Finally I turned the page over so that we were again looking at the original grid. I had Pa'a lay her overlapping hands on top of the grid and pointed out to her that the grid was really our two drawings superimposed: The vertical and the horizontal axes created the cells in the grid just as her overlapping fingers made windows in the lattice created by her hands.

When Pa'a seemed to grasp the notion of overlap, I took her two index fingers and drew down one of the columns with her right hand and across one of the rows with her left, until both fingers were located in the cell defined by that row and that column. We looked at the labels for the two columns and I asked her what to write in the cell. She didn't know, and a hurt, almost panicky look came into her eyes. I told her the answer and traced her two fingers back to the respective labels in the margins of the rows and columns. At that point she suddenly saw the relationship between the row and column labels and the concept I had written in the cell. She eagerly moved her index fingers to two other headings and traced them down and across to another cell, where she filled in the right answer. Pa'a continued to work on the task independently and eventually joined her classmates in the discussion of their grids.

Here's the lesson I learned: Pa'a had understood my English, and she had certainly been paying attention. What she had not understood was the formal framework of a two-dimensional grid—how two intersecting concepts create new concepts represented by and recorded in the individual cells of the grid. It was the framework she didn't understand and its connection to the writing and speaking activity the class was doing. Switching to a kinesthetic and visual explanation, using our hands to draw and model the grid, served Pa'a's learning style and conceptual development better than relying on the more abstract, academic aural channel (Bailey, 1998a, 43–45).

Pa'a's moment of awareness came when she understood how a grid depicts concepts through the interaction of two separate ideas. She became aware of a concept outside herself. For me as the teacher, however, there were several layers of awareness.

First, I was aware of some annoyance on my part that Pa'a had not begun the task on schedule with the other students. (I hope I kept this annoyance to myself and was therefore working in the "secret self" quadrant of the Johari Window.) Then as she revealed what I perceived to be sincere confusion, my annoyance changed first to feeling puzzled and then to befuddlement. Then it seemed possible to me that Pa'a had understood the English of my instructions but she didn't know how a grid works. Next, I wondered if changing to a kinesthetic and visual teaching mode (rather than an aural mode only) would help, since I was aware that Pa'a did not have a typical academic background. At another, more abstract level, I was aware that various learners favor different learning styles, and so a switch in teaching modality might help.

After the fact, while writing about the experience later, I realized that the concept of *formal schemata* explained the gap in Pa'a's understanding. *Formal schemata* are our existing knowledge structures about the form or shape a certain bit of discourse takes. (We know, for instance, that a newspaper want-ad is different from a newspaper editorial, and that both of these differ from other genres, such as sonnets, haiku, limericks, acceptance speeches, eulogies, etc.) *Content schemata*, on the other hand, are our existing knowledge structures about certain topics or subjects. (So, for example, one might read a newspaper editorial about taxes, capital punishment, the environment, the pros and cons of increased tourism, and so on. For each of these areas, we would have more or less knowledge about the topics.) While Pa'a had understood the basic English of my instructions, she lacked the formal schemata for using a grid.

2.4 *TASKS FOR DEVELOPMENT*

It is especially difficult to deny awareness gained though self-initiated data collection. For this reason, professional development practices based on such data collection are especially powerful (Bailey et al., 1998, 548–549). Throughout this book we will develop the themes of self-awareness and self-observation as the cornerstones of professional development. The following tasks are designed to help you integrate the ideas presented so far, whether you are working on your own or with a group of colleagues or classmates.

1. Revisit the story of Pa'a and identify any instances of Kathi's "reflection-in-action" and "reflection-on-action" as the story unfolds. Next, think of a salient teaching experience you have had in which some event during the lesson caused you to think attentively about what you were doing. What reflection-in-action occurred at that time? What reflection-on-action occurred after the lesson?

2. As noted above, Leo van Lier (1998, 131) has described four levels of consciousness. Using van Lier's definitions, try to identify an instance of each level of consciousness in Kathi's story about Pa'a.

   Level 1: *Global ("intransitive") consciousness,* "just being alive and awake"

   Level 2: *Awareness,* or consciousness of something

   Level 3: *Metaconsciousness* (awareness of the activity of the mind)

   Level 4: *Voluntary action, reflective processes,* and *mindfulness*

3. Sometimes we can gain awareness about the classroom by leaving it behind, and we can gain important insights about teaching by concentrating on learning. It can be very instructive to observe someone learning something outside the environment of a formal classroom, and that is the focus of this investigation. In this activity you will

observe one person who is the knower and who provides guidance to the person(s) learning the skill or knowledge, but there should be no classroom teacher involved and the learning event should take place outside the typical classroom setting. Here are some examples of the types of things that would be appropriate foci for this investigation:

- a small child learning a physical skill such as catching a ball or flying a kite;
- children learning a new computer game, a craft, a song, or a physical game;
- a coaching situation (swimming, a team sport, golf, etc.);
- people learning to play a card game, mah-jong, or a board game;
- people at a Senior Citizens' Center learning a dance step or doing handicrafts;
- people learning tai chi in a park;
- someone in a physical therapy context (learning to walk again, learning to use a brace or a prosthetic device);
- and someone in an on-the-job training context, or serving an apprenticeship.

There may be one learner or several in the situation you observe, so long as you are not one of the participants.

Watch the person(s) learning for at least 30 minutes. Document the observation in some contextually appropriate way (e.g., through fieldnotes, audiotaping, videotaping, etc.). Try to see how people learn when they are not in classrooms. What are the apparent psychological processes involved in the acquisition of new knowledge and/or skills?

Next, document your thinking about the learning you observed. Write as many statements as you can to complete the phrase "People learn when...." If you are working with a group, each person should complete this statement. Compare the various points of view. Are there notable similarities or differences? What generalizations can be drawn from these statements?

4. Appendix A of this book contains a transcript of a lesson David taught (pages 249–261). Please read through the transcript and look for information about the teacher's awareness, attitude, skills, and knowledge. Make notes about each of these topics on the transcript.

Of course, in this case you have access only to the transcript. As a result your understanding of the lesson may feel somewhat limited. Imagine that you had a chance to talk with David about this lesson. Think of one question about each of the four levels of awareness listed above that you would like to ask him.

Suggested Readings

Diane Larsen-Freeman's (1983) and Donald Freeman's (1989a) articles are both seminal papers in this field. If you are interested in the interplay of awareness, attitude, knowledge, and skills, reading these two articles is a great way to start expanding your horizons.

The *Language Teaching Matrix* (Richards, 1990) contains several chapters about professional development for language teachers. The one closest to our topic here is Chapter 7, "The Teacher as Self-Observer: Self-Monitoring in Teacher Development."

Joseph Luft's and Harry Ingram's (1969) book, *Of Human Interaction*, while not related to language teaching, is a very interesting treatise about human development. Like Richards (1990), we have found the "Johari Window" to be a useful heuristic device.

Katherine Samway (1994) has written a very helpful article entitled "But It's Hard to Keep Fieldnotes While Also Teaching." She describes three convenient systems for accurately noting observations in our own classrooms.

Leo van Lier's little book *Introducing Language Awareness* (1995) is a very helpful, user-friendly introduction to the topic. The background information he provides about awareness in general has influenced our thinking in this chapter.

3

REFLECTIVE TEACHING: LOOKING CLOSELY

...The process of learning to teach continues throughout a teacher's entire career....[N]o matter how good a teacher education program is, at best, it can only prepare teachers to begin teaching. When embracing the concept of reflective teaching, there is often a commitment by teachers to internalize the disposition and skills to study their teaching and become better at teaching over time, a commitment to take responsibility for their own professional development. This assumption of responsibility is a central feature of the idea of the reflective teacher (Zeichner and Liston, 1996, 6).

This chapter is about *reflective teaching*, a concept that underpins the rest of the book. It is structured around a series of questions that we hope will enhance your understanding of what has become a complex and widely discussed topic, in both first and second language education. We begin with the question of what is meant by reflective teaching. We will see that there are many different definitions available in the teacher cognition literature today, but all of them build upon the ideas of self-awareness and self-observation introduced in Chapter 2.

3.1 *WHAT IS REFLECTION?*

If one of your students asked you the meaning of reflection, *what would you say? Take a moment to write your definition(s) of* reflection. *How many different definitions can you write? It will be helpful if you write your definitions before you read further. (Save your list, because the end-of-chapter Investigations will lead back to these issues.)*

Mark Manasse

MARK STARTS TEACHING

Kathi: So Mark, congratulations on your new teaching job. Who are your students and what are you teaching?

Mark: Thanks, Kathi! I am very excited. I have six ESL students, four from Japan, one from Vietnam, and one from Korea. It's challenging because they all have varying degrees of experience, from an extreme beginning level to high intermediate. They are fun to teach, though—outgoing, friendly, and extremely willing to learn.

Right now, I'm teaching several classes, which is hard because I'm still going to school myself. I'm teaching two reading classes, a TOEFL grammar class, an autobiographical writing class, and a community experience class where I take them on field trips. For instance, I took them to the Monterey Police Department this morning, and they got to try on handcuffs and bulletproof vests. They loved it, and so did I!

Kathi: Have you had any teaching experience in the past?

Mark: I have very little experience teaching. Last semester I volunteered in a conversation class where I now work. After that, I taught a creative writing class for a month. I started teaching regularly a month ago, and I have really enjoyed it. It's a challenge, but I feel like it has taught me so much about what works and what doesn't work in a real classroom setting. Experience is definitely the key.

Kathi: I understand you decided you wanted to add an element of reflective practice to your teaching. What is it exactly that you are doing?

Mark: Well, I thought it would be good to keep a journal of my teaching from the outset of my professional development. What better way to improve myself than to start thinking about my teaching practice at the beginning, right? So I decided to keep a journal in combination with opening up my class to observers on a regular basis. That way, I can get a good idea of what others see in me as a novice teacher and what it is I see in myself. Comparing these two kinds of information, I feel, will propel me into becoming a better teacher much faster than if I just went to class every day and didn't think about what I was doing.

Kathi: What have you learned so far by doing this?

Mark: So far I have found that I am concerned with reaching (or not reaching) my lowest level student. Looking back through my journal, I notice that I mention him often. I feel like I am leaving him behind so that the rest of the class isn't bored. I'm trying to find ways to keep everyone involved. I think I am going to do pair work with him personally, and let the others work with each other instead, because they seem frustrated when they're placed in a group with him.

Some observers have told me that I look very organized and experienced, which is hilarious to me since those are the two things I worry about most: being unprepared and appearing like a novice. It is so helpful to get outside feedback because, as with most aspects in life, teaching included, we are our own worst critic and can dwell on parts of ourselves that are already developed. Because of this feedback, I feel more confident in my abilities, and more willing to focus on other areas of my teaching, like board work, which I might have not even thought about when I was preoccupied with my preparation.

Kathi: How often do you make entries in your journal?

Mark: I try to write in my journal after every class session, but there isn't always time. If I can't write immediately after class, I try to do so within the next few days so the class period is still fresh in my mind. I usually write for at least half an hour. I look forward to getting written feedback from my observers so I can start comparing that to what I have written. I have enjoyed the oral feedback, but I am excited to see what the observers have to say when they have had a chance to reflect a bit more.

DEFINITIONS OF REFLECTIVE TEACHING

Some definitions of reflective teaching emphasize a rather solitary process of introspection and retrospection, focusing specifically on a teacher's actions and thoughts before, during, or after lessons. Cruickshank and Applegate, for example, define reflective teaching as "the teacher's thinking about what happens in classroom lessons, and thinking about alternative means of achieving goals or aims" (1981, 4, as cited in Bartlett, 1990, 202). This version of reflective teaching could be practiced in isolation.

Richards and Lockhart's definition (1994,1) also suggests that reflective teaching can be carried out by individuals working alone. They say that in reflective teaching "teachers and student teachers collect data about teaching, examine their attitudes, beliefs, assumptions, and teaching practices, and use the information obtained as a basis for critical reflection about teaching." These authors note that reflective teaching can be practiced by both inservice and preservice teachers, so long as the persons have some current, ongoing teaching experience that can serve as the basis for reflection. (For example, in Mark Manasse's Teacher's Voice, we see a new teacher who is reflecting on his current teaching by keeping a journal and getting feedback from observers.)

Other definitions take a broader stance and embed the concept of reflection within the social and political contexts of programs, schools, and communities. For instance, a more socially oriented definition of reflective teaching comes from Zeichner and Liston, who work as elementary school teachers and teacher educators. For them, reflective teaching involves "a recognition, examination, and rumination over the implications of one's beliefs, experiences, attitudes, knowledge, and values as well as the opportunities and constraints provided by the social conditions in which the teacher works" (1996, 6). While the cognitive processes of recognition are still carried out by individuals, this definition emphasizes the social contexts in which our teaching occurs.

Zeichner and Liston were influenced by the work of John Dewey. They quote Dewey's definition of reflection as "active, persistent and careful consideration of any belief or practice in light of the reasons that support it and the further consequences to which it leads" (Zeichner and Liston, 1996, 9).

Leo Bartlett says reflection has a double meaning involving "the relationship between an individual's thought and action and the relationship between an individual teacher and his or her membership in a larger collective called society" (1990, 204). This analysis clarifies the apparent contrast between individual and social processes. Bartlett continues, "The first relationship involves the subjective meanings in teachers' heads. The second relationship explores consciously the relationship… between individual teaching actions and the purposes of education in society" (ibid., 204–205).

Another view of reflection is found in the work of Stephen Kemmis (1986, 5), who has been instrumental in promoting action research (see Chapter 8). He says,

> Reflection is not just an individual, psychological process. It is an action oriented, historically-embedded, social and political frame, to locate oneself in the history of a situation, to participate in a social activity, and to take sides on issues. Moreover the material on which reflection works is given to us socially and historically; through reflection and the action which it informs, we may transform the social relations which characterize our work and our working situation.

Here again we see the influence of the social context, but Kemmis highlights the added connection to action.

As mentioned in Chapter 2, a key distinction is often made between *reflection-in-action* (during our teaching) and *reflection-on-action* (before or after our teaching). Russell and Munby point out that reflection-on-action, which includes planning, preparation, and follow-up, is more familiar than reflection-in-action (Russell and Munby, 1991, 164; see also Munby and Russell, 1989). The former concept "refers to the ordered, deliberate, and systematic application of logic to a problem in order to resolve it; the process is very much within our control" (ibid.). In contrast, reflection-in-action happens very quickly as we are teaching.

Reflection-in-action can trigger on-line decision-making (Woods, 1996). When we are planning our lessons, we make *pre-active decisions*, but as we teach we are constantly engaged in making *interactive* or *on-line decisions*, because most lessons are "co-produced classroom conversations" (Allwright and Bailey, 1991, 25). Not all of the teaching and learning that occurs in classrooms happens according to our lesson plans, and certainly not everything we plan gets taught. To take this logic one step further, not everything we teach gets learned. This is partly because language teaching and learning are interactive: In order to be effective we must be able to respond to unexpected questions, to students' errors, to learning opportunities that arise.

The following Teachers' Voices section describes an event that took place when Kathi was a student in an intermediate Spanish class in California. The incident illustrates a teacher's on-line decision to incorporate a learner's comment as part of the lesson.

Teachers'
Voices

Kathi Bailey

One day, while we were rolling our double *rs* by repeating words like *ferrocarril* (railroad) and *herrero* (ironmonger), I remembered a Latin American proverb: *En casa de herrero, cuchillo de palo.* Although I muttered this proverb to myself, the teacher overheard me and asked me to explain it to the class. A rough translation is, "In the ironmonger's house, there are knives of wood." The actual meaning is that one's professional skills are not necessarily put to use in solving one's own problems. After I explained this idea to my classmates (in Spanish), they generated several examples—the crazy psychiatrist, the dentist whose children have rotten teeth, the shoemaker's barefoot children, the linguist who is a poor communicator, and so on. We chatted about this paradoxical phenomenon in Spanish for about five minutes in all.

When the lesson was over, I realized that the teacher had spontaneously allotted 10 percent of the 50-minute lesson to this unexpected topic, which I had unintentionally suggested. Because *I* accidentally nominated the topic, I *know* the instructor had not planned on this excursion from her pronunciation lesson. Later it occurred to me that this responsiveness was one of the things that we most appreciated about our teacher, so I began to watch for examples of such flexibility in my own teaching and in that of other teachers I observed (adapted from Bailey, 1996, 15–16).

Investigations

3.2 *DEPARTING FROM A LESSON PLAN*

If you have teaching experience, think of an occasion when a student's contribution caused you to depart from your lesson plan. What was the contribution? What did you do? Why did you choose this course of action? What was the result?

If you do not have any teaching experience, can you recall an occasion, like the event in Kathi's Spanish class, when you were aware of your teacher changing the lesson, based on the students' input? If so, try to answer the questions above, as you think your teacher might have answered them.

If you are working with a group of peers, it may be useful to collect several such stories and compare them. If you do, what are the common themes? Why do teachers choose to depart from their lesson plans?

In completing these tasks, you are engaged in reflection-on-action. Ironically, the focus of that reflection is reflection-in-action.

Frameworks

WHAT DO REFLECTIVE TEACHERS DO?

One way to understand something is to ask what is not an instance of the construct. Zeichner and Liston (1996, 1) point out that simply thinking about teaching does not necessarily constitute reflective teaching: "If a teacher never questions the goals and the values that guide his or her work, the context in which he or she teaches, or never examines his or her assumptions, then it is our belief that this individual is not engaged in reflective teaching." In other words, simply planning our lessons or thoughtfully marking papers does not necessarily entail reflective teaching. By definition, this practice involves critical examination of our motivation, thinking, and practice.

What do teachers do when they engage in reflective teaching? Claire Stanley (1998, 585) contends that

> ...developing of a reflective teaching practice can be represented as a series of phases: (a) engaging with reflection, (b) thinking reflectively, (c) using reflection, (d) sustaining reflection, and (e) practicing reflection. The phases do not represent a sequence that is followed but rather moments in time and particular experiences that constitute a particular phase.

These phases are not strictly linear. At "certain points in time, given personal and contextual circumstances, teachers may find themselves in any of the phases" (ibid.). Stanley's research with preservice and inservice teachers indicates that we can become more adept at reflective teaching. It is a skill that can be developed over time.

According to Zeichner and Liston (1996, 11), a reflective teacher:

- examines, frames, and attempts to solve the dilemmas of classroom practice;
- is aware of and questions the assumptions and values he or she brings to teaching;
- is attentive to the institutional and cultural contexts in which he or she teaches;
- takes part in curriculum development and is involved in school change efforts;
- and takes responsibility for his or her own professional development.

This practice must include "reflection about the unexpected outcomes of teaching because teaching, even under the best conditions, always involves unintended as well as intended outcomes" (ibid.). This element of unpredictability can lead us into troublesome areas. Sometimes reflection leads us to uncomfortable awareness:

> ...[T]eachers need to be able to consider their practice in an informed and dispassionate way. This implies an extensive knowledge base and an attitude of mind that is sufficiently courageous to face the reality of one's own teaching, which may at times be unpalatable (Birch, 1992, 284).

In other words, a certain level of maturity and openness is needed to address aspects of our "blind selves" (Luft, 1969).

Indeed, John Dewey (1933) felt that three key attitudes are necessary in order for teachers to be reflective: open-mindedness, responsibility, and wholeheartedness. Building on his work, Zeichner and Liston state that "open-mindedness and responsibility must be central components in the professional life of the reflective teacher." Wholehearted teachers "regularly examine their own assumptions and beliefs and the results of their actions and approach all situations with the attitude that they can learn something new" (1996, 11). Zeichner and Liston (ibid.) further cite Dewey as saying that reflection "emancipates us from merely impulsive and routine activity…[and] enables us to direct our actions with foresight and to plan according to ends in view of purposes of which we are aware" (Dewey, 1933, 17). That is, in order to be reflective, we must be open-minded, responsible, and wholehearted in our desire to improve.

3.3 *What Do You Think?*

How important are the three attitudes identified by Dewey (1933) for reflective teaching? Circle the number that best represents your view of each construct:

	Not Important				Very Important
Open-mindedness	1	2	3	4	5
Responsibility	1	2	3	4	5
Wholeheartedness	1	2	3	4	5

Now assess the extent to which you think you possess these attitudes:

	Not at All				To a Great Extent
Open-mindedness	1	2	3	4	5
Responsibility	1	2	3	4	5
Wholeheartedness	1	2	3	4	5

If you compare the same attribute on the two scales above (e.g., responsibility as rated on the two scales), how do your judgments of the importance of these traits match up with your assessment of these traits as part of your own attitudes?

FIVE DIMENSIONS OF REFLECTION

Zeichner and Liston describe five dimensions of reflection. The behaviors that characterize these dimensions range from split-second on-line decision-making to long-term reformulation of our practical theories. These five dimensions are depicted in Figure 3.1, which is reprinted from Zeichner and Liston (1996, 47):

Figure 3.1: Dimensions of Reflection

1. RAPID REFLECTION	Immediate and automatic Reflection-in-Action
2. REPAIR	Thoughtful Reflection-in-Action
3. REVIEW	Less formal Reflection-on-Action at a particular point in time
4. RESEARCH	More systematic Reflection-on-Action over a period of time
5. RETHEORIZING and REFORMULATING	Long-term Reflection-on-Action informed by public academic theories

We have added a double line between levels two and three to emphasize the fact that the first two dimensions occur during reflection-in-action, while the remaining three are part of reflection-on-action. We will examine each dimension in turn.

The first level, *rapid reflection*, is a type of "reflection-in-action," to use Schön's (1983) term. This is part of our on-line decision making while we are teaching. Of necessity, such decision making happens very fast, almost constantly, and often privately. This kind of rapid reflection happens so quickly that such responses are thought of as "routine and automatic" (Zeichner and Liston, 1996, 45).

The second dimension is called *repair* (not to be confused with *repair* in the sense of communication breakdowns or error treatment). Like rapid reflection, repair is a form of reflection-in-action, which occurs while we teach. In this case a teacher makes a decision to alter his or her behavior in response to cues from students (e.g., novel ideas that they contribute, evidence that they didn't understand, and so on).

Review, the third dimension, moves us into what Schön has called "reflection-on-action" (1983), which occurs before or after our teaching. In review, a teacher thinks about, discusses, or writes about some element of his or her teaching or the students' learning. As Zeichner and Liston note (1996, 46), review "is often interpersonal and collegial." Review can be as simple as an after-class conversation with colleagues, or it can be more systematic, such as writing a report on a child's progress.

The next dimension is called *research*. At this level "teachers' thinking and observation become more systematic and sharply focused around particular issues" (ibid.). This type of reflection is a long-term process that involves collecting data over time. Action research (see Chapter 8) and teaching journals (see Chapter 4) are two professional development procedures that entail this level of reflection.

The last dimension in Zeichner and Liston's model consists of *retheorizing and reformulating*. These processes are described as "more abstract and more rigorous than the other dimensions" (ibid.). In this dimension, "while teachers critically examine their practical theories, they also consider these theories in light of public academic theories" (ibid.). (In later chapters we will revisit this contrast when we discuss the interplay of teachers' experiential knowledge and the received knowledge of the field.) Retheorizing and reformulation are long-term processes that can continue for years.

Investigations

3.4 YOUR OWN USE OF REFLECTION

Review Figure 3.1 above, which Ziechner and Liston entitled "Dimensions of Reflection" (1996, 47). Which of these five dimensions of reflective teaching have you used? Write an example of each from your own experience.

If you feel you would like to utilize some of these dimensions more fully, which one(s) would you like to address? How would you begin to do so?

PENNY'S REFLECTIONS

As noted above, reflection-in-action sometimes leads us to depart from our lesson plans. The following example is from a writing lesson for lower intermediate ESL learners taught by Penny Partch. The students had brainstormed about their topics in groups, and then they explained to the class their group's preferred sequence for organizing the essay. At a certain point the students were having difficulty with the prepositions *in*, *on*, and *at*, so Penny drew three concentric circles on the chalkboard (like a bull's-eye or a target). She then quickly explained on the blackboard when to use each preposition, using the simple drawing as a framing device. The students copied the drawing from the board and then the writing lesson continued.

Kathi observed the lesson. Later, when she asked the teacher about this episode, Penny explained her decision to insert the mini-grammar lesson into the writing lesson. She was aware that the grammar explanation was a departure from her lesson plan, and even referred to it as "getting sidetracked." Yet she was also able to return to her lesson plan and to explain her choice to digress. Here is a part of the conversation after the lesson, when Kathi asked Penny about her decision to draw the target. Bracketed comments describe the speakers' nonverbal behavior during the conversation. Italics indicate a heavy stress on a particular word.

Penny Partch

Penny: Uhm [she pauses], it was a narrative that they were doing and it had a lot of prepositions in it.... They were born *in* this country, *on* this day, *at* this place. And it was just [she pauses] messy....I had devised my own little mini-lesson on how to present these prepositions...as a target with the largest circle being the *in*, the next circle *on*, and the most precise being the *at*. And so I just stopped what we were doing.... I did the bull's-eye and would write it around the circle. So *in* is a place, a country, a state, a town. *On* is a street or a corner. *At* is the address. Then the time, the month, the year....

Kathi: When you say you had done a little mini-lesson with your bull's-eye model...had you prepared *that* for that day, or was it something you'd done in the past...?

Penny: I've had it. I just had it in my mind.

Kathi: Okay. So, when you went into class, did you know you were going to do that—

Penny: No.

Kathi: Or you decided to do it in class?

Penny: I decided to—I had no idea I was going to do that....When you think about it, it's the same level year after year. It's always the same level. They have predictable problems. So I have my little grab bag of activities that I know might come up. I just, you *know* that. I didn't prepare for, for it for *that* lesson. Uhm, I was looking for something else. I wanted to work on, pretty much on the thesis statement. That's what I had in my mind to do that day. But they couldn't get beyond that. They were very frustrated with the surface level problem, and I think that's appropriate, to stop when they want to stop....

Kathi: Yeah. Did you get any reactions from it?

Penny: Yeah, they love that, that kind of stuff. They love grammary, pencilly, writey-down things. [We both laugh.]

Here we see Penny's in-class decision to focus briefly on the prepositions *in*, *on*, and *at* as an example of reflection-in-action—specifically of repair (Zeichner and Liston, 1996, 47). The teacher utilized the visual model of the target as an aid in explaining the relative specificity of *in*, *on*, and *at* as a result of her judgment of how the lesson was going (Bailey, 1996, 29–30). In discussing the lesson with Kathi later, Penny engaged in collaborative reflection-on-action.

Frameworks

WHY BOTHER?

Why should we bother with reflective teaching? The best reason is stated in the introduction to Zeichner and Liston's book:

> [M]any educational issues engage and affect our heads and our hearts. Teaching is work that entails both thinking and feeling and those who can reflectively think and feel will find their work more rewarding and their efforts more successful (Zeichner and Liston, 1996, xii).

Being successful involves continually improving our practice, but reflective teaching goes beyond the level of acquiring new techniques. As Bartlett points out, "[A]s teachers we have to transcend the technicalities of teaching and think beyond the need to improve our instructional techniques" (Bartlett, 1990, 205).

Improvement entails change—from a less desirable to a more desirable kind of practice. Such change demands that we look critically at ourselves: "Becoming reflective forces us to adopt a critical attitude to ourselves as individual second language teachers—to challenge our espoused personal beliefs about teaching" (ibid., 213). Richards and Nunan note that "experience alone is insufficient for professional growth, and that experience coupled with reflection is a much more powerful impetus for development" (1990, 201).

Throughout this book we will discuss practices that we as teachers can undertake on our own as we pursue professional development. However, we want to be clear from the outset that there is tremendous value to collegial communication in the development process. In highlighting the value of working with colleagues, Gary Birch draws a helpful analogy between practicing reflection and learning a new language:

> Reflection is potentially threatening. It involves the possible deconstruction of a belief system with which one has become familiar and its replacement with an alternative that may, in the initial stages, prove uncomfortable. In this it is analogous to the learning of another language, where an habitual system is discarded, to be replaced by an alien system of equal complexity, for which attempts at mastery may be traumatic (Birch, 1992, 290).

Under these circumstances, Birch adds, "the support of colleagues who are undertaking a similar process is highly desirable" (ibid.). In the next Teachers' Voices section, we hear John Fanselow's (1997, 166–167) ideas about the value of colleagues in our own professional development.

Teachers' Voices

John Fanselow

BLADES OF THE SCISSORS

…[S]eeking to find out for myself by myself, alone, is like trying to use a pair of scissors with only one blade. Simultaneously asking what difference my work with teachers makes in my own teaching and beliefs about teaching and the way I live provides the other blade of a pair of scissors for me. Scissors, to cut, like the tango, require two: a pair of blades. Without others, neither I nor anyone can find out much, as learning must be giving up as well as gaining.

The need I have for others to enable me to travel roads on my own at first seems to be paradoxical, if not contradictory. But I feel I need others to have experiences with so I can make choices. The insights, knowledge, and advice of others provides me with choices as well as stimulation. With choices, I can compare. Information and insights from others can also serve as benchmarks to see what degree the changes I perceive I am making in words I am, in fact, making in actions as well. Finally, I can make discoveries others might have already made my own.

CLOSING COMMENTS

So we return to the paradox highlighted in the various definitions of reflective teaching with which we began this chapter. Reflection consists largely of affective and cognitive processes practiced by individuals. Yet, such reflection, at least as part of reflective teaching, operates within and is about social processes: teaching and learning. This intertwining of individual and collegial efforts surfaces as a recurrent theme throughout the remaining chapters of this book.

3.5 *TASKS FOR DEVELOPMENT*

These end-of-chapter Tasks are intended to make the concept of reflective teaching less abstract. We hope that these and the Suggested Readings will be helpful in your exploration of reflective teaching.

1. The following list is adapted from Zeichner and Liston (1996, 6). It describes what reflective teachers do. For each item write two or three things that you do yourself (or would like to start doing) to practice reflective teaching.

   A. Examine, frame, and attempt to solve the dilemmas of classroom practice.

   B. Be aware of and question the assumptions and values you bring to teaching.

   C. Be attentive to the institutional and cultural contexts in which you teach.

   D. Take part in curriculum development and get involved in school change efforts.

   E. Take responsibility for your own professional development.

2. When Kathi first began thinking about reflective teaching, she was surprised to find how many definitions of *reflection* served as apt metaphors for the concept as it is used in reflective teaching. Here are some typical dictionary definitions (from *The Oxford English Dictionary*, 1994, 1541): (1) reflexive influence on the mind; (2) the action, on the part of surfaces, of throwing back light or heat; (3) the action of a mirror or other polished surface in exhibiting or reproducing the image of an object; (4) the action of bending, turning or folding

back; (5) the action of throwing back, or fact of being thrown or driven back; (6) reference, relation, connection; (7) the action of turning back or fixing the thoughts on some subject; meditation, deep or serious consideration; and (8) a thought or idea occurring to or occupying the mind (reprinted from Bailey, 1997, 3). Which of these items were also in your list from Investigation 3.1 (page 34)? Which of these definitions appeal to you as meanings of *reflection*, as the concept is used in reflective teaching?

Figure 2.1 is on p. 23.

3. You will recall that Figure 2.1 portrays *awareness, attitude, knowledge,* and *skills* as the constituents of teaching. How can the practice of reflective teaching promote professional development in each of these areas? Your replies may be speculative and abstract, or they could draw upon your own experience (or both).

Figure 2.2 is on p. 25.

4. Look back at the Johari Window, which is reprinted as Figure 2.2. How can reflective teaching promote change in each of the four quadrants of the model?

5. According to Dewey (1933), three key attitudes are needed in order for teachers to be reflective: open-mindedness, responsibility, and wholeheartedness. Think of an example in your teaching, planning, or follow-up when you exhibited these attitudes.

6. If you have teaching experience, you may have also had times when you felt a distinct lack of one or more of these attitudes. Think of a situation when it was difficult or impossible to be open-minded, responsible, and/or wholehearted. What were the conditions in which you were working? How does the instance differ from the context(s) described above, when you feel you did experience these positive attitudes?

7. Stanley (1998) discussed five "phases" of reflective teaching, while Zeichner and Liston (1996) described five "dimensions" of reflective teaching:

Five Phases of Reflective Teaching *(Stanley, 1998)*	**Five Dimensions of Reflection** *(Zeichner and Liston, 1996)*
1. Engaging with reflection	1. Rapid reflection
2. Thinking reflectively	2. Repair
3. Using reflection	3. Review
4. Sustaining reflection	4. Research
5. Practicing reflection	5. Retheorizing and reformulating

Based on what you've been reading in this chapter, what are the similarities and differences in the concepts embodied in these two frameworks? In other words, how do you compare and contrast these two lists? (Of course, your answer to these questions will be much richer if you read the authors' original accounts.)

8. As a next step, we suggest you compare the framework provided by Stanley's work and that of Zeichner and Liston with van Lier's four levels of consciousness (1998, 4), which were discussed in Chapter 2: (1) global (intransitive) consciousness, (2) awareness, (3) metaconsciousness, and (4) voluntary action, reflective processes, and mindfulness.

See p. 25 for van Lier's four levels of consciousness.

9. Which of the three frameworks identified in Task 8 above (van Lier's, Stanley's, or that of Zeichner and Liston) can be used to analyze the anecdote about the teacher utilizing Kathi's unexpected contribution in the Spanish class? (See page 38.)

10. Imagine a staff room conversation among John Dewey, John Fanselow, and Gary Birch about collegiality versus individuality in professional development. What would they agree on? Where would they disagree? (Try role-playing the conversation.) What would happen if Julian Edge (introduced in Chapter 1) entered the conversation? Who would agree with whom and on what issues?

Suggested Readings

Several authors in general education have written about reflective teaching as a key to teacher development. We have been particularly influenced by Dewey (1933), Zeichner and Liston (1987, 1996), and by Schön (1983, 1987, 1991). As a starting place we recommend Zeichner and Liston's book, *Reflective Teaching: An Introduction* (1996).

Claire Stanley's (1998) article about the development of teacher reflectivity provides much more information about her research than we have been able to reproduce here. We recommend it for both teachers and teacher educators.

Jack Richards and Charles Lockhart have written a book entitled *Reflective Teaching in Second Language Classrooms* (1994). It includes chapters on investigating classrooms, teachers' beliefs, teachers' decision making, teachers' roles, the structure of lessons, classroom interaction, learning activities, and language use in classrooms.

Teacher decision making has been studied in language classroom research. See, e.g., Bailey (1996), Johnson (1992a, 1992b), Nunan (1992a, 1996), Richards and Lockhart (1994), and Woods (1996).

Karen Johnson (1999) examines teachers' knowledge, beliefs, and reasoning in action. She talks about the processes of critical reflection in connection with the idea of "robust reasoning" (10–11) in teacher development.

Andy Curtis (1999a) has written about teachers' increasingly important roles as experts, researchers, and reflective practitioners.

4

TEACHING JOURNALS:
PIECES OF THE PUZZLE

*There are few novelists among us, and only a small number will
have their works published in any form. But we all have the desire
to learn more about ourselves and the children who call us Teacher.
My way has been to resurrect the daily journal to help me study
the most complex society ever assembled in a single place: the
school classroom (Paley, 1997, 122).*

Many of us who make regular entries about our teaching in a personal diary
have found that the process can be very beneficial in furthering professional development. As Bartlett notes, the act of writing begins a reflective, analytic process that helps the writer view teaching more clearly. He says that
recording our practice can be "done by audio or visual means (tape-recording a
lesson, using photography, etc.), but the best means would seem to involve some
form of writing. In writing, we begin not only to observe, but we take the first
step in reflecting on or about our practice" (1990, 209). So keeping a teaching
journal can be both a form of data collection and the first steps in data analysis. Like arraying the jumbled pieces of a jigsaw puzzle on a table, keeping a
journal gives us a place to lay out and examine our questions (Bailey et al.,
1998, 548–549). In the process we find the borders of the puzzle, the splashes
of light and the dark patches, and begin to group the pieces in clusters.

Over time, reading the journal entries allows us to see patterns in our teaching—what Lynette Murphy-O'Dwyer (1985) has called "recurring regularities."
Discovering these patterns may suggest areas to change; it can also affirm successful practices. This chapter describes some options for keeping journals for
professional development purposes and gives examples of things we (and other
teachers) have learned in the process.

Why should we bother to write in a teaching journal? Let us begin to answer
this question with the following Teachers' Voices section, which is an extended
quote from Vivian Paley, a kindergarten teacher who works in the United States.

REFLECTIONS OF A KINDERGARTEN TEACHER

Vivian Paley

It is useful to discuss [classroom] matters with colleagues, especially
those who work in the same classroom, but talk is not enough.
Only as we write down our thoughts and observations may we
question and argue with ourselves about the things we do and say.
Note: Question and argue with ourselves.

If I were principal of your school or mine, this is what I would announce next September: "Hear ye, hear ye! There will be no faculty meetings this year. And no committees or in-service programs. I am calling a halt to official groupthink for a whole year."

Those who had not already dozed off would clap and cheer, until they heard the rest of my message. "Using the time thus made free, you are to keep a daily journal or write letters to a close friend. You are to write about the things that you do not understand, that didn't work, and try to imagine why. It is only with yourself or perhaps with a good friend that you can learn to be completely honest. Once you begin to bring out the first errors and misjudgments the dam will burst with revelations. One idea will flow into another, reaching deeper into that reservoir of impressions, anxieties, and fragile connections we all keep bottled up beneath the surface."

"But," you will argue, "this can happen when I talk."

"Seldom. You are interrupted and distracted before you can carry any thought very far. Furthermore, when you become too self-revealing or too critical of accepted notions and practices—even of your own—your audience is likely to turn away."

"Wait, not so fast," you urge. "I need my colleagues, their ideas and support."

"True. But you also need to know your own ideas more intimately; you need to know what makes you different from your colleagues. You have your own inner support of memories, feelings, and instincts. Through these you will find your own questions and follow through in your own ways. It is quite euphoric, really, to see yourself revealed on paper" (Paley, 1997, 120).

DIARY STUDIES

Teaching journals can be used as data collection devices in practicing reflective teaching, in conducting action research, or as the basis for a diary study. For many years, intensive journals have been kept by language *learners*, for purposes of research on second or foreign language acquisition (see Bailey, 1991, for an overview), but in this chapter we will focus solely on teachers keeping journals for the purposes of professional development. In other words, here journal writing is viewed "as an opportunity for teachers to use the process of writing to describe and explore their own teaching practices" (Ho and Richards, 1993, 8).

We begin the frameworks section with Figure 4.1, which is adapted from Bailey and Ochsner (1983, 90). This figure distinguishes between simply keeping a journal and doing an actual diary study, which entails some sort of systematic analysis of the journal entries. A diary study would typically also include a language learning or teaching history. We contend that even keeping a private, unanalyzed teaching journal (without completing the extra steps of conducting a diary study) can be very informative. However, many teachers have found it useful to analyze their journal entries, looking for patterns over time. Some have even published their diary studies.

Figure 4.1: Conducting a Language Learning or Teaching Diary Study

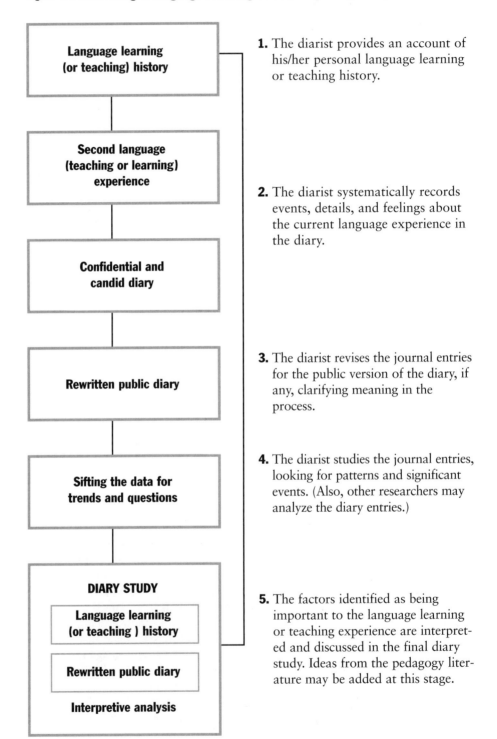

Language learning (or teaching) history	**1.** The diarist provides an account of his/her personal language learning or teaching history.
Second language (teaching or learning) experience	**2.** The diarist systematically records events, details, and feelings about the current language experience in the diary.
Confidential and candid diary	
Rewritten public diary	**3.** The diarist revises the journal entries for the public version of the diary, if any, clarifying meaning in the process.
Sifting the data for trends and questions	**4.** The diarist studies the journal entries, looking for patterns and significant events. (Also, other researchers may analyze the diary entries.)
DIARY STUDY **Language learning (or teaching) history** **Rewritten public diary** **Interpretive analysis**	**5.** The factors identified as being important to the language learning or teaching experience are interpreted and discussed in the final diary study. Ideas from the pedagogy literature may be added at this stage.

What exactly is a diary study then? An early definition is found in an article by Bailey and Oschner (1983, 189):

> A diary study in second language learning, acquisition, or teaching is an account of a second language experience as recorded in a first-person journal. The diarist may be a language teacher or a language learner—but the central characteristic of the diary studies is that they are introspective: The diarist studies his own teaching or learning. Thus he can report on affective factors, language learning strategies, and his own perceptions—facets of the language learning experience which are normally hidden or largely inaccessible to an external observer.

The diary studies are thus "first-person case studies—a research genre defined by the data collection procedures" (Bailey, 1991, 60). When the journal author also analyzes the data, the process is called *introspective analysis* (Matsumoto, 1987), or *direct analysis* (Bailey, 1991). In some published diary studies the journal entries have been analyzed by researchers who were not the original diarists. Matsumoto (1987) has called this *non-introspective analysis*. However, we prefer the terms *indirect analysis* (Bailey, 1991) or *secondary analysis* (Numrich, 1996), because the original diary entries, the data, were still derived through teachers' introspection, even though someone else did the analyzing. For example, Carol Numrich (1996) provides a quantitative and qualitative analysis of journals kept by 26 novice teachers as they completed their practice teaching experiences. Numrich comments on what she learned as a teacher educator from the process of analyzing her students' journals:

> By reading their diaries and analyses of their teaching, I was able to discover what was most important to these teachers in their own process and to uncover recurrent "cultural themes" (Spradley, 1980, 140) particular to them during their early teaching experiences. Without this analysis, I would have been unaware of some of the early preoccupations of novice teachers (Numrich, 1996, 148).

Numrich felt that these realizations helped her develop her own teacher education curriculum. Her analysis of the novice teachers' journals made her "more aware of their discoveries about effective teaching and their continued frustrations" (ibid.).

One of the values of keeping a journal is that the process allows us both to vent and to examine the sources of our frustrations. Joachim Appel, a secondary school EFL teacher in Germany, kept a teaching diary for six years. Later he published a book based on the journal entries and his analyses of his experiences. We will cite several comments from Appel's journal in this book, but here we have selected four entries that reveal his reactions to a few students.

15th September: Oliver

The spot I can't look away from is Oliver. He constantly disturbs my lessons and drains me of all my energy. Oliver is choleric by nature. Handing back a test to someone seems, in theory, to be a straightforward task. Not with Oliver. When he doesn't like his grade—and he usually doesn't—he scrunches up the paper, takes

Joachim Appel

his notebook and hammers on the table with it. When I gave back their word test yesterday, he put his head on the table and kept drumming on it with his fists (Appel, 1995, 3).

20th June: Drama

Today's bit of drama had, of course, never been planned. [A particular class] kept looking for my weak spots. They found them. It was the afternoon lesson. It had taken a long long time to establish any order and I had just about succeeded in getting them to do an exercise, when a boy from the second row of seats got up to open the window. The windows are, admittedly, difficult to open. The boy was pulling it very hard but did not manage to open it. Meanwhile the class's interest had switched to him. They started to laugh. The more he struggled with the window, the more hysterical their laughter became. At that point I lost my nerve. I just could not face another round of calming them down. Something drastic had to be done. I wrote the name of the boy who had gone to the window in the register (which means there will be some disciplinary consequence) and sent him out of the classroom. His neighbor burst into more hysterical laughter. At which point Oliver joined in the action, protesting I was being grossly unjust. While I was at it I wrote down his name as well and sent him out, too. Others came to his aid, telling me I had picked on the wrong person. By this time rationality had gone. I shouted that there was going to be no more discussion (ibid., 8).

10th January: Michael

Tried a similar procedure in [a certain class] today and read out a passage of student writing. I read it in a completely neutral tone of voice, correct sentences as well as incorrect ones. Students were to write down the correct version. I started to dictate sentences from Michael's text. He took exception, saying the others would laugh at his mistakes. I only just persuaded him. In the event the others found some of his mistakes but accepted a lot of the others as correct. After the exercise he looked satisfied. He had seen that the majority of the class would have made the same mistakes (ibid., 38).

20th June: Jens

Decided to test some of the pupils individually. Jens was an obvious candidate. We had had a little show-down at the beginning of the year when I told him either to take part in the lesson or to leave the room. He never said a word in class again. Now I had to assess his spoken English. In his interview this afternoon, Jens suddenly began to speak in fluent English. He told me that he had been to the US several times. I resisted the urge to ask why he had never told me his English was so good (ibid., 40–41).

Discipline and classroom management are often major concerns, especially for new teachers. For example, Appel describes the student called Oliver as "the spot I can't look away from" (1995, 3). We three authors find Appel's diary entries about particular learners to be compelling and candid. We related to them easily because we have had similar struggles.

> If you have teaching experience, perhaps you know the feeling—the worry about a student who is "the spot you can't look away from." If so, write a paragraph or two about such a student. What were the issues you struggled with? What did you actually do?

> Think about how the situation finally worked out. In the long run, what happened? How did your relationship with that student evolve over time? Write a paragraph about the resolution. If you are a novice teacher, ask an experienced colleague to answer these questions for you.

Teachers' Autobiographies

Figure 4.1 on page 50 shows that a language learning history is a component in a diary study. Writing a language learning autobiography can also be a useful professional development exercise for language teachers or teachers-in-training.

Dan Lortie (1975) has written about what he calls the "13,000 hour apprenticeship of observation." This phrase refers to the fact that, in North American education at least, before becoming teachers, most of us have watched approximately 13,000 hours of teaching. From observing all this teaching we develop—by internalizing the models presented to us by our own teachers—implicit concepts of how teaching is done. As Kennedy notes, "Teachers acquire seemingly indelible imprints from their own experiences as students and these imprints are tremendously difficult to shake" (1990, 17). Think about the time factor involved in learners watching teachers. Here's Kennedy's analysis (ibid., 4):

> By the time we receive our bachelor's degree, we have observed teachers and participated in their work for up to 3060 days. In contrast, teacher preparation programs usually require (about) 75 days of classroom experience. What could possibly happen during these 75 days to significantly alter the practices learned during the preceding 3060 days?

What's needed is a way to make these out-of-awareness assumptions explicit. Otherwise we end up teaching as we were taught, unknowingly participating in an unquestioned cycle that contributes to the inherently conservative nature of education.

This problem is directly related to reflective teaching. As Zeichner and Liston point out, "Not only do students walk into schools with expectations and assumptions formed as a result of life experiences, but so do their teachers. Practicing and prospective teachers can benefit from thinking about their expectations and assumptions" (1996, xiii). You will recall from Chapter 3 that one of the characteristics of a reflective teacher is that he or she "is aware of and questions the assumptions and values he or she brings to teaching" (ibid., 11). Zeichner and Liston note that reflective teaching makes "more conscious some of this tacit knowledge that we often do not express. By surfacing these tacit understandings, we can criticize, examine, and improve them" (ibid., 15). As teachers, if we write retrospective accounts of our own language learning, we can "surface these tacit understandings" (ibid.) about teaching and learning. Drawing a simple timeline can be an effective way to start your language learning autobiography.

4.2 YOUR OWN EXPERIENCES

The purpose of this investigation is to help you understand how your experiences as a language learner have influenced you (or will influence you) as a language teacher. Here are the guidelines for completing the task:

1. Draw a timeline as the basis for documenting your history as a language learner.

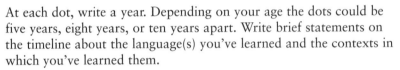

   At each dot, write a year. Depending on your age the dots could be five years, eight years, or ten years apart. Write brief statements on the timeline about the language(s) you've learned and the contexts in which you've learned them.

2. Using your timeline as a memory aid, write a prose summary of your language learning history that answers the following questions:

   A. What language learning experiences have you had and how successful have they been? What are your criteria for judging success?

   B. If you were clearly representative of all language learners, what would someone learn about language learning from reading your autobiography?

   C. What can be learned about effective language teaching by reading your autobiography?

3. Think in more depth about the assumptions you hold regarding how people learn and about your value system (e.g., your assumptions regarding effective teaching). What has your own history as a language learner led you to believe about language teaching?

We firmly believe that examining our own language learning histories, whether or not we complete a full diary study, is a valuable exercise in developing self-awareness. In the Teachers' Voices section below we have quoted the comments of a group of language teachers who wrote autobiographies about their own language learning experiences.

LEARNING FROM OUR AUTOBIOGRAPHIES

Teachers' Voices

Various teachers

- While writing and revising my language-learning autobiography I learned that I am a highly motivated language student, able to learn from a wide variety of instructors.

- I saw that my experience with language learning influenced my teaching, i.e., what I considered to be effective teaching was based on the "good models" I'd experienced.

- I learned that those experiences I had always considered to be "failures" were actually successes, because they taught me valuable lessons about my language learning style.

- I learned that I want to teach the way I learned best—e.g., using authentic materials, because I found them most useful when I was learning a foreign language.

- I learned that I actually have many relevant language-learning experiences that will be useful to me as a language teacher, which I hadn't realized before.

- I realized how important the role of the teacher is in motivating students to learn a foreign or second language, as well as how delicate motivation is in contributing to one's success.

- I learned that I should probably be running a cross-cultural dating service instead of a school in order to promote real acquisition of a language. But seriously... a student's emotional needs must be met before any real learning can be achieved.

- I realized that at times my experience as a learner did not mesh with my own students' needs and expectations, thus having a negative effect.

- I learned that I've been limiting myself from using teaching methods that may be available, due to my limited exposure to different kinds of methods as a language learner.

4.3 *COMPARING EXPERIENCES*

Investigations

Look at the comments made by the teachers who wrote their language learning and teaching autobiographies. How do these comments relate to your own experience? Put a plus "+" beside those that ring true, or seem particularly apt in your case. Put a check "✓" next to those that are plausible, but not necessarily reflective of your experience, and a minus "–" beside those that are definitely not true in your case or seem very unlikely. Compare your responses with your peers'.

INTROSPECTION AND RETROSPECTION

The timing of journal entries is a methodological issue in keeping a journal, whether for research or professional development purposes. When does the writing occur relative to the event about which the teacher is introspecting? According to Fry the term *introspective data* refers only to information "gathered from subjects while they carry out a task" (1988, 159), while *retrospective data* are those "collected after the event" (ibid.). Of course, the difficulty here is that true introspection can take place only while the process is occurring, so the introspection can actually disrupt the process.

In contrast to true introspection, which is concurrent with the task, retrospection involves a very broad timespan, ranging from immediately after the event (following a language class, for example) to years later (as is the case in the language learning autobiographies and language teaching histories). Cohen and Hosenfeld (1981) distinguish among three types of introspective data collection, each of which represents a band rather than a point: *concurrent introspection* (during the event), *immediate retrospection* (right after the event), and *delayed retrospection* (hours or more following the event). Thus the cover term *introspection* entails all three zones, as depicted in Figure 4.2 (adapted from Bailey, 1991, 64):

Figure 4.2: Introspection Immediacy Continuum

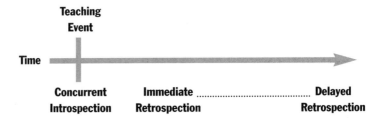

Presumably for most teachers, the process of keeping a teaching journal would fall somewhere on the continuum of immediate to delayed retrospection, with the immediacy of the writing often being determined by largely practical factors. But whether you are keeping a diary for research purposes or purely for professional development, we recommend that you write your journal entries as soon as possible after the teaching event you are describing.

If you think you might like to keep a teaching journal but aren't sure, we suggest you try out three different approaches, over about a month's time, to see which (if any) works for you:

1. For two weeks, write just a weekly summary at the end of the week. (This would be an example of delayed retrospection.)

2. If your schedule permits, make an entry in your teaching journal for at least five or ten minutes every day for one week, but do it right after you teach your classes. (This process would be closer to immediate retrospection.)

3. For the final week of the month, make a commitment to write in your teaching journal for at least 30 minutes every day.

At the end of the month, compare these three experiences. What worked best for you—the weekly summary, the brief daily writing session, or the more intensive daily writing sessions? What were the similarities and differences among these three approaches in terms of both the processes you were using, as well as the resulting product?

PRIVATE VERSUS PUBLIC JOURNALS

Journal entries are typically a combination of records of events and interpretations of those events (Bailey, 1991). Their value lies in the fact that the teacher's introspection often reveals aspects of language teaching that are normally hidden from the view of an outside observer. These include teachers' decision making, moments of uncertainty, worry, or confusion, and private triumphs—all grist for the professional development mill.

Introspection includes "self-report, self-observation, and self-revealment," according to Grotjahn (1987, 55). Self-revealment, in terms of the Johari Window (see Figure 2.2 on page 25), involves moving from the "hidden self" quadrant to the "open self" quadrant if you share your realizations with others. However, journals are also helpful in changing from the "hidden self" to the "secret self" if you choose to keep private what you discover by writing and reading your journal. As Numa Markee has noted (1996, 139), "journals are primarily private records of individual [teachers'] insights into the processes of language teaching. But they can also become more public documents." Thus, another question is whether you wish to keep a journal as an entirely private activity, or as part of a more collegial or even public process. A range of options is available, as depicted in Figure 4.3:

Figure 4.3: Private Versus Public Teaching Journals

Private Account

LEVEL 1 Making entries privately in your teaching journal and rereading them alone

LEVEL 2 Making entries privately and reading some of those entries to known and trusted colleagues and classmates

LEVEL 3 Making entries privately in your teaching journal and allowing some known colleagues or classmates to read your entire teaching journal (either after it's finished or while it's in progress)

LEVEL 4 Making independent entries in a journal but sharing the journal with known colleagues and class-mates (who also share their journals) and collabora-tively discussing both the process and the product

LEVEL 5 Making collaborative entries in a teaching journal with known colleagues or classmates and discussing both the process and the product

LEVEL 6 Keeping a collaborative journal with a team teaching partner, where the teaching, the recording, the reading, and the analysis are all shared tasks

LEVEL 7 Reporting on the results of a diary study (regardless of how the data are generated) to an unknown audience, in print or at a conference, using your teaching journal as a data base

Public Account

If you undertake journal writing as a professional development exercise on your own initiative, the choice to "go public" or remain private is up to you. Jo McDonough made the following comment (1994, 64) after keeping a teaching journal:

> The diary itself is an entirely private endeavour; the diary study, on the other hand, means going public, and adds on stages of revision, looking for patterns, interpretation, and public discussion. A diary study, then, can by its nature reach a wider professional audience, ideally encouraging other teachers to try out this and other techniques for investigating and understanding their own classrooms.

This distinction between the initial teaching journal and a possible later analysis for a formal diary study should be kept in mind. But even if you plan to "go public," the initial journal entries should usually be written to yourself (or to your most trusted colleagues) in order to avoid prematurely editing or cleaning up the data, or censoring your reflections. It is possible to slant the data, either intentionally or inadvertently, in the direction of an external audience.

WHO SHOULD READ A TEACHING JOURNAL?

Imagine sharing a teaching journal you had written (privately and candidly). Think of a person with whom you would definitely be comfortable sharing your journal. What skills, personal attributes, or professional expertise of this person led to your selection?

Now think of someone with whom you would definitely not want to share a candidly written journal of your teaching. What are the particular attributes of this person that would make you reluctant to reveal your journal entries?

Finally, think about yourself as a potential reader of your colleagues' teaching journals. Which of your qualities would make you a valued reader? Which of your characteristics might make someone hesitate to choose you as a reader?

BENEFITS OF KEEPING A TEACHING JOURNAL

In our experience there are four key benefits of keeping a teaching journal. These include (1) articulating puzzles or problems (including posing hypotheses for further research), (2) venting frustrations, (3) clarifying and realizing, and (4) stretching ourselves professionally. (A teaching journal can also be a place for celebrating our triumphs.) Almost invariably, articulating puzzles and problems, and venting our frustrations if we so desire, lead to clarification and possibly to realization, which can result in professional development.

When we write in confidential journals to and for ourselves, we can acknowledge and describe those aspects of our teaching that may puzzle or worry us. Because there is (at least initially) no other intended audience, we can be completely candid in reporting on our teaching and our reactions thereto. This private context provides freedom from the potential loss of face involved with sharing our concerns with others in a more public forum.

Keeping a teaching journal can provide helpful distancing—what van Lier has called an "estrangement device" (1988, 37)—that lets us view our teaching somewhat more dispassionately than we can right after teaching the classes. MaryAnn Telatnik, who kept a journal about teaching her ESL class, put it this way:

> After having analyzed myself daily I tended to see other people's analysis of my own teaching more objectively. Having learned to be honest and objective in my own recording, I found it easier to be more honest and objective about others' comments.... With Observer X, who criticized my authoritarian, teacher-dominated approach, I began to become less defensive. My resentment passed when I accepted the fact that I did run a teacher-dominated classroom and that was exactly what I wanted. I no longer secretly raged through our discussions. I even managed to glean from our sessions a few techniques on encouraging student participation (Telatnik, 1978, 7–8).

Thus, the privacy of the journal also allows us to vent our frustrations—even to rant and rave if we wish. Teaching is high-pressure, demanding, face-to-face work that necessarily involves human interaction—not all of which is pleasant. Expressing annoyance in a contextually appropriate way, outside of the class-room, can keep it from building up and splashing onto our students, colleagues, or families.

Finally, by articulating a teaching problem or puzzle, laying out our respons-es to our teaching, and clarifying our understandings, we can stretch ourselves as teachers. We can hypothesize and wonder, speculate about alternatives, note gaps in our linguistic knowledge, generate new teaching ideas, and make tenta-tive commitments to try new things. (We know that "tentative commitments" is an oxymoron, but that's one of the beauties of journal keeping.)

Deciding to keep your journal entries private or to share them with others may relate to why you make them in the first place. If your journal is primarily used for venting your frustrations, you may not wish to share the record with any but your most trusted colleagues. If your purpose is to stretch yourself pro-fessionally, then you might benefit from sharing your teaching journal with oth-ers. And, of course, doing so could make a contribution to the field.

Entries in a teaching journal can also validate our work. The clarification derived from writing may not lead to a particular change in our teaching. It may simply lead to a better understanding of why we do what we do, or why particu-lar activities work well. As Donald Freeman has pointed out, "Change does not necessarily mean doing something differently; it can mean a change in awareness. Change can be an affirmation of current practice" (1989a, 38). Here is an exam-ple, from a journal entry written by Deborah, a novice ESL teacher:

> Today, for the first time, I really felt like a "teacher." This is
> because I was able to integrate everything to a degree that was
> smooth, confident, and well-received. I felt comfortable with my
> presentation, I was energetic but relaxed, I had a good lesson plan
> that was fully accomplished in the hour, my structuring went well,
> I was able to keep everything on track and choose what was a
> meaningful use of my time and which to throw away.... I remem-
> ber feeling like this when I was taking tennis lessons and that mar-
> velous moment, after eight hours of swatting air, running up and
> down the court and performing incredible feats of contortion in
> pursuit of yellow balls, when everything came together (for the first
> time, for a moment) and I was coordinated and graceful. I was still
> a beginner, but for that class I felt like a tennis player (Deborah,
> quoted in Numrich, 1996, 149).

Like Deborah, all of us have teaching moments that feel like "swatting air." But we also have moments of brilliance, when everything works well for us and our students. Keeping a teaching journal lets us document both the dark patch-es and the light.

If you are an experienced teacher, or if you've done some practice teaching, think about a time when you had a successful lesson. Or, as an alternative, you could recall an unsuccessful lesson. Tell a peer about the event, or write a paragraph about the event if you are working alone.

> How do you think the story would differ if you had written it as a journal entry within a day of the event? Think back and see if you can add any details to the story. Where are the notable gaps in your recollection?

PROBLEMS WITH JOURNAL KEEPING

Of course, there are also pitfalls in keeping a teaching journal. In fact, one of the advantages can lead to one of the potential disadvantages. That is, the privacy of the initial journal entries and the fact that we ourselves are the intended audience allow us to write candidly and extensively, without premature culling or editing of the data. However, choosing not to share our issues and/or insights with other teachers does little to break down the sense of isolation that many teachers feel. Not talking to colleagues can also prevent us from gaining valuable teaching ideas—whether these are insights about our own behavior, practical tips about teaching, or useful new understandings of our subject matter.

Some people feel that keeping a daily journal of their teaching experiences is too time-consuming. Certainly keeping a journal should not interfere with our time for teaching, for preparation, or for follow-up. Likewise, it should not detract from other professional development opportunities, or even from the general quality of our lives. Gillian Palmer (1992, 243) has suggested that diaries can be written on alternate days or on a weekly basis, though she acknowledges that this practice might disrupt the continuity of the entries.

Another strategy for managing the time involved in journal keeping is to decide in advance how much time you are willing to commit, and then use that amount of time religiously to structure the writing process. For instance, if you can only devote five minutes per day to making journal entries, you could limit yourself to five minutes after class and focus on the most salient event of the day, or on a persistent puzzle you are facing. You could get a pack of large index cards and write on just one card, front and back, every evening. Or you may wish to start a computer word processing file and write just one page, or for just five minutes, every day after class. Perhaps you can only write in your journal during the bus or train ride home from work. Many limitation strategies can be used to circumscribe the time you spend keeping a journal.

Some people have preferred to talk their journal entries into a tape recorder instead of writing them. If you have a lapel microphone for your portable cassette recorder, you might find you can make oral journal entries while walking, or while driving to and from school. If you choose this option, consider how you will analyze the data if you wish to do so later. Will it be necessary to transcribe your tapes, or parts of them, in order to access the information you need? No matter how much or how little time you spend writing (or speaking) in a teaching journal, the important thing is to be systematic and constant in making regular entries.

Not only is timing an issue in terms of when we write, how often we write, and how long we write at each sitting; there is also the question of the duration (days, weeks, months, or years) of the journal-keeping process. There seems to be a benefit to keeping up the effort long enough for patterns to emerge. As Brita Butler-Wall noted in her teaching journal,

> Much of the time I actually did not know what was going on in the classroom. Because I tended to equate positive affect with learning, I looked no further to find out if any learning was in fact taking place. A review of the diary entries suggests that this would have been wise. It seems that a diary is more than the sum of its parts; although I was the one who recorded every item, I did not realize what I had recorded until I had recorded many items (Butler-Wall, 1979, 10, as cited in Bailey, 1990, 225).

Of course, the duration of your journal-keeping project is up to you. We suggest, however, that you try to continue making entries for the length of the course you are teaching if you can.

Another alternative to intensive journal keeping is to write a weekly summary instead of making daily entries. For example, Kathi was once faced with a difficult class composed of students with very different levels of preparation, including some students who had not completed the prerequisites. As a way of documenting her strategies for dealing with the problems that arose, she spent about 15 minutes a week writing an e-mail to her dean, Ruth Larimer, whose judgment about teaching Kathi trusted. In the process, Kathi learned some things about the course and her interaction with the students that she might not have realized without the experience of writing. For instance, she was able to examine her own time management issues in terms of covering the material and trying to meet the course objectives with ill-prepared students. This benefit developed by systematically writing her ideas to Ruth on a weekly basis, even though Ruth did not overtly respond to or analyze the data in any way.

Shelley Wong (1994, 13) has also commented about time pressures and keeping a journal. She offers the following advice:

> I had trouble finding time every day, so my journal was catch-as-catch-can....After the year of teaching was over, I had many regrets about the inadequacies of my journal entries...I cannot overemphasize the importance of setting and sticking to a minimum weekly writing goal for yourself, perhaps once a week, one thoughtful, reflective entry, or 15 minutes of writing three times a week.

Wong stresses that "whatever you write—even if it is not polished—will be valuable as you reflect upon your teaching in the future" (ibid.).

Some teachers may simply feel that journal keeping is not worthwhile for them. Perhaps they are not naturally introspective, or they are not comfortable writers. As Jo McDonough has noted, "[T]he use of a diary to record and reflect on one's own classroom is not necessarily a technique that will suit everyone" (1994, 57). For instance, one of McDonough's colleagues initially felt that keeping a teaching journal didn't have "any real purpose" because "it is too much like the kind of things we might say to each other in passing at the end of a class or even in a meeting, but writing it all down gives it too much importance.... Looking back over what I have written I can't find anything unexpected or surprising" (ibid.). But we believe, like Vivian Paley in the first Teachers' Voices section of this chapter, that systematically writing about our teaching over time can lead us to more substantial realizations than do most informal chats, partly because most such chats evaporate. We feel that "many practicing teachers will find the keeping of a personal-professional diary of interest and value from a number of perspectives" (McDonough, 1994, 57). As Ho and Richards point out, "The goal of activities such as journal writing is... to engage teachers in a deeper level of awareness and response to teaching than they would obtain by merely discussing teaching in terms of teaching procedures and lesson plans" (1993, 15).

4.7 *WHAT DO YOU THINK ABOUT IT?*

What is your opinion? What are the advantages and disadvantages of talking to your colleagues about teaching versus writing in a teaching journal? Write your thoughts, substantiating them with examples where possible, and exchange your paper with a colleague or fellow student for discussion of the pros and cons.

SUGGESTIONS FOR KEEPING A JOURNAL

The following suggestions are intended to make writing your diary entries pleasant and easy. You should set up the conditions for writing so that the journal-keeping process does not require a great deal of effort. The writing process should be (or should become) relatively free—not a chore you dread or avoid, or one that interferes with your teaching.

First of all, it is important to realize that focusing on your own teaching practice (your behavior, your planning, your motives, the lessons that just don't work) can be an uncomfortable process. And at times, writing can be hard work. Many diarists have reported great difficulty in getting started. For example, MaryAnn Telatnik wrote,

> At first it was very slow work. For almost two weeks I used only 10 or 20 minutes of my hour. It was difficult both to write and to know what to write. Without realizing it, I was editing my thoughts before I put them down on paper....It was not until the fourth or fifth week that I was able to read the journal and say, "Oh, so that's what I do" (Telatnik, 1978, 2).

In spite of her initial difficulties, Telatnik continued to use the time she had set aside for making her journal entries and eventually found a rhythm for writing that she could sustain.

Our experience has shown that the time spent writing about our language teaching experiences can easily equal or exceed the time we spend teaching a class. If you are teaching several hours each day, you will find you cannot possibly write about everything that happens, so you may want to focus your diary on some particular aspect of your teaching that interests or puzzles you. However, you may also discover that a teaching journal can be an unruly beast. Sometimes it will go off in unexpected directions, compelled by unanticipated issues. For instance, when Kathi began teaching at the Chinese University of Hong Kong, she decided to keep a journal for only the first two or three weeks of the first and possibly the second semester, in order to examine her concerns about starting a new class (in a new culture, at a different school, with students whose L1 she did not speak and who were much younger than the students she normally teaches—see Bailey, 1998b). But new questions quickly emerged, and she soon found herself keeping a teaching journal for the entire academic year.

We also recommend that you keep your diary (or your diskette) in a safe, secure place—a locked drawer, a file cabinet, a secure briefcase. The idea is for you to be able to write anything you want without feeling uneasy about someone else's reaction to what you have written.

When you record entries in the original uncensored version of your diary, don't worry about style, grammar, and organization—you are the audience to whom the diary entries are addressed. The idea is to get complete and accurate data at a time when the information is still fresh in your mind. The original diary entries sometimes read like "stream of consciousness" writing, but that's not a problem. You can polish your presentation of the data at a later time if you decide to revise your journal or write a diary study for public consumption.

Many language teaching journals are full of fascinating but unsubstantiated insights. In keeping your diary, try to support your insights with examples from your class sessions, your daily interactions with the students, or from your planning and follow-up sessions. Each time you write an assertion, ask yourself, "Why? Why did I write that?" In other words, what evidence do you have for the statement you just made?

The opposite problem can also occur. Merely reporting on class activities without reflecting on them produces a flat factual account (which might be better captured by a video). As Ho and Richards point out, "The mere fact of writing about teaching does not necessarily involve critical reflection, since teachers can write largely at a procedural level focusing on trivial details rather than underlying or deeper issues" (1993, 15). In making diary entries, you should not limit yourself to objective observations alone: Your inferences and opinions should also find a home in your journal. On the other hand, when you draw an inference or state an opinion, you should also try to document the facts and events that led to your position.

At the end of each diary entry, it's a good idea to note thoughts or questions that have occurred to you to consider later. This is one way to narrow your focus somewhat during the diary-keeping process, in case you find you want to work on a certain aspect of your teaching, or conduct a diary study about a particular topic.

LEARNING ABOUT A "FROZEN" LEARNER

Our emerging questions can also lead to new ideas and awarenesses. Jo McDonough, whose comments are cited above, decided to keep a journal about a course she taught. First she describes her motivation for keeping a teaching journal (McDonough, 1994, 58–59):

> I first wrote a teaching diary two or three years ago, initially out of no higher-minded motivation than to express frustration about an apparently "frozen" learner in my group, and in a minor way to complain to myself about the way in which some of the classroom observation literature seemed to talk down to and past me rather than tap into my own reality.... But then the diary-writing became a valuable routine, and over the months I was led—directly through the diary as a reflective instrument—into a number of areas of personal professional development and meta-exploration, as well as ending up with a formulated case study of my problem student, and a fresh perspective on evaluation and assessment.

McDonough concludes her article with the following comment:

> A diary alone will not cope with all possible questions, and other methods and data sources will need to be used depending on what we wish to investigate. There are also many issues that can perfectly well be examined without recourse to a diary. What a diary can do, I have suggested, is to help us document and formalize the everyday working experience that might otherwise be lost (ibid., 64).

We believe that there is much to be gained by attending conferences and workshops, taking courses, reading articles in professional journals, and so on. But, like McDonough, we believe that we can learn a great deal, in terms of our own professional development, by documenting and examining "the everyday working experience that might otherwise be lost" (ibid.).

Jo McDonough

JOURNALS AND REFLECTION

Belinda Ho and Jack Richards used Schön's (1983, 1987), Zeichner and Liston's (1987), and Dewey's (1933) ideas about reflection as the theoretical basis to investigate journals kept by 10 secondary school English teachers in Hong Kong. The diarists were enrolled in a university-based teacher education program and were completing a unit on reflective teaching. (Their journals were kept as a program requirement, so the intended audience was not just the teachers themselves but also their university professors.) Ho and Richards asked, "If journal writing is useful, what evidence can we look for to confirm its usefulness?" (1993, 9).

Ho and Richards located five main patterns among the topics discussed in the teachers' journal entries: (1) theories of teaching; (2) approaches and methods used in their lessons; (3) evaluations of their teaching; (4) self-awareness about their own strengths and weaknesses; and (5) questions (used, e.g., to speculate about why things happened or to ask for advice). In these data, comments in the self-awareness category were the least frequent (20 instances out of 483 topics coded, or just four percent). Ho and Richards concluded that "...teachers differ considerably in the extent to which their journals evidence traits of reflectivity" (1993, 18). This study points out that simply writing about teaching may not lead to reflection.

We can see that Jo McDonough's (1994) work with her colleagues' journals and Ho and Richards' (1993) analysis of the Hong Kong teachers' journals are both examples of Level 3 on the continuum of totally private to totally public journals in Figure 4.3 on page 58. Although these authors published diary studies, the teachers whose journal entries comprised the data have remained anonymous. In the following Teachers' Voices section, we see a more collaborative use of teaching journals (Level 4 on the private-public continuum in Figure 4.3).

COLLABORATIVE JOURNAL KEEPING

Mark Brock, Bart Yu, and Matilda Wong wrote about their experiences with collaborative journal keeping as EFL teachers. Here's how they framed their report (1992, 296):

Mark Brock,
Bart Yu,
Matilda Wong

> This paper describes our experiences keeping diaries of two of our classes throughout a ten-week term at City Polytechnic of Hong Kong. Each week we read one another's diary entries, made written responses to each of those entries, and discussed our teaching and diary-keeping experiences for one hour. Our report draws on our individual entries, our written responses to one another's entries, and transcripts of our weekly discussions.

As you can imagine, the steps they took together added substantially to their time commitment. They describe their collaborative journal process as follows:

> Each of us wrote three diary entries each week of a ten-week term.... Our entries concerned different classes, including business, technical, and supplementary English classes....[We] wrote our diary entries immediately following the lessons so that we could remember classroom events and our responses in as much detail as possible.... We wrote freely in almost a stream-of-consciousness style, paying little attention to grammatical correctness or stylistic coherence. In addition, we attempted to be as honest in our diary entries as we possibly could. The fact that our entries often included issues of frustrations or feelings of failure may indicate that we were indeed honest in what we wrote (Brock et al., 1992, 296–297).

These authors' first data collection process involved three teachers writing parallel but independent journal entries. It is in what they subsequently did with these entries that their work became truly collaborative:

> To maximize the effects of interaction among the three diarists, our diary-keeping was coupled with written responses and group discussions. These three steps formed a kind of triangulation which offered us more than one way of exploring teaching issues and concerns. After writing each diary entry, we made copies and gave them to one another to read. We then wrote brief responses to one another's entries and gave copies of these responses to one another before our one-hour discussion time on Friday afternoon. These group discussions were audio-taped and later transcribed. At the end of the

term, we analyzed the diary entries, our written responses, and transcripts of discussions to determine how these three interacted and what issues occurred most frequently (Brock et al., 1992, 297).

In other words, Brock, Yu and Wong conducted a diary study based on their journal entries combined with other data. When these authors mention "triangulation" they are talking about an important validation process used in qualitative research. *Triangulation* is a term borrowed from navigation and land surveying as a metaphor. It refers to "the inspection of different kinds of data, different methods, and a variety of research tools" (van Lier, 1988, 13) to make sure that multiple possible interpretations are considered. (See also Denzin, 1970.)

The excerpts reproduced below reveal what these colleagues learned through this intensive process of journaling together and triangulating their data. They found that their written responses were full of questions and requests for more information, as illustrated in the following comments written by Bart to Matilda (Brock et al., 1992, 297):

> I am interested in knowing how the change of the classroom
> atmosphere is taking place and did you do anything to make them
> participate more fully in class? I remember you saying this class
> was very disappointing last week but how come, one week later,
> the class changed rapidly?

These colleagues' written responses to one another set an informal agenda for their Friday afternoon discussions. For example, after reading one of Bart's journal entries, Mark wrote,

> I want to hear more of what you are discovering. I think if I can
> just see more clearly some things that are going on in my class and
> in my thinking, then I can put words to it and that will help me to
> understand it. I think hearing you talk more about this will help me
> along the way (ibid.).

By sharing their journals, these teachers opened the typically closed doors of their classrooms and began to ask one another questions and make connections. Their written responses to one another's diary entries helped to clarify their positions about teaching issues, identified recurring themes, and encouraged each of them to write about similar experiences (ibid.).

The report specifically addresses the issue of awareness, which was discussed in Chapter 2. In his first journal entry, Mark wrote:

For awareness, see Figure 2.1, p. 23.

> My mirror is clouded. I hope that by reflecting further on my teaching
> I can polish up my mirror and see myself clearly in the light of day.
> I probably won't like some of what I see. But at least I can see it and
> with that vision have before me then some possibility of change (ibid).

These authors agreed that "this evolving self-awareness and the urge to improve seems to be a natural part of the reflection process" (ibid., 301). They connected their work to that of Cheryl Brown (1985, 131), who observed, "it may be that the awareness would have come without the journals, but writing it down made it very evident." Another comment from Brock, Yu and Wong connects journal keeping directly to reflective teaching:

Although diary-keeping may not yield any answers, at least at the beginning, the fact that many questions are raised as a result of the reflection diary-keeping requires is significant in itself. Thinking about and evaluating what we do in the classroom, examining whether it is effective, and considering some of the variables affecting teaching and learning processes has the potential of moving teachers beyond mechanistic, non-reflective teaching (Brock et al., 1992, 301).

The fact that so many questions emerge in the process of writing journal entries may partially account for the fact that journals tend to grow in unexpected directions.

In spite of the perceived benefits, these colleagues did feel the time crunch of keeping up such an intensive process. Their feelings embodied "several conflicting emotions" (ibid., 300):

On one hand we saw the project as valuable in providing insights and some measure of awareness-raising that we previously had not experienced. In addition, we collected what we called a list of issues, concerns, and questions related to our teaching that we each could choose to investigate at some future time through diary-keeping or other research methods. Along with these positive reflections on the diary-keeping process, there were negative sentiments as well. Our enthusiasm dimmed as the term neared the end, and at times we saw the discipline of diary-keeping as a burden on our time rather than as a tool with which to enhance teacher development (ibid.).

In spite of these problems, Brock, Yu and Wong acknowledge that the process had its value:

Collaborative diary-keeping brought several benefits to our development as second language teachers. It raised our awareness of classroom processes and prompted us to consider those processes more deeply than we may otherwise have. Collaborative diary-keeping also provided encouragement and support; it served as a source of teaching ideas and suggestions; and in some sense it gave us a way to observe one another's teaching from a "safe distance" (ibid.).

So there is a tradeoff to consider in the continuum represented in Figure 4.3: To what extent does the value of sharing your journal entries offset the time needed for collaboration?

As noted earlier, these three colleagues wrote weekly responses to each other's entries and they met for one hour per week to discuss their journals. Did they think the results were worth all this extra collaborative effort?

[T]he additional experiences of reading and responding to one another's diary entries and then discussing what we had read served to enhance this awareness-raising process. Receiving responses from one another and seeing ourselves through another's perspective helped us discover some of our "blind selves" and discover what we might have overlooked (ibid., 301).

The comment about "blind selves" here refers to the Johari Window (see Figure 2.2 on page 25).

Another factor to consider is that these teachers were on equal footing. They stress the value of working with peers in a collegial relationship on an equal-power basis:

> As teachers of approximately the same professional level, our relationship was not marked by the discomfort that can attend relationships of power, such as that of a supervisor and teacher or that of a master-teacher and novice-teacher. As Mark expressed during one group discussion: I think we've come at this not as experts who tell people how to teach, "I'm going to tell you how to teach and you're going to tell me how to teach," but more as people trying to learn and be supportive of each other (ibid., 305).

We will return to this issue of equal-power status in professional development activities when we discuss coaching in Chapter 11.

These authors note that collaborative diary-keeping can also be an effective development tool if the teachers focus the scope of their journals more narrowly: "Such an approach would allow participants opportunity to choose and investigate in depth two or three issues of common interest rather than attempting to explore many issues at one time" (ibid., 306). They warn, however, that teachers who undertake collaborative diary-keeping should be comfortable sharing both positive and negative experiences in order to "gain a clearer picture of classroom teaching and learning processes" (ibid.):

> …[E]ach of us believes that there is potential for using collaborative diary-keeping as a tool for teacher development. This sentiment is reflected in our final entries in which we summarized our experiences. In his entry, Mark recollected, "Overall I think that our project has been worthwhile. I think that I have learnt something about myself as a teacher. I really have enjoyed our discussions and I've enjoyed hearing particularly about the teaching experiences of Bart and Matilda." Bart expressed that "through diary-keeping, we raised our consciousness of what happened during our teaching and for the first time I began to be aware of many of the interesting points during the class flow." Matilda stated that "on the whole I think journal writing enables me to clear some of my doubts through getting responses from my partners…sharing journals with the others…widens my vision." It is with this widened vision that possibilities for teacher development come into clearer focus (ibid.).

4.8 *TRY IT YOURSELF*

If you are team teaching with a colleague or a practicum partner, or if you can co-teach even one lesson, it may be interesting for you and your teaching partner to make journal entries on the shared teaching experience. These entries could be made under two conditions:

1. You could plan and teach the lesson together and then independently record your reactions to the session in totally separate journal entries.

2. You could plan and teach together and then write a joint journal entry in which you co-construct the record of the teaching event.

As an alternative, if you have the opportunity, you and your teaching partner(s) could try both Option 1 and Option 2 above and compare the two journal-keeping experiences. (See Chapter 10 on team teaching for examples of diary entries that Kathi and Andy made independently but that were based on shared teaching experiences.)

INTERACTIVE GROUP JOURNALS

Brock, Yu, and Wong made their original journal entries independently but read them, responded to them in writing, and discussed them collaboratively (Level 4 in Figure 4.3). But teachers can also collaborate on the actual writing of the journal entries (Level 5 in Figure 4.3). An example of this process appears in an article by four language teachers who wrote about their use of interactive group journals as graduate students in a teacher education program.

Robert Cole, Linda McCarthy Raffier, Pete Rogan, and Leigh Schleicher define an *interactive group journal* as "a written document that takes the idea of reflective practice and merges it with social interaction by recording active dialogue among peers in a journal format" (1998, 556). They describe the process as follows:

Robert Cole,
Linda McCarthy
Raffier, Pete
Rogan, and
Leigh Schleicher

> …[W]e passed a computer diskette from person to person, each member writing about any issues, concerns, questions, or insights that seemed appropriate at the time. Other members could choose to respond to previous entries or to branch off on new topics. We began by electing a group member to write the journal's first entry. Next, we established the order in which the [Interactive Group Journal] would be passed among group members. Given the size of our group, our individual and collective goals, and the constraints of the academic time frame, we decided to strive for one-week journal-writing cycles, meaning that each group member would be able to read and respond to the [journal] at least once a week. Due to computer compatibility issues and for the sake of access, we also decided to pass around both computer diskette and hard-copy versions (ibid., 560).

These four teachers felt that the process of keeping an interactive group journal helped them to build a professional community. This happened because "a group journal moves beyond a storage device for minutes or other reports of group activity to include the opportunity for reflection in order to collaboratively extract meaning from shared experiences" (ibid., 562).

This concept of community was directly related to the equal-power basis of their communication. Because these teachers were writing to their peers (rather than their professors), they were able to express themselves candidly. For this reason, the journal became "a means of building confidence within members of the journal-writing group, enriching the notion of a learning community" (ibid.,

564). Like Brock, Yu, and Wong, these authors related this intra-group communication directly to their development as professionals. They felt that the interactive group journal provided a means to "reflect on experiences, formulate and reformulate ideas, and gain autonomous membership in the professional discourse community" (ibid., 566). They concluded that the journal itself provided a much needed bridge from being students together to engaging in reciprocal professional relationships (ibid.).

4.9 *TASKS FOR DEVELOPMENT*

In this chapter we have tried to explain the benefits and problems of keeping a teaching journal for professional development purposes. Doing so can be largely private or very public, in terms of both the process and the product. Although journal keeping can be time-consuming, and even uncomfortable at times, we believe it to be a potentially valuable professional development procedure. The following investigations are intended to help you address these issues further.

1. Triangulating your data can help you have confidence in your findings, since they can be verified (or challenged) by two or more different sources. If you are planning to keep a teaching journal, what additional data could you collect in your context to help you investigate your teaching? (The chapter titles in our Table of Contents may give you some ideas.) Which of these data types would be most appropriate and most interesting to you?

2. We claim that the main benefits of keeping a teaching journal are that the process allows us to (a) articulate puzzles or problems, (b) vent frustrations, (c) clarify and realize, and (d) stretch ourselves professionally. If you have kept a teaching journal, try to think of an example of each of these benefits based on your own experience. If you have not previously kept a teaching journal, try to find a teacher who has done so and ask him or her for an example of each of these benefits. Are there other benefits that we have not discussed here?

3. As noted in a Teachers' Voices section above, Jo McDonough began keeping a teaching journal "initially out of no higher-minded motivation than to express frustration about an apparently "frozen" learner in [her] group" (1994, 58). Identify a learner whom you are concerned about, or one who seems to be learning slowly, or even one whom you find to be annoying, perhaps as Joachim Appel found working with Oliver to be particularly challenging. Make journal entries about your interactions with this student over a period of time—e.g., for two weeks if you see him or her every day, or for a month if you see the student only two or three times a week. At the end of that time period, reread the journal entries to see what patterns you can find in your relationship to this learner. What strategies for change might you develop? (Please note: In posing this task we are not

suggesting a "witch hunt" or an opportunity to belittle the student in writing. Our focus here is on the awareness we as teachers can gain by systematically examining our own practices.)

4. If you are contemplating keeping a teaching journal, would you prefer to keep a private journal, or to share the process and/or the product with other people? It may help you to consider the pros and cons of varying degrees of privacy versus sharing. Set up a grid like the one that follows and then fill in the boxes.

	PROS	CONS
Making journal entries individually and not sharing the results		
Making individual entries but sharing some of the entries with trusted colleagues		
Making joint entries in a teaching journal and sharing and discussing the results with trusted colleagues		
Making either individual or joint entries in a journal but then "going public" by sharing the results with unknown colleagues in a publication or at a conference		

Suggested Readings

Kathi Bailey (1990) discusses the use of teachers' journals in teacher education and summarizes the outcomes of several teachers' diaries. Many of the journals cited are unpublished, but the excerpts are informative examples of other teachers' experiences.

Jo McDonough (1994) wrote the article from which we took one of the Teachers' Voices sections in this chapter. That paper was based on the experiences she and three colleagues had in keeping journals. All four were experienced teachers of English working in the United Kingdom

We recommend the paper by Brock, Yu, and Wong (1992) for anyone considering undertaking a collaborative journal project. We have used a number of quotes from this article, but there are several valuable parts of the original text that we have not reproduced here.

A potentially useful reference is Kathi Bailey and Robert Ochsner's (1993) paper entitled "A Methodological Review of the Diary Studies: Windmill Tilting or Social Science?" Those authors were writing primarily about language learning diaries, but many of the principles they discuss would pertain to diary studies based on language teaching journals as well.

Sometimes journals have been kept by teachers participating in preservice or inservice training programs about their participation in those programs. In these cases the journal entries were not based on their teaching, but rather on what they were studying, how they learned, and how the material connected to their teaching. Two reports have been written about such "learning records," as they are called by Jennifer Jarvis (1992), or "academic journals" by Pat Porter, Lynn Goldstein, Judith Leatherman, and Susan Conrad (1990). The paper by Cole, Raffier, Rogan, and Schleicher on interactive group journals (1998) adds a collaborative dimension to diary-keeping about coursework during a teacher education program. The Ho and Richards (1993) article contains a helpful list of journal-keeping procedures and questions to promote reflection among teachers in formal training courses. Numrich (1996) analyzed the journals of 26 teachers-in-training who were completing their practice teaching.

Bailey, Bergthold, Braunstein, Fleischman, Holbrook, Tuman, Waissbluth, and Zambo (1996) collaborated on an article about what they learned by writing and then sharing their language learning autobiographies.

Karen Johnson (1999) discusses the "apprenticeship of observation" (Lortie, 1975) and offers many ideas for entries in reflective journals.

Allwright and Bailey (1991, 190–193) describe a project you can do in which your students keep journals of their language learning experiences. The insights derived from the learners' diaries can be very helpful in teachers' professional development efforts.

As we mentioned in one of the Teachers' Voices sections above, Joachim Appel (1995) has published a book based on the journal he kept while teaching EFL in Germany. The book relates his experiences to current literature on language teaching. We thought you might like to read his final entry about Oliver:

5th May: Oliver at 26

Met Oliver in the supermarket. Outwardly he hasn't changed much, although he is wearing glasses now. He has, like myself, a baby daughter. Recently he started his own business as a designer. I tell him about the book I am writing. He is amused. At the same time interested. School is over, yet it is never over. We talk about the "episodes" that happened between us ten years ago. He tells me his sister-in-law is training to be a teacher. He says he feels almost embarrassed thinking about his past as a pupil (Appel, 1995, 134).

5

USING CASES: STORIES IN THE AIR

We tell stories for many reasons: to entertain, to gossip, as evidence for our arguments, to reveal who we are. Sometimes we tell stories, especially about experiences that are puzzling, powerful, or upsetting, in order to render those experiences more sensible. Telling stories offers one way to make sense of what has happened. We may even catch a level of meaning that we only partially grasped while living through something (Mattingly, 1991, 235).

KATHI'S MONDAY STORY

Kathi Bailey

One day my friend Les (himself a teacher) picked me up at the Chinese University of Hong Kong, after what had been a particularly long and discouraging Monday. My two EFL classes had not gone well at all. I had felt disorganized and confused in both, even though I had prepared a lesson plan and extensive teaching materials in advance. I loaded my bags of papers and books into the car and collapsed into the passenger seat, obviously exhausted.

"How was your day?" asked Les.

I then proceeded to tell him about what I had tried to accomplish, how several little things had begun to go wrong, how the materials had confused my students, and finally how the entire lesson plan had fallen apart. Les listened patiently to my Monday tale of woe (as he always does). Then he said, "It sounds like you were over-prepared."

"No, I—I wasn't. I got so confused! I didn't feel prepared at all! I was—" I paused, stuck for a diagnosis. He was right—I had spent a lot of time over the weekend preparing the materials for my classes. What had gone wrong?

Suddenly, like the pieces of glass in a kaleidoscope tumbling into place when the cylinder is turned, a new awareness emerged: "Oh! No. I wasn't over-prepared. I was under-prepared. But I was over-supplied." I had had too much stuff, and I hadn't figured out how to use it well. The students and I were all overwhelmed by the materials. Les's interpretation—that I had been over-prepared—had given me a hypothesis to bump up against.

Reflecting on this simple story-telling experience, I saw a pattern in my teaching that had characterized thousands of unsuccessful lessons in a 25-year career: I often have more stuff to cover (both physically and conceptually) than I or the students can deal with in the time available. I am often aware that I haven't finished with my lesson plan. But telling Les about my unsuccessful Monday classes, hearing his interpretation of the events I had recounted, and then trying to create an alternative interpretation gave me a new insight about a pattern in my teaching. "The verbalization of a story in spoken discourse creates awareness… and better understanding… of tacit issues" (Olshtain and Kupferberg, 1998, 187).

5.1 *WHAT'S YOUR STORY?*

The Teachers' Voices section above is a story about telling a story. We don't actually hear the story about the Monday classes—we are only given a synopsis. Until she told the story, Kathi was stuck with her disappointing day. But telling the story and hearing her listener's quiet response gave her a different way of seeing the events. She didn't agree with Les's assessment that she had been over-prepared, but hearing him say it gave her one plausible explanation. Before hearing his comment on her story she had no explanation—just a disappointing day.

Think of a situation in which telling someone a story about your teaching led you to a realization. Then answer the following questions:

1. What was the story about?

2. Whom did you tell?

3. What did you realize?

4. In that situation, what were the factors that enabled you to learn something?

(It will be helpful for later Investigations if you save the answers to these questions.)

DEFINITIONS

What is a case study? According to Nunan (1992b, 75), a case study involves an "instance in action. In other words, one selects an instance from the class of objects and phenomena one is investigating (for example, 'a second language learner' or 'a science classroom')" and "investigates the way this instance functions in context.…[T]he case study is generally more limited in scope than an ethnography.…" It represents a "bounded system" (ibid.). In our field, case studies are a familiar genre in second language acquisition research. But more recently, they have been used in teacher development contexts as well.

Our thinking in this chapter has been influenced by Lee Shulman. In his framework, a case has "a narrative, a story, a set of events that unfolds over time in a particular place" (Shulman, 1992, 21). According to Shulman, a case is not just a report of an event or incident:

To call something a case is to make a theoretical claim. It argues that the story, event, or text is an instance of a larger class, an example of a broader category. In a word, it is a "case-of-something" and therefore merits more serious consideration than a simple anecdote or vignette. It implies an underlying taxonomy or typology, however intuitive or informal, to which a given case belongs....To call something a case, therefore, is to treat it as a member of a class of events and to call our attention to its value in helping us appreciate more than the particularities of the case narrative itself (ibid.).

Cases, Shulman says, can be either "documented (or portrayed) occasions or sets of occasions with their boundaries marked off, their borders drawn" (ibid., 12). So for instance, in the Teachers' Voices section above, we heard Kathi's meta-story (a story about a story). The original story was about two EFL classes that didn't go as planned. The generalizable interpretation was about having too much stuff, which led Kathi to understand the difference between being over-prepared and over-supplied—a long-term problem in her teaching.

In recent years a great deal of jargon has been associated with case-based methods of teacher preparation. Here are some of the key terms you may encounter:

Case materials are the raw data from which cases are constructed, whether by the original author or by a third party. They are diaries, personal letters, student work samples, videotapes, observer's notes, and so on.

Case reports are first-person accounts, reports written by someone who is reporting her or his own experiences, activities, and interpretations. When the author is the protagonist of the narrative, we are reading a case report.

Case studies are third-person accounts—the anthropologist's write-up of a native ritual, the psychologist's portrayal of a classroom episode, the teacher's presentation of the story of a child.

Teaching cases are original accounts, case reports, or case studies that have been written or edited for teaching purposes....Teaching cases can vary enormously in length, from the quite brief vignettes (a paragraph or two) used in teaching medical problem solving, through the lengthier narratives (two or three pages) employed in ethics courses (Shulman, 1992, 19).

Casebooks are collections of case reports, case studies, or teaching cases selected, sequenced, organized, and glossed for particular educational purposes (ibid., 20).

Decision cases are "cases which focus on dilemmas or critical incidents in teaching and are most often presented from the perspectives of individuals or organizations that must make decisions related to those dilemmas" (Jackson, 1997, 4). This type of case is typically open-ended and the readers are supposed to "make their own decisions while providing analyses and rationales to support their positions" (ibid.).

The story of Pa'a starts on p. 28. So, for instance, Kathi's story of Pa'a, the young woman who didn't understand the grid, is an example of a *case report*, because it is a first-person account of the incident.

5.2 *What Appeals to You?*

Throughout the rest of this book you will encounter examples of the case types defined above. At this point, which ones sound the most appealing to you as a reader of cases? If you were to try to write a case, which of the types listed above would you prefer to write?

We will argue here that creating cases (whether through talking or writing) and reading and discussing cases are all valuable forms of professional development. In the following Teachers' Voices section, Julian Edge explains why it is particularly important to tell our stories.

Julian Edge

> A lot of what we think we know is a jumble of unexamined information and feelings. When I try to put my thoughts into a coherent shape, as I have to if I am going to communicate them to someone else, I often find that my ideas are less clear than I thought they were. And I find that my opinions are not always as solidly founded as I wish they were. I find, then, that my ideas need developing, my plans need sharpening.

> There is another, more positive angle on this experience. Sometimes, it is exactly when I am trying to formulate my ideas that I see properly for the first time just exactly how they do fit together: By exploring my thoughts, I discover something new. That "something new" may well be the basis for a new plan of action that will move me along in an interesting direction.

> Finally, it is in my attempts to express—to express my self—that I bring together intellectual knowledge and my experiential knowledge in a way that obliges me to fuse the two into one person's integrated statement: mine. Experience and book-learning can drift along their separate ways indefinitely, but a serious attempt to articulate an individual opinion or position will bring the two together, and when I have made the statement that brings together my intellectual comprehension and my experiential understanding, I shall also have a much clearer idea of what I need to do next, whether that means gathering more experience or reading another book (1992, 7).

5.3 *Tell Us About It*

If you have teaching experience, think of a situation that you found perplexing, puzzling, upsetting, or annoying. What was the context (subject matter, physical environment, materials, etc.)? Who were the students (ages, genders, first language[s], goals, etc.)? What aspect of the event was puzzling, upsetting, or annoying to you? In other words, what happened? What did you do in response? What was the outcome? How did the episode end? (If you make notes in answering these questions, you will have the beginnings of a case report.)

Cases don't have to be written about problems (though they often are, since unsolved problems tug at our minds and we grow by grappling with them). Think of a teaching/learning experience in which you felt successful. Try to tell or write the story of the successful teaching event. (If you tell the story, tape-record the narration for possible transcription later.)

THE VALUE OF CASES

There is great pedagogical value in using cases. According to Shulman, cases can be used "to teach (1) principles or concepts of a theoretical nature, (2) precedents for practice, (3) morals or ethics, (4) strategies, dispositions, and habits of mind, and (5) visions or images of the possible" (1992, 2). Cases can also help in

> increasing motivation for learning, providing unique benefits to practitioners who participate in writing as case authors or commentators, providing specific antidotes to the dangers of overgeneralization from either the learning of principles or from prior cases, and serving as the instructional material around which participants can form communities for discussion or discourse (ibid., 2–3).

So in general education, as Shulman notes, cases have many potential uses. Recently, cases have been used in language teacher education as well.

Where do such cases come from? According to Richards, in language education, "[U]p to now little of this literature has been developed by teachers themselves or deals with teachers' accounts of how they resolve issues in teaching" (1998, xi). Richards feels that case studies are useful precisely because they "can provide a rich source of teacher-generated information that is both descriptive and reflective" (ibid., xii). We believe that the use of cases—reading them, writing them, and discussing them—can be very valuable in professional development.

One reason why cases (and particularly *case reports*) are useful is that they yield insiders' insights. Anthropologists, especially those who work in ethnography, draw a distinction between *emic* and *etic* explanations. *Etic explanations* come from the external theoretical framework of outsiders (usually researchers) who try to interpret the behavior of members of the culture they are studying. *Emic explanations*, in contrast, are based on the insiders' interpretation of events, physical artifacts, or belief systems (see Watson-Gegeo, 1988). Richards points out that cases written by teachers derive their power from the emic perspective:

> Case studies are a good example of how "insider" accounts of teaching can be used in teacher education.... Case accounts by teachers can illuminate the kinds of issues teachers deal with on a daily basis and how teachers deal with problems such as classroom management, student motivation and attitudes, and teaching strategies. Case accounts allow access not only to accounts of the problems teachers encounter but to the principles and thinking they bring to bear on their resolution (1998, xii).

Cases, then, are certain kinds of stories about teaching and learning. Shulman (1992, 21) states that such "teaching narratives" share a number of particular characteristics:

- Narratives have a plot—a beginning, middle, and end. They may well include a dramatic tension that must be relieved in some fashion.

- Narratives are particular and specific. They are not statements of what generally or for the most part is or has been.

- Narratives place events in a frame of time and place. They are, quite literally, local—that is, located or situated.

- Narratives of action or inquiry reveal the working of human hands, minds, motives, conceptions, needs, misconceptions, frustrations, jealousies, faults. Human agency and intention are central to those accounts.

- Narratives reflect the social and cultural contexts within which the events occur.

The connection of experience and narratives gives cases instructional power: "cases instantiate and contextualize principles through embedding them in vividly told stories" (ibid., 5).

5.4 *ANALYZE AND IDENTIFY*

Using Shulman's (1992, 21) characteristics of teaching narratives listed above, analyze the story of Pa'a in Chapter 2 (see page 28). Identify the elements of the story that illustrate the features of teaching narratives. If you are working with a group, it may be useful to share your ideas about these points with your classmates or colleagues.

WHY CASES WORK

A number of features seem to make cases useful in learning about teaching. Shulman identifies two: "their status as narratives and their contextualization in time and place" (1992, 21). They are also useful and applicable in teacher development for the following reasons:

> Cases show little respect for disciplinary boundaries. They are messy and recalcitrant. They rarely admit of a single right answer. They are therefore ideal for inducting the neophyte into those worlds of thought and work that are themselves characterized by unpredictability, uncertainty, and judgment (ibid., 8).

One of the characteristics of narratives that makes cases memorable is the fact that they include some action. Kathy Carter elaborates on this point:

> The action feature of story would seem to make it especially appropriate to the study of teaching and teacher education. Teaching is intentional action in situations, and the core knowledge teachers

have of teaching comes from their practice, i.e., from taking action as teachers in classrooms (1993, 7).

Jack Richards would agree. He thinks that preservice teacher preparation should focus on how teachers think, how they conceptualize issues, and how they use their beliefs, their experiences, and their pedagogical knowledge. Although methodology texts are useful, he feels, we also need:

> a complementary source of information on what teachers do when they actually enter classrooms and begin teaching, for it is then that issues arise that have often not been dealt with in a teacher preparation course. In responding to such issues, teachers draw on a wide variety of sources of knowledge: previous teaching experience, their own experience as learners, the knowledge they have acquired from training, as well as their own personal philosophies of teaching and learning.... (Richards, 1998, xii).

Cheryl Mattingly says that such narratives give meaning to our experiences, but they "also provide us a forward glance, helping us anticipate meaningful shapes for situations even before we enter them, allowing us to envision endings from the very beginning" (1991, 237). Narratives are powerful because we can relate to them, and because the development of the plot often parallels our development as persons (ibid., 248):

> Events in a story are construed as a passage, a movement from some initial situation through various twists and turns to some final situation....[N]arratives... nearly always contain an evocative element that draws listeners into an empathic identification with the protagonist that allows them to experience something of what being in this sort of situation would feel like if they were actually there.

This being drawn into a situation leads us to wonder, "What would I have done? What would I do, faced with a similar situation?" Such reflection can be promoted by reading cases others have written, but we also see great potential in writing case studies, and discussing case studies—both our own and those written by others. We will discuss each of these options in turn.

Reading Cases

The case study method of teaching is often associated with schools of law or business. Shulman (1992, 11) explains that a typical practice in business schools is to prepare a case in two versions. In the *A case,* background information is provided and alternate courses of action that might be taken are described. After the class has had a thorough discussion of the *A case,* the *B case* is unveiled. This version provides more information, including what the actors did and what the outcome was. According to Shulman, the incomplete nature of the *A case* is very important because the case itself should not limit the group's opportunity to analyze and discuss the situation by presenting an already complete account (ibid.).

Jack Richards has edited a volume of case studies written by language teachers from many different countries (*a casebook,* in Shulman's terms). Richards says that these case studies are not necessarily intended to be models of excellent teaching (1998, xiii):

Rather they are examples of significant teaching incidents and responses to them, as reported by teachers themselves, that can be used to explore and better understand how teachers work, to reflect on strategies that may work in different situations, as well as to consider alternative modes of thought and action.

Each case is followed by a comment from a teacher educator. Such comments can be helpful, but Richards acknowledges that they may also prematurely close the discussion. According to Shulman, proponents feel that "commentaries 'layer' cases by providing additional perspectives or lenses through which to view the events of the case. Skeptics fear that commentaries will function as verdicts that proclaim the one best way to interpret a case" (1992, 12).

Writing Cases

Writing original cases can be as helpful as reading them. Elite Olshtain and Irit Kupferberg explain that telling stories and creating cases are useful professional development endeavors because these processes allow us "to impose order and coherence on the unpredictable classroom reality where there are always alternative solutions to cope with similar problems…" (1998, 187). These authors continue (ibid.), "When teachers reflect on their professional world, they often retrieve relevant, well-remembered personal memories of past events. This process of reflection constitutes a reunderstanding of these events in the present circumstances…." Shulman feels that writing cases can lead us as teachers to be more reflective and more analytic about our teaching. In addition, he notes that writing such cases can "instill deserved pride in practitioners, especially teachers, whose own professional insights are rarely afforded the respect they deserve" (1992, 9).

Carter adds the idea that teachers' knowledge is "event structured" and for this reason, creating stories gives us access to such knowledge:

> [S]tories are especially useful devices for dealing with situation, conflict or obstacle, motive, and causality. In creating stories, we are able, therefore, to impose order and coherence on the stream of experience and work out the meaning of incidents and events in the real world (1993, 7).

This idea is related to Shulman's point that the field of teacher preparation now has a "growing understanding of narrative ways of knowing, of the local and situated character of cognition, and of the conditions needed for the development of cognitive flexibility to cope with unpredictable and fluid domains" (1992, 26). Language teaching is just such a domain, and we believe that writing cases about our experiences as teachers is a way of articulating the challenges we face.

The value of teaching narratives is not limited to storytellers and their listeners or readers. Cases have broader potential impact in terms of research. Terry Denny explains why storytelling is valuable in educational research:

> Weak theory comes and goes, but superb description survives the test of time…. Without good documentation, good story telling, we'll never get good educational theory, which we desperately need. Simply put, if you know what the problem is, you don't need a storyteller or an ethnographer…. Telling can contribute to our under-

standing of problems in education and teachers can help. Folks are forever calling for and proposing nifty solutions to problems never understood. Story telling is unlikely to help in the creation or evaluation of educational remedies, but can facilitate problem definition. Problem definition compared to problem solution is an underdeveloped field in education (Denny, 1982, 5).

So talking or writing about an event can help us to pinpoint issues of concern, whether for our own professional development, for the benefit of our immediate colleagues, or for the field.

Discussing Case Studies

One value of reading and/or writing cases lies in the kind of discussion they can promote. We can, of course, simply read (or write) case studies privately and think about them, or we can review and interpret the cases with classmates or colleagues. In such discussions there are two types or "layers" of discourse (Shulman, 1992, 15):

> In the first, the text or case itself is the object of inquiry as the group moves toward the... elaboration of multiple alternative readings. In the second layer, the dialogue becomes reflexive. The students begin to work reflectively on their own dialogue and analyses, treating them as a form of second-order text. They thus alternate between cognition and metacognition, between addressing the case and analyzing their own processes of analysis and review.

Although Shulman refers specifically to "students" (teachers-in-training), we believe that his statement also holds true for inservice teachers working in discussion groups.

Jane Jackson (1997, 7) has suggested using the following questions to focus the analyses of decision cases: (1) Why is this case a dilemma? (2) Who are the key players? (3) What are the main issues/problems? (4) What, if anything, should X do to resolve the dilemma? (5) What are the consequences of each solution? (6) What would you do if you were the decision-maker? and (7) What did you learn from this case?

These questions are most appropriate to use with open-ended decision cases. But they can also be used with case reports or case studies that contain resolutions, if you stop reading and answer questions 1 to 6 before reading the author's resolution to the problem. Jackson states that these questions "are intended to encourage creative and critical thinking, rather than suggest predetermined views about the case" (ibid.).

5.5 *FROM STORY TO CASE*

Think of a teaching situation that puzzled or worried you—perhaps based on an incident described in your teaching journal. Tell your story to a sympathetic colleague or friend. Ask the person in advance to listen quietly without interrupting or asking any questions until you are finished. It may be useful if you tape-record the story and the questions or comments that follow. It can also be helpful for the listener to retell or summarize the story, so the original author can see what points the listener considered most memorable or significant.

Next try to write your story as a case. Play the tape of your story if you feel it will help you to write the case. When you are happy with your draft, check to see if it embodies all of Shulman's (1992, 21) characteristics of narratives. If you are working with a group of classmates or colleagues, it will be instructive to read one another's cases.

Shulman's list is found on p. 79.

Finally, discuss the case you have written with two or three trusted colleagues. How does the experience for you, as the case writer, change if you (1) participate actively in the discussion of your case, or (2) listen without talking while your colleagues discuss the case?

We have argued above that there is a value in reading, writing, and discussing case studies. By definition, discussion involves at least one other person, while reading and writing can be solitary activities. Of course, there are advantages and disadvantages to both working individually and working collaboratively. The following grid provides a place to map out the pros and cons of either approach. On a separate sheet of paper, set up a similar grid. Then, in each cell, write one advantage and one disadvantage:

	Reading Cases	Writing Cases
Working on the Case Individually	*Advantage:* *Disadvantage:*	*Advantage:* *Disadvantage:*
Discussing the Case Collaboratively	*Advantage:* *Disadvantage:*	*Advantage:* *Disadvantage:*

If you are working with a group, it may be useful to share your impressions with your peers.

A TYPICAL DAY

While cases are often written about critical incidents or memorable events, there is also a value in documenting the commonplace. It can be very useful, in trying to understand our teaching contexts, to describe a typical day or a typical class period. Describing a typical class period, for instance, demands that we identify and articulate repeated elements in our teaching, thereby discovering patterns that cut across the individual lessons, days, courses, and semesters.

Because lessons, days, courses, and semesters are—by definition—units of time, trying to describe the prototype of any of these units is inherently a chronological proposition. To do so entails identifying the following:

1. typical openings (warm-up exercises in a lesson, or first-class sessions in a course);

2. typical next steps (presenting information or structuring a task in a lesson; covering discipline-based assumptions or introductory modules in a course);

3. usual application or practice opportunities;

4. common ways of checking learning, understanding, or progress;

5. procedures for reviewing; and

6. regular mechanisms for bringing about closure.

Depending on the fluidity or the structure inherent in our teaching contexts, such categories may arise from the system (e.g., describing a typical home room, second period, third period, recess, etc.), or they may be more intuitive and personal. For instance, in the Teachers' Voices section below, David describes a typical class period. He does not work from an institutionally mandated lesson plan format, but he does have clear sequences of events in mind in terms of how he chooses to realize instructional time with his learners in order to achieve the course objectives.

DAVID'S TYPICAL EFL CLASS

David Nunan

In my present teaching situation, I have to work very hard to build and maintain the trust and confidence of my students, as well as breaking down their inhibitions and reservations. The students come to my class from a variety of other classes. There are generally 18 to 21 students per class. They wander in over a 5- to 10-minute period, and I make sure that I'm in the room early to chat with them, and to get them to relax. As soon as all of the students are assembled, I take the class register, and then begin the class. I try to begin each class with a warm-up activity that gets the students interacting, and communicating with each other in English. I do this even in my academic essay-writing class.

The bulk of the class consists of small group interactive tasks that involve the students in learning experientially. During the small group tasks, I try to monitor the students as unobtrusively as possible. If I don't monitor, then I know that they will slip back into using their native language. If I monitor them too closely, then they'll stop talking altogether. From time to time, I might provide them with input on some aspect of the material that they're working on, but I try to keep this teacher-fronted teaching to a minimum.

Toward the end of the lesson, I ask representatives from the small groups to report on their work. Occasionally, I formalize this step by having each group summarize their discussion, or the outcome of their work, on a transparency. If there is homework to submit, I collect it at this point. If there is an assignment to be done, I remind students of what they are required to prepare for the next class.

5.6 *"A Typical Day"*

If you are a preservice teacher (or even an experienced teacher moving to a new setting), it can be useful to ask someone who is working in the position to which you aspire to tell you about a typical day. We suggest the following steps:

1. Arrange to interview a practicing teacher whose job seems interesting to you.

2. Ask that person to describe a typical class period. Make notes or audiorecord these ideas (with the teacher's permission).

3. Ask any questions you may have about the class, the curriculum, the school or program, and the students.

4. Give the teacher the opportunity to add to the description, in case any new ideas arose during the questioning.

5. Ask the teacher what the most rewarding aspects of this typical day are. In other words, what is it that keeps this person teaching, day after day, year after year?

6. Ask the teacher if there are any parts of the typical lesson (or day, or course) that he or she would really like to alter. If there are, what does the teacher think could be done to bring about such changes?

If you are an experienced teacher who is currently working, choose a unit of analysis (a lesson, a day, a course, a semester, etc.), and describe what is typical (either in speech or in writing). Think of your audience as a new person coming to work in your school or program. What would be the key things (both positive and negative) that person would need to know?

RESEARCH FINDINGS

Olshtain and Kupferberg conducted research on EFL teachers' knowledge in Israel. The authors state, "Telling stories enables teachers to impose order on the unpredictable classroom reality where each teacher formulates her own rules out of her own narrated experience" (1998, 185). They elicited data with a questionnaire that included both problem-solving and narrative items. The former described a teaching problem for which the teachers were to provide a solution. The latter required the teacher to tell a story related to the problem (ibid., 190). Three groups responded to this questionnaire: student teachers (still in their preservice training), new teachers (in their first few years of service), and more experienced teachers who had been designated as "experts." The expert teachers' discourse was longer and more elaborated than that of the less experienced teachers, but it was also qualitatively different:

> The differences between the three groups indicate that domain-specific professional knowledge develops gradually, and this development is conditioned, on the one hand, by the amount of class-

room experience and, on the other hand, by the ability to relate to this experience reflectively (ibid., 196).

They conclude that "the study of teachers' discourse provides us with a peep-hole into the practitioner's ongoing narrative thinking, illustrating how knowledge develops…" (ibid., 195).

5.7 *EXPLAINING OR NARRATING*

The following activities are loosely based on Olshtain and Kupferberg's research. Here are two tasks related to student participation in language classrooms. The first requires an explanation and the second elicits a story:

1. Some teachers believe that students should be required to speak in language classes. Others believe that students should not be forced to participate orally. Which position do you hold? Explain your reasoning.

2. Tell a story about a time when a typically passive student (or class) participated eagerly in a class discussion or activity.

Try to address these two tasks yourself before moving on to the next part of the investigation.

Do you think of yourself as a student teacher, a new teacher, or an experienced teacher? Olshtain and Kupferberg's research revealed differences in the way more experienced teachers dealt with tasks of explaining about teaching and telling stories about teaching. If you are an experienced teacher, try to find a student teacher and/or a new teacher to do these same tasks. (If you are a student teacher, try to find a new teacher and/or an experienced teacher, and so on.) What differences do you find in the resulting texts—the explanation versus the storytelling—for teachers with varying levels of experience? It may be helpful to make notes in a grid like the one below:

	Explanation	Story
Student Teacher		
New Teacher		
Experienced Teacher		

Returning to the earlier investigation (p. 85) in which you or another teacher described a typical lesson (or day or course), did you use explanation, or story, or both?

EXPLANATION AND EXPRESSION

The Investigations above contrast explanation and storytelling among more or less experienced language teachers. Peter Reason and Peter Hawkins, working in psychology and psychotherapy, used a similar approach in a cooperative inquiry process. They wrote about "storytelling as inquiry" (1988, 79), and proposed a model of "two basic modes of reflecting on and processing experience" (ibid.), explanation and expression, which are described as follows:

> *Explanation* is the mode of classifying, conceptualizing, and building theories from experience. Here the inquirer "stands back," analyses, discovers or invents concepts, and relates these in a theoretical model.... *Expression* is the mode of allowing the meaning of experience to become manifest. It requires the inquirer to partake deeply of experience, rather than stand back in order to analyse. Meaning... needs to be discovered, created, or made manifest, and communicated. We work with the meaning of experience when we tell stories, write and act in plays, write poems, meditate, create pictures, enter psychotherapy, etc. (ibid., 79–80).

Reason and Hawkins note that expression is often connected to producing beautiful or entertaining things (ibid., 81). But they also view expression as a "mode of inquiry, a form of meaning-making, and a way of knowing" (ibid.).

Explanation, in turn, can be realized through two approaches. The first consists of observation and description, as they are used in sciences such as botany and astronomy:

> [T]he inquirer senses the world either directly or through instruments, and endeavours to describe and then map out that which is experienced. This is essentially an analytical approach: dividing holistic experience into manageable components (ibid., 80–81).

The second approach to explanation is based on experimentation, in which the inquirer manipulates variables in order to test a theory. Reason and Hawkins themselves have proposed a more elaborate model (ibid., 84) depicting the relationship between explanation and expression. It is reprinted below as Figure 5.1:

Figure 5.1 **Explanation and Expression**

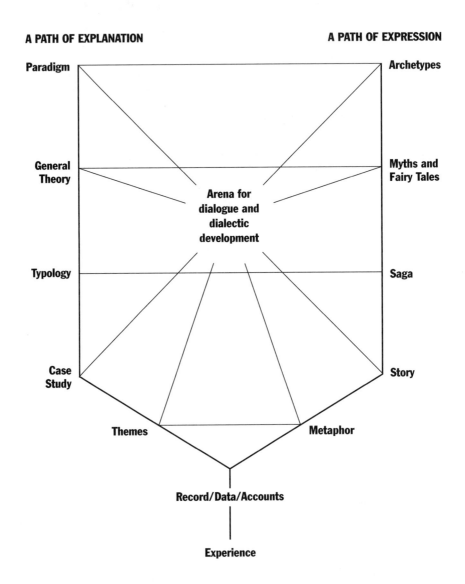

A PATH OF EXPLANATION

A PATH OF EXPRESSION

Paradigm

Archetypes

General
Theory

Myths and
Fairy Tales

**Arena for
dialogue and
dialectic
development**

Typology

Saga

Case
Study

Story

Themes

Metaphor

Record/Data/Accounts

Experience

Reason and Hawkins view explanation and expression as poles of a dialectic, rather than as competing approaches to knowing. The result is "two paths of inquiry: from experience through explanation to general theory; and from experience through expression to myth and archetype" (ibid., 85). Between these two paths lies the connection between stories and case studies.

In their work, Reason and Hawkins noticed that stories were powerful and efficient means of communicating: "[W]hen we wanted to share our practice with each other the best way was to tell each other stories. We also noted how we used stories for a variety of purposes in teaching, when working in groups and in therapy" (ibid.). Reason and Hawkins describe how they utilized the concept of story in a workshop about relationships (ibid., 89–90):

> [A]t the beginning of the workshop there was almost a "hunger" for stories; and yet people saw themselves much more as listeners than as storytellers. We kept being asked, "But what do you mean by a story?"; and we kept responding that any event retold from life which appeared to carry some meaning, however small, is a story.... What is needed is the development of easy, concrete ways to start the storytelling off, to create an inviting space that may then be filled.

They found that different ways of phrasing an invitation to talk led to different kinds of accounts: "Instead of asking 'Tell me about…', which leads to an explanatory account, one can ask, 'Tell me the story…', which invites more expression" (ibid., 100). Thus this exploration parallels that of Olshtain and Kupferberg's (1998) investigation of language teachers' knowledge.

POETRY AS EXPRESSION

Poetry is one form of expression that is seldom associated with teachers' reflection. Ann Carlson wrote this poem about a third-grade ESL student who came to her ESL class in tears (1992, 108):

Ann Carlson

THE CARD GAME

I shuffle the game cards again as
the small brown face
across the table crumples,
shameful tears sliding down his chin.

More shuffling, more
tears. I wait, calculating the time
I have for this
latest international
crisis.

What happened?, I ask.
Cards slap the table.
He stares as from a dream.
I know he has no English
Words for one more Anglo face today.

We are both shuffling now.

I trade another five minutes
for a smile,
a familiar joke.
There is so little time.

I can't fix it for him or
any of them but
I can shuffle the cards.

I have no gifts for this
child but a smile,
a joke, a language
that will never speak to his heart.
Such gifts!

5.8 *USING FORMS OF EXPRESSION*

What is your response to this poem? Have you ever been in a situation where your words could not help a student—where only your time and your patience would serve?

Try using some form of expression to tell about a teaching or learning experience. You could write a poem, or sketch, or paint. You could also try scripting an incident as a scene from a play. If you try this investigation, what do you learn or gain in the process?

We would like to encourage you to share the outcome of your efforts with trusted colleagues or classmates and ask them to write their responses. In doing so, you will be starting what Reason and Hawkins have called "cooperative inquiry" (1988, 100).

STORIES AND COOPERATIVE INQUIRY

Reason and Hawkins collected a number of the stories that had been told at their workshop, along with the other participants' responses to those stories. They found that these responses fell into four types: *replies, echoes, re-creations,* and *reflections*:

1. A *reply* is "my reaction to your story": an expressive way of giving shape to the feelings and ideas arising while listening to the story.

2. An *echo* or sharing response is "your theme in my story": here the listeners tell their own stories on the same theme.

3. A *re-creation* is "your story as re-created by me": here the listeners take the story and reshape it into another form, finding their own way of telling the tale. This could be a poem, a fairy tale, or some other kind of story.

4. A *reflection* is "my story about your story": essentially the reflection involves standing further back, it is more "about-ist," pondering the story (ibid., 91).

By labeling these four types of responses, Reason and Hawkins are employing explanation to describe different kinds of expression (ibid., 90). The uses of explanation and expression are not mutually exclusive. Indeed, they can be complementary processes:

[A]s one moves along the path of expression one may need to call on the clarity of explanation in order to see the available choices.... Similarly as one moves along the path of explanation one needs to call on forms of expression to give meaning to what may otherwise become arid and ungrounded concepts (ibid., 96).

Reason and Hawkins worked with storytelling as interactive, collaborative events. We believe such a process works well in teacher development contexts too. Their description of a workshop about relationships could just as easily be about a teachers' workshop:

As we told stories and listened to responses we became aware how quickly a story seemed to move from belonging to an individual to becoming part of the collective.... The responses were both intensely personal, and at the same time put alongside each other evoked the archetypal aspects of their relationship. At these points we felt that we moved on to, and evoked, a higher or deeper level of expression, that there was "something in the air" in the shared consciousness of the group, that we could feel but not yet touch, we could experience but not tie down. In later storytelling we have tried to find ways to express this collective story in the air, and found it almost palpable and at the same time elusive (ibid., 93).

Reason and Hawkins add that "One obvious application of storytelling is to the co-operative inquiry process" (ibid., 100). One of the Teachers' Voices sections in Chapter 2 contains Kathi's account of Pa'a, the ESL student who didn't understand the grid, and how the event led Kathi to a realization. In a sense, Kathi's recounting of the episode provides us with a case. But what is it a case *of*? Reason and Hawkins suggest that it can be helpful to *story-associate*; to ask the question, "What stories and myths does this tale bring to mind?" (ibid., 89). We illustrate this point in the following Teachers' Voices section, which gives us Andy's reactions to the story of Pa'a.

The story of Pa'a starts on p. 28.

ANDY READS THE STORY OF PA'A

The beginning of the story (Pa'a's background) triggered this response from Andy:

Memories of my mum talking about what life was like for a 12-year-old girl in British Guiana (now Guyana). She didn't sell flowers, but her schooling was stopped when she was 12 because she was a girl, and had to take care of the menfolk. Even with mum's tendency to exaggerate, if even half of what she said is true, it must've been a pretty terrible life.

Andy Curtis

Andy read a bit further in the story of Pa'a and then wrote:

Memories, this time much more recent, of when I am tempted to get impatient with students who don't do as I've asked them to, after carefully repeated and reformulated instructions or requests.

"Phoenix," I said to a student last week, "why did you have to check with Vincent whether you have started filming for your video project before you answered my question?"

"Because you talk so fast," replied Phoenix.

Bang! Thank goodness I had kept calm about the lack of response from Phoenix, and noticed the momentary glance at Vincent and his quick nod. "I'm sorry," I said. "Please let me know when I do that."

In Andy's recounting of the brief exchange with Phoenix, we see that he has indeed made a connection between the story of Pa'a case and his own teaching experience. He continues,

Now I really am intrigued. What's going to happen in this story next? What will be Pa'a's reason for not getting on with the task?

Andy read the story to the point where Pa'a finally began to do the task:

Thank heavens for that—a happy ending! And a sigh of relief from me! I read "Here's the lesson I learned" and then put down the book, to prevent myself from reading further, so I could complete the thought myself, and see how it compared to Kathi's.

By setting the book down at this point, before he read the resolution to the story of Pa'a, Andy has, in effect, created what Shulman called an *"A case"*—one in which the solution is not provided (1992, 11). This action allowed Andy to respond to the problem on his own before hearing how someone else dealt with the situation in the case report:

So, I would've learned, I think, that concepts that I might label in my mind as simple, are not necessarily easy for my students. OK, let's see. What did Kathi learn? I think she said it was a "profound lesson"—the teacher as learner, full role-reversal switchback....

At this point Andy finished reading the case. Then he wrote,

What Kathi learned is different from what I learned, but it's true, I did have to sit here with my own hands overlapped to see what she was describing.

These moments of revelation that we jointly experience with our learners in class often seem to happen when a student gives me a "wrong" answer, but one that shows a way of looking at the question I posed that I would never have imagined. This makes me think to myself (and say to them), "Great!" These moments are, for me, one of the best things about teaching.

5.9 TASKS FOR DEVELOPMENT

We agree with Jane Jackson, who states, in her discussion of decision cases, that "cases can help novice teachers develop the skills needed by professional ESOL teachers or sharpen the skills of experienced teachers" (1997, 9). But whether you are just beginning your career as a language teacher or you have many years of teaching experience, we hope this chapter has interested you in the uses of cases and other teaching-related narratives for professional development purposes. The following tasks are intended to expand your understanding of the value of cases in particular, and narrative ways of knowing in general.

1. Consider these questions about teachers' learning, framed in the context of Kathi's story about Pa'a and the grid:

    A. What did Kathi learn by interacting with Pa'a and trying to explain the grid activity to her in class that day?

    B. What did Kathi learn later, by thinking about and writing the story of the incident?

    C. What, if anything, did you as an individual learn by reading about Pa'a?

    D. If you are working with a group, what did you learn by discussing the case with your classmates or colleagues?

2. How do you think Pa'a felt and what do you think she learned from the event recounted in Chapter 2? Try to retell the story from the learner's point of view. You could either do this in a role play (in which you, as Pa'a, talked about the episode to a friend) or in writing. For instance, you could write a letter (as Pa'a) to a friend, explaining what happened in your ESL class.

3. You could also try *to explain* the event from the point of view of an observer who was not participating in the interaction (Kathi's team teaching partner, for instance, or a peer observer). Remember if you take this stance, however, that you do not have direct access to either Kathi's or Pa'a's thoughts. What questions might arise in your mind about the teacher's and the student's interaction if you were to observe it? If you write the case from an observer's vantage point, you will have an example of what Shulman calls a *case study* (1992, 19).

4. In the last Teachers' Voices section of this chapter you saw Andy's response to the story of Pa'a. Using the definitions from Reason and Hawkins (1988, 91), would you say Andy's response was a *reply*, an *echo*, a *re-creation*, or a *reflection*? Why do you think so? If you are working with a group, compare your analysis with those of your classmates or colleagues.

5. Try writing your own reactions to the story of Pa'a using one or more of the types of response identified by Reason and Hawkins (*reply, echo, re-creation,* or *reflection*) as Andy did. If you are working with a group of classmates or colleagues, it will be helpful if different people select different response modes so you can compare and contrast what you write.

6. Shulman's (1992, 21) characteristics of teaching narratives are listed again below. Using a case that you or one of your colleagues has written, identify the elements of the story that illustrate these features: (A) Narratives have a plot—a beginning, middle, and end. (B) They may well include a dramatic tension that must be relieved in some fashion. (C) Narratives are particular and specific. (D) Narratives place events in a frame of time and place. (E) Narratives of action or inquiry reveal

the working of human hands, minds, motives, and emotions. (F) Narratives reflect the social and cultural contexts within which the events occur. If you are working with a group, share your ideas about these points with your peers.

7. If you have kept a teaching journal, you may find that rereading your entries provides a rich source of background data for describing a typical lesson or a typical day. We would like to encourage you to write such a description and then to address the following questions:

A. In describing your typical day (or lesson or course), are there any regular recurring elements that you would like to change?

B. If so, what motivates you to change these factors?

C. How could you bring about the desired changes?

It may be helpful if you use a chart such as the following grid to help you structure your ideas:

	A. Elements to Be Changed (What to Change)	B. Motivation for Changing (Why to Change)	C. Ways to Bring About Change (How to Change)
1.			
2.			
3.			

8. In Chapter 2 we encouraged you to tape-record yourself telling someone about how you learned something about teaching. You could now replay the tape and see if you used explanation, expression, or both. Could your recording be developed into a written case report?

Suggested Readings

The case study approach to professional development can focus on many different sorts of topics. An individual learner, a certain class session, a particular problem, or even an entire course can serve as the "case." For example, Martha Clark Cummings (1996) wrote about teaching writing to a group of immigrant adults in New York City. All of her students had failed the writing course at least once before, so she faced a number of challenges in teaching them.

Tom Russell and Hugh Munby (1991) have examined the practice of two teachers—Deane, who teaches elementary school, and Roger, a junior high school science teacher. The case study uses direct quotes from the teachers to investigate reflection-in-action (Schön , 1991, 165).

James Cooper's (1995) book, *Teachers' Problem Solving: A Casebook of Award-Winning Teaching Cases*, is a collection of nine cases that won a national competition on case writing in the United States. The cases are not specific to language teaching, but they are useful nonetheless.

Ted Plaister (1993) published a book of case studies about ESOL teaching and administration, including 35 cases on vocabulary, tutoring, writing, reading, and listening comprehension, and 18 case studies related to administrative concerns.

Jerry Gebhard (1996, 9–14) compares two EFL lessons (written as case studies) to introduce the concept of self-development for language teachers.

As noted above, Jack Richards (1998) has edited an international volume of cases from language classrooms representing nearly 20 countries. Each chapter documents a problem and a solution written by a practicing teacher, followed by comments by another teacher or teacher educator.

Jane Jackson (1997) discusses the benefits and limitations of case-based learning in preservice training for ESOL teachers. This article contains a list of case method distribution centers for teacher education. (See also Jackson, 1998.)

Leo van Lier (1996) has written about a Spanish-Quechua bilingual program in Peru. He begins with a description of a typical day in the lives of the teachers and the students.

Richard Watson Todd has argued that poems can be used in teacher education: "Poetry in general is more open to interpretation than closely-argued articles, and thus allows trainees to find their own meanings and understandings…" (1998, 11).

Horace's Compromise: The Dilemma of the American High School (Sizer, 1983) begins with a prologue that describes a typical day in the life of Horace, an experienced secondary school English teacher somewhere in the United States. This brief description demonstrates, without editorializing, the value of the "typical day" genre.

If you want to work more with original case studies, we recommend an article by Richard Ackerman, Patricia Maslin-Ostrowski, and Chuck Christensen (1996), which provides a clear description of a workshop in which teachers write and discuss their own cases.

6

LANGUAGE LEARNING EXPERIENCE: ROLE REVERSAL

I've been teaching for ten years, making assumptions about how my students felt, which ones were nervous and which ones weren't, and it's really rather frightening for me to realize how much was going on, important things that were happening to people in the class, that I really didn't know about (Lowe, 1987, 93).

The comment above was made by Martin Parrot, a teacher who had participated with a group of colleagues as a student in a Mandarin class. The goal of the course was to "give teachers a chance to renew their connection with language learning, and thereby to become more sensitive to the problems and processes confronting their learners" (Lowe, 1987, 89). Such language learning experiences can be very powerful, and can lead to interesting insights about language and teaching, whether or not we are native speakers of the language we teach.

Indeed, one of the best opportunities for a language teacher's professional development is to get into a language learning situation. Whether you are taking a class or just studying a language on your own, whether you begin a new language or try to increase your proficiency in one you've already studied, the experience of putting yourself in the learner's shoes can be incredibly illuminating (and sometimes even humbling). This chapter suggests ways that we as language teachers can enhance our professional development by traveling, taking classes, or participating in "shock" language lessons. Even eavesdropping on conversations or listening to radio broadcasts in languages that are not our own can be very revealing.

Being aware of our own mental processes and affective responses to foreign or second language learning experiences can help in at least three ways: First, the experience can lead us to understand the challenges our learners face. Second, it can help us to better understand language, and specific languages. Finally, taking the learners' role and attending to both effective and ineffective teaching can subsequently help us to develop our own actual teaching strategies.

6.1 *HEAR AN UNKNOWN LANGUAGE*

Spend at least 30 minutes watching a television program or listening to a radio broadcast in a language you do not understand. What is the experience like? What can you say about the broadcast language after listening for half an hour?

At what point, if at all, do you feel your attention wavering? How do you feel during and after the experience?

KATHI'S WORKSHOP IN BRAZIL

One summer I was working in Brazil, doing workshops for EFL teachers there. The participants (native speakers of Portuguese) got into a heated debate about whether language lessons should use the learners' first language (L1). About a third of the group thought that it was acceptable to use the L1 to explain tricky grammar points and so on. One third was undecided, and the remaining third was adamant that teachers should NEVER use the learners' L1 in a lesson. Reflecting upon this class that evening, I decided that as a group we needed some common experience to ground our discussion of the merits and demerits of using the students' home language in a foreign language classroom. So the next day I started our class with a "shock language lesson." I walked into class and spoke nothing but Korean (a good trick, since I recall only about 30 vocabulary items from my life as a US Army wife in Korea in the early 1970s).

Kathi Bailey

The Brazilian teachers' reactions ranged from intrigued to amused to befuddled to horrified. As I greeted them and got them to respond in the target language, I continued to speak only Korean, gradually introducing a couple of useful verbs, the equivalents of house, car, man, and woman (with pictures representing these nouns), as well as thank-you, you're welcome, and a few other basic phrases. It was amazing to me that some of the teachers who had been most vocal about not using the learners' L1 in the classroom were among those most frustrated and intimidated by the experience of being restricted to the target language. After about half an hour of nothing but Korean, I asked the group (in English, our common language) to respond individually in writing to two questions:

1. What do you think you know about this language? (Think about morphology, vocabulary, pronunciation, word order, etc.)

2. How do you feel right now?

The Brazilian EFL teachers worked quietly by themselves for a few minutes to answer these questions. They then shared their answers in small groups. In our plenary discussion following the group work, several interesting patterns emerged, including the following:

- Each group was able to make correct generalizations, based on the data, about word order and how questions are formed in Korean.

- They were able to make some accurate statements about Korean phonology.

- They correctly identified *thank-you* and *you're welcome*, but often confused these phrases.

- They had discerned two different verbs that roughly equate to the English *to be*, but they had not figured out the distribution rules that govern the choice of one form over the other.

- They thought they knew the noun equivalents of *man, woman, car,* and *house* (and indeed, it appeared that they had learned these lexical items).

- They thought that [+ human] nouns end with the marker /ja/. On the basis of the available nouns, this assumption was well founded. However, it is not true of Korean nouns in general, so this point provided an opportunity for an interesting discussion about how language learners make inferences on the basis of the available input.

- No one in the group knew what language I had been speaking.

The Brazilian EFL teachers in this course all agreed that it was very unnerving to be completely without L1 guidance in a foreign language lesson and to have to rely on context, gestures, pictures, and modeling by the teacher and one's classmates to derive understanding. Some found this situation amusing and intriguing; others found it humiliating and disorienting. After this experience, those participants who had felt that language teachers should never use the students' first language in class were not quite so sure. The experience of being confused, lost, and perhaps even embarrassed in an initial language lesson had caused them to reconsider their position.

We are not suggesting here that all language teachers must know the first language(s) of their students (though it certainly can be helpful). We are focused instead on the potential for awareness raising that language learning experiences can offer us as language teachers.

6.2   OBSERVING A LESSON IN AN UNKNOWN LANGUAGE

Observe a language lesson in a language you don't speak. Try to remain in the role of a nonparticipant observer for this activity. In this case, it may be useful if you DO NOT ask the teacher anything about the lesson plan in advance. Try to be aware of your inferences about the target language and the teaching/learning process as you watch the class.

If possible, go with a colleague or classmate to observe a class taught in a language that neither of you speaks. Again, maintain the role of a nonparticipant observer. Or watch a video of such a language lesson with a group of colleagues or classmates. Afterwards take a few minutes to write your individual responses to the experience and then compare your reactions to those of your colleagues or classmates.

Set up a "shock language lesson" for yourself and a group of trusted colleagues. Find someone who can offer your group an introductory language lesson for at least 30 minutes. Remember that the intended focus here is not to critique the teacher or the method. Instead the purpose is for you to experience foreign language learning firsthand. Immediately after the lesson, the "learners" should each write at least a paragraph in response to two questions:

1. What do you think you know about this language? (Think about morphology, vocabulary, pronunciation, word order, etc.)

2. How do you feel right now?

We have found this experience to be most powerful when the group members are exposed to a language that is not one—and not even similar to one—they have previously studied.

EXPERIENTIAL AND RECEIVED KNOWLEDGE

No matter how you feel about the use of the students' L1 in the classroom, the point of Kathi's story is that the experience of being confronted with a completely foreign language, with no recourse to explicit mother-tongue equivalents or explanations, challenged some of the Brazilian EFL teachers' beliefs about L1 use in the classroom. We believe that experiencing an issue, concept, or event firsthand leads to different types of awareness and understanding than does simply reading about the issue, or even discussing it with colleagues.

Michael J. Wallace has written a book called *Training Foreign Language Teachers: A Reflective Approach*. The basic premise underlying this approach is that what teachers know consists of (at least) experiential knowledge and the received knowledge of the field (Wallace, 1991, 14–15). *Received knowledge* is "the vocabulary of the subject and the matching concepts, research findings, theories and skills which are widely accepted as being part of the necessary intellectual content of the profession..." (ibid.). *Experiential knowledge* relates to the "knowledge-in-action by practice of the profession" (ibid.)—in other words, the knowledge we amass through our personal experience with teaching. The relationship of those two types of knowledge is depicted in Figure 6.1 (ibid., 49):

Figure 6.1 **Reflective Practice Model of Professional Education/Development**

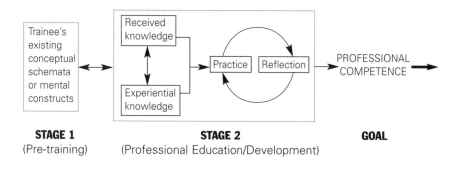

STAGE 1   STAGE 2   GOAL
(Pre-training)   (Professional Education/Development)

As this figure shows, both experiential knowledge and received knowledge are key components of teachers' expertise. The problem for us as teachers (in blending these two types of knowledge) is twofold. First, it's often difficult to incorporate the received knowledge of the field into our day-to-day classroom activities. On the other hand, we often use our experiential knowledge to make decisions without realizing that we are doing so. The following quote from a teacher in Australia (from Brindley, 1991, 103–104) illustrates this delicate balance well:

> Practically speaking I knew a lot—I was very much involved in it as a practitioner....I was quite confident that I had a good understanding of what was going on because I was actually involved in doing it. But then I sort of realized the further and further I got into it that that was on a different level, that experiential level, and that there was a whole other level that I was really unaware of. And once I started reading the literature, then I realized... how much I didn't know about it all. And so it was just completely different levels. I was operating at a practitioner level... this other body of work that's in the... literature...I didn't really delve deeply into....

The two "levels" referred to by this teacher represent experiential knowledge and the received knowledge of the field, in Wallace's terms. Julian Edge (1992, 6) has referred to these two kinds of knowledge as *experiential understanding,* and *intellectual comprehension,* respectively.

6.3 *WHAT'S THE SOURCE?*

Write three principles of language learning and teaching that you firmly believe. (This list will be useful when you read Chapter 12 about Teaching Portfolios, so please save it.) Now look at Figure 6.1 (on p. 99), about experiential knowledge and received knowledge. What is (or are) the source(s) of your three beliefs? That is, how did you come to hold these three principles to be important and true—through experiential knowledge, received knowledge, or both?

CHRIS LEARNS JAPANESE

Our purpose in this chapter is to illustrate the value of language learning experiences as avenues to professional development. Such experiences might be as brief as a single "shock language lesson" or as lengthy as the lifelong efforts of nonnative speaking teachers improving their own proficiency. Even learning a new phrase can trigger our awareness in important ways. For instance, in this Teachers' Voices section, we see what Chris Wenger realized about asking permission to use a telephone in Japanese, while he was working as an EFL teacher in Japan.

Chris Wenger

> I think the level of complexity and variety that we bring [to language lessons] can be tempered by the learners' level to some extent. For example, when I was learning Japanese I remember wanting to know how to ask to use someone's phone in their apartment. I ended up saying "Denwa o tsukaitai" (I want to use the phone) because that was the closest thing in meaning that I knew how to produce. Eventually in the same situation I heard someone else say, "Denwa o tsukatte mo ii desu ka?" (Is it OK if I use your

phone?). Then I was able to recognize its meaning, and I was at a point where I was able to understand its makeup and reconstruct it, so I incorporated the correct phrase from then on.

My point is that as a low level learner at that time, it probably wouldn't have done me much good to see five to ten different ways to ask for permission, analyze them, and then think I'd be able to remember them all in order to recognize them, much less produce them.... With Krashen's "i+1" in mind, I would try to choose a number of expressions using language that was just enough beyond the learners' comprehension that it would awaken their ability to recognize, and reconstruct the expressions, but not overwhelm them so that the goal became unachievable. (At the outset we can give more models and input to develop listening than we can at the same level for speaking, though eventually the former feeds into the latter.) How can we judge this? Ahh, that's the sweet mystery of life.... In any event, where production is concerned, confidence-building is key, especially in Asian EFL!

So just remember that not all input is appropriate input at all levels and for all purposes. Sure, every once in a while we might even run the risk of de-authenticating the language somewhat (by simplifying, using low-frequency vocabulary, bringing the speed down, etc.), but just because we've taught learners how to step on the gas, turn the wheel, and use their mirrors doesn't mean they're ready for the Indy 500 (or to drive a bus in Manila).

6.4 BRIDGING THE GAP

When Chris Wenger refers to "Krashen's i + 1" in the Teachers' Voices section above, he is talking about Stephen Krashen's comprehensible input hypothesis— the idea that people learn language when the input they receive is somewhat above (represented by "+1") their current level of interlanguage development (represented by "i" for interlanguage) (Krashen, 1982, 20). Think of an instance when you have been faced with input in another language that was just a bit challenging for you. Did that input help you learn? If so, how?

In the Teachers' Voices section above, Chris's experience of noticing the gap (Schmidt and Frota, 1986) between his request to use a telephone and someone else's way of expressing the same need led him to reflect about important constructs in the received knowledge of the field. Think of a situation in which you noticed the gap between what you said or wrote and the form that was produced by a native (or a more proficient) speaker of the target language. What were the circumstances? Were you able to incorporate the correct form in your own language use at that time? Did you remember the correct form later when you wanted to use it?

DEANNA LEARNS BAMBARA

In this Teachers' Voices section, Deanna Kelley talks about how a total immersion situation in Africa influenced her teaching ESL to secondary school students in California.

Deanna Kelley

Peace Corps training was great. What more could a language junkie like me want? I got a free ticket to West Africa, room and board, some really interesting people to meet, and hours and hours of free language lessons. I was in Mali, a country in francophone West Africa, so I got to continue to study French, but what really caught my attention was Bambara—a language whose name I didn't even know how to pronounce before I embarked on my adventure. I had never heard a single word of this language before in my life—so very different from the French and Spanish I had studied before. It seemed so exotic and exciting!

The way that I was taught Bambara was new and exciting too. I still see in my mind, clear as if it were yesterday, the brilliant smile of my first instructor, Hawa, as she patiently pulled my first Bambara words from my mouth within 24 hours of my arrival in Mali.

My beliefs about language teaching are the reflections of my language learning experiences. They are ongoing and recent enough that I remember my struggles, I remember the revelations I had, I remember the activities that helped me learn.

One part of my Bambara learning experience that was quite different from my previous Spanish and French learning was that I was not allowed to sit at a desk and quietly observe the language lesson and only answer an occasional question, as was my earlier tendency—not stretching my comfort zone. Instead, we were all active participants in the classes, we were strongly encouraged to speak in Bambara outside of class, and every Friday we had an interview with one of the instructors to see how we were progressing.

One Friday, a few weeks into the training, I was being interviewed by Mamadou, an enthusiastic instructor with a mischievous glint in his eye. After struggling through a few very basic questions, I gave an exasperated sigh, saying *"Mamadou, je ne peux rien dire, je ne peux pas parler le Bambara!"* (Mamadou, I can't say anything, I can't speak Bambara!) Much to my surprise, rather than sadly agreeing with me, he boldly said *"Si! Tu peux!"* (Yes! You can!) and continued to patiently remind me of all that he knew that I knew. He asked me, "How do you say *I*"? And I responded correctly. Then "How do you say *go*"? I could answer that as well. "And *school*?… and *every day*?" I knew these words. "Now put them in a sentence," he told me. Suddenly, I realized that I could speak Bambara: *"N be taa lakoli la don go don!"*

Mamadou had stretched my belief of what I could do, stretched my comfort zone a bit. I was used to being a student who always sat silently taking in the language for years, learning how to read and write it rather well, but leaving my speaking ability way behind.

That was what I found to be easy and what teachers seemed to expect from me—the quiet one sitting in the corner. It wasn't lack of motivation or interest in language learning. I was fascinated by it and dreamed of the day when I would be able to speak easily, but I didn't challenge myself to speak.

The results of the style of teaching I experienced in Peace Corps training were amazing to me. Before I knew it, I could have conversations in Bambara. My host family grinned with approval when I took the risk of speaking to them in Bambara instead of French. I had become convinced that, even with limited resources, I *could* communicate by putting together the pieces that I did know. I had found the confidence I needed in order to continue taking the risk of speaking with others in Bambara as much as I could. As a result, I was finding more opportunities for meaningful interaction that helped me to learn even more.

So, now I am working with a high school ESL class of native speakers of Spanish in California. They're learning to read and write and to listen to me and each other. I'm also trying to push them to speak more than just isolated words or memorized dialogues. I recently interviewed many of them individually, and it was exciting to hear them put together the pieces of language that they know, forming longer, more complex discourse and showing me what they can say—that they *can* speak English.

6.5 LISTENING TO YOURSELF

Participate in a conversation in your second language, either with a native speaker of that language or with a nonnative speaker who is more proficient than you are. With that person's permission, tape-record the conversation. If you made many errors, how did your interlocutor respond to them? How did the person teach you (or just supply you with) new words, if there were gaps in your vocabulary? What syntactic elements were difficult for you and how were they negotiated in the conversation? How did you feel during and after the conversation? (You could try this task with two different people—one who is a language teacher and one who is not.)

You can also use the taped conversation as the basis of a stimulated recall experience. In *stimulated recall*, some data (usually audiotapes, videotapes, photographs, transcripts, or an observer's notes) are used to prompt, or stimulate, a person's memory of a situation he or she experienced (see Nunan, 1989, 66–70). The data typically elicit more vivid and trustworthy recollections than would be possible working from memory alone. As you listen to the audiotape of your conversation, record several brief reactions in three columns as follows:

What was said	What I was thinking	What I was feeling

Your data may reveal some interesting information about the language learner's cognitive and affective responses to language processing.

As an additional step, you could play the tape for your conversation partner and ask that person to write comments in these three columns as well. If you are able to do this, it should be quite interesting to compare the records resulting from the two stimulated recall processes. Again, you can look at what the data suggest about teaching.

CONTEXT

Being immersed in a new language can be a revealing experience. It can provide us with insights about language, nonverbal behavior, cultural contrasts, and human interaction, whether or not we are taking language courses. What we gain from the experience will depend on various factors including our prior experience, our attitudes toward language learning, our personality, and the context in which the language learning experience takes place.

Context is particularly important. Does the experience take place in a second or a foreign language situation? Is it an immersion experience or a foreign language classroom in which the teacher uses our first language as well as the target language? (Learning Thai in the United States will be a different experience from learning it in Bangkok. Learning Spanish in Madrid in an intensive program will be different from learning it in an evening class in Chicago.)

The following Teachers' Voices segments are from two experienced language teachers who put themselves into total immersion experiences for a brief time. In the first case, Andy Curtis was traveling in Thailand and was not formally studying the language. In the second case, Laura Latulippe, the director of an Intensive English Program, enrolled in a two-week intensive Spanish program as a beginner in Costa Rica.

ANDY IN THAILAND

Andy Curtis

The first thing I noticed while traveling in Thailand was the tonal quality of the Thai language, which has five tones, compared to Cantonese, which I think has up to nine. I also noticed how much I preferred the tones of Thai to Cantonese, which reminded me of how much of what we filter of another language and culture is based on what we feel, no matter how irrational those feelings might be. Even our best attempts at being objective about learning a language are influenced by our positive or negative disposition toward that language and culture.

With my sense of direction, I was constantly getting lost and having to rely on the patience and goodwill of people on the streets to put up with my miming and gesticulating, as I tried to find my way back to the hotel. Not only were people very helpful, but I noticed that the more open I was, the more open they were. So if I smiled or laughed and thanked them, whether they were able to help me or not, that did help, as, on more than one occasion, the person who couldn't help me called on someone else who could.

Once or twice, I even pretended to be more lost than I was, just as an excuse to interact with people on the streets and in shops, most of whom didn't speak any English (and I spoke no Thai). Time and again, the interaction was friendly, which gave me the courage to ask someone else. This reminded me of all that research on language learners' anxiety in the classroom and how things as simple (and as complex) as a genuine smile, nonverbal encouragement, friendliness, and openness can really affect our willingness to go on and continue the journey.

Another thing I noticed was how little spoken language is actually needed in brief, uncomplicated interactions and exchanges. As teachers, and perhaps particularly as language teachers, we may forget this. But spending a while in a country in which you don't speak the language and the people don't speak yours is a wonderful reminder of how much can be achieved without any words, and of the value and power of nonverbal communication.

6.6 WHAT ABOUT YOU?

Think about Andy's experience of traveling in Thailand without being able to speak Thai. If you have had a chance to travel to a region where you don't speak the language, what did you notice about trying to communicate with the people there? If the language was written in a script that you don't read, how did the experience of being illiterate affect you?

LAURA STUDIES SPANISH IN COSTA RICA

Laura Latulippe has written a brief but informative article called "Lessons Learned from Being a Student Again." Here's how she framed the experience of studying Spanish as a beginner in Costa Rica (Latulippe, 1999, 17):

> Having spent 25 years as an ESL professional, I wanted to gain new perspectives on language learning while renewing my energy. I decided to enroll in an intensive Spanish program in Costa Rica. My interest in Latin American culture and the usefulness of knowing Spanish also influenced my decision. I embarked on this adventure with apprehension as I don't consider myself a good language learner, and I knew that I would experience a loss of status by trading the role of intensive English program (IEP) director for that of a beginning language student. Although I followed the advice I give ESL students, I encountered familiar difficulties.

Laura
Latulippe

Laura encountered three major problems during her two-week intensive course: (1) the pressure to speak one's first language, (2) frustration with the pace of learning, and (3) the loss of self-esteem. Here are her descriptions of each:

Pressure to Speak One's First Language

I wanted to be the perfect language student but quickly encountered my first problem: Many of my English-speaking classmates wanted to speak English outside of class, even the Japanese students. At first, I resisted, not saying much but speaking only Spanish. Every evening I studied vocabulary and structure for hours to have something to say the next day.

After four days, exhausted from speaking only Spanish, I planned an evening of English conversation with a classmate. When she arrived at the restaurant with her host family, she understood the look on my face. "I'm sorry," she whispered, "they insisted." Despite my initial response, the evening was a turning point. In addition to speaking Spanish, we laughed a lot and I began to feel more comfortable with the language. I slept happily exhausted that night, waking with a determination to keep trying (ibid.).

Frustration with the Pace of Learning

Frustration with the pace of learning is the second familiar problem I encountered. Despite studying and practicing every evening, each day I forgot vocabulary learned the previous day. Having to relearn as well as learn new things each day, it seemed I would never acquire enough Spanish to survive, let alone communicate ideas. To beginning students, the final goal seems nearly impossible to achieve.

I tackled this problem by setting daily goals, such as being able to describe my son's recent wedding in Spanish. For this goal, I learned the necessary vocabulary and structures, then practiced by telling the increasingly more complex story to each of the school's teachers (ibid.).

Loss of Self-esteem

Humor is one solution for the third problem, an important one for older students: the self-esteem loss that occurs when students find themselves in a status they perceive to be lower than that at home. I knew barely enough Spanish to get through daily tasks. Often I saw impatience on the face of my host mother, and waitresses spoke to me with the tone of voice used for children or frowned as I spoke. I wanted to tell people, "Listen, I may not be making much sense to you, but I got some of the words right and that's pretty good for me." After a few days, I was embarrassed to tell anyone my profession.

I kept up my own morale by including funny comments in my homework and speech, showing my teachers that, despite my inadequate Spanish, I am a likable person. I also laughed at my own mistakes, happily telling stories illustrating my errors. Everyone heard me say I had 51 children, thinking I was asked my age...(ibid.).

Latulippe ends her article by saying that before she went to Costa Rica, she anticipated problems. Her conclusion capsulizes our point in this chapter: "I was surprised at my initial reactions to these obstacles and gained new insights into how our IEP students must feel and how we can help them" (ibid.).

6.7 *TURNING POINTS*

Laura Latulippe describes an evening that was a "turning point" in her lan-guage learning. As a learner, have you ever experienced a turning point? What was the situation?

She also discussed three factors that influenced her experience in Costa Rica. Drawing upon your own experience or that of other language learners, give an example of each: pressure to speak one's first language; frustration with the pace of learning; and loss of self-esteem.

Now think of yourself in your role as a language teacher. If some of your students came to you and voiced their concerns about these three factors, what would you say to them? How could you alter your lessons, or facets of your program, to account for these concerns?

LANGUAGE LEARNING IN TEACHER EDUCATION

Language learning experiences are often used as components in preservice and inservice teacher education programs. For instance, Larsen-Freeman (1983, 269–270) describes how a language learning experience is used in the teacher preparation program at the School for International Training. For a week or so, the teachers-in-training study a language they have not studied previously. At the end of the language course they write about the experience, focusing partic-ularly on how they learn. For example, one participant wrote, "I was very aware of how much I as a learner depended on the teacher's input, approval and cor-rection. When I no longer needed to look to the teacher for help or at the black-board or at my own notes was when I felt I had learned. I was my own measure of correctness at this point" (ibid., 270).

Gary Birch has described how the language learning experience is built into the Graduate Diploma program for language teachers at Griffith University in Australia. Teachers enrolled in this program may either opt to stay in Australia and study Mandarin as a foreign language, or they may go to Thailand, teach EFL, and study Thai while they are immersed in the target culture. In either case, this component of the program required the teachers:

> to begin the study of a language, to keep a diary in which they recorded their reflections on their language learning, and to use this diary to produce a case study which brought together themes which the learner considered particularly significant. They were free to focus on any aspect of the experience which they considered to be particularly important to their development as a second language teacher (Birch, 1992, 285).

Birch emphasizes the need for language teachers to have a current language learning experience as they undergo professional preparation:

> Most second language teachers have some personal experience of learning another language, but often it was undertaken well before

they became second language teachers and their memories of the experience are too hazy to be reliable as a guide to second language learning processes. In planning the Graduate Diploma it was felt that it would help teachers to clarify their own beliefs about the nature of second language learning if they were required to undertake the study of a foreign language (ibid., 287).

This setup allowed Birch to systematically investigate and contrast the experiences of those teachers who studied Mandarin in Australia with those who went to Thailand. As Birch points out, the immersion situation was quite powerful: "[T]he important dimension of the impact of the culture on language learning and personal adaptation in general cannot be appreciated when studying a foreign language in the safety of one's own cultural environment" (ibid., 285). The key difference, of course, between the two contexts was that the EFL teachers in Thailand could not entirely retreat to the safety of their first language after the classes were dismissed:

> [T]he language learning experience in Thailand played a significant part in providing the teachers with insights to inform their reflections on many aspects of their development as second language teachers. The experience went beyond the formal Thai classes and permeated every aspect of the teachers' lives (ibid., 287).

By studying Thai, "many teachers experience second language learning for the first time and, as a result, are in a better position to engage in informed reflection" (ibid., 289).

Both groups of teachers (those in Thailand and those who stayed in Australia) wrote language learning journals. Birch notes that all the EFL teachers who studied in Thailand "make some reference to the effects of culture shock upon their language learning. This is in marked contrast to the … teachers who learnt a language in Australia" (ibid., 291).

One interesting cross-cultural element that emerged in the diaries of the teachers studying Thai was the contrast between the predominant teaching style of the host culture Thai instructors and the preferred learning styles of the EFL teachers (ibid., 291–292):

> …[A] teaching and learning style which focuses on formal aspects of language is common in Thailand. The project gave the teachers the opportunity to experience the reality of being on the receiving end of a teaching style which was contrary to their beliefs about what constituted desirable practice in language teaching.

Here again we see an important connection being made between experiential knowledge and the received knowledge of the field. Birch also notes the value of the immersion experience in connection with the teachers' formal coursework at the university:

> …[T]he teachers arrived in Thailand with a strong belief in the benefits of communicative language teaching. As a result of this language teaching and learning experience, they emerged with a much more complex view of the nature of the approach and its

relationship to the social, psychological and cultural context of language teaching (ibid., 289).

Thus, learning Thai in Thailand provided these teachers with an important experiential basis for their reflections. According to Birch (ibid., 293),

> The teachers were not meeting any of these issues for the first time. They had encountered the discussion of relevance and authenticity in a number of the courses they had already studied; they had read about the importance of attitudes on the part of the host culture to the learners' progress and the need to practice using the language with sympathetic native speakers. These notions took on a new significance in the light of their Thailand experience and it became a natural progression to relate them to the practice of language teaching in Australia.

In terms of professional development, the connection to our own teaching is most important. Birch notes, "...[T]eachers reported that the experience of reflecting on their own language learning enabled them to understand better the language learning experience of their second language students and that consequently they had modified their teaching" (ibid., 285).

It seems clear that the teachers who were immersed in Thai also benefited from working in a group, instead of as isolated individuals. Birch continues:

> Teachers engaged as a group in the reflective cycle described by Bartlett (1990). In doing this they were developing reflective procedures which would be available to them beyond the life of the project. In addition, they had the opportunity to reflect as a group on aspects of the language teaching and learning process with an immediacy which would not have been possible in a different context (ibid., 290).

These collaborative discussions about language learning and teaching parallel the collaborative use of teaching journals (Brock et al., 1992; Cole et al., 1998) discussed in Chapter 4.

6.8 *WHAT WOULD YOU CHOOSE?*

Think about the choice of staying at home and studying Mandarin as a foreign language or going to Thailand to study Thai in an immersion environment. What are the benefits and drawbacks of each choice?

Which situation would you choose if practical issues (money, time, housing, childcare, etc.) were not matters of concern? What factors most strongly influence your choice?

JOACHIM'S LANGUAGE LEARNING EXPERIENCE

Joachim Appel, whose teaching journal we quoted earlier, put himself in two situations in which he was taking language classes—once in Italian and once in Chinese. Here are some of his reactions to these experiences:

Joachim Appel

25 March: An Italian Class

Several of us teachers are attending an Italian class a colleague teaches. After the lesson, Ralph, who was sitting next to me, said it had been a long time since he last experienced a lesson from a pupil's perspective. Pupil conversation during the lesson, we agree, was less disruptive than it would have seemed to us had we been standing in front. We probably would not have tolerated it if we had been teaching. Yet we had to admit that despite all the talking the lesson was still clearly comprehensible to us (Appel, 1995, 39).

1 April: Chinese Intensive Course

I am going to take the role of a student for the next few days. This is day one. The teacher turned spectator: I am very disappointed when I don't get a turn to say something because the teacher has decided the exercise is taking too long. As a teacher I would have done the same. As a student I'm addicted to praise. My fears: being called on to say something, mistakes, corrections, irony, ridicule. I keep comparing myself to the others. Even more important for my well-being than I thought: comprehension of what is said in class (ibid., 68).

2 April: Outside the Teacher's Field of Vision

I didn't get a chance to speak for an entire ninety minutes because I was sitting outside the teacher's field of vision. She never once moved during the lesson. It takes her ages to find the right place on the tape. Worse still, while playing the tape she does other admin tasks, like sorting out papers, which makes me feel I am just plugged in and then left on my own. The group had no control over the tape. It would have been so easy to have given it to us.

Over lunch we were cooking a Chinese meal. We were to speak only Chinese. I saw little use in speaking the language to others who speak the language as badly as I do. I want a native speaker to listen to me (ibid., 68).

3 April: A Good Teacher

Today the joy of being taught by a good teacher. At no point does any boredom creep in. It just doesn't. Maybe this is what good teaching does to you. It leaves you with a feeling of having spent an agreeable morning that has passed quickly. Interestingly, C, the teacher, uses basically the same method for about four hours. Nor is there a lot of variation in terms of the material he uses. It is probably his flexibility. There is something improvised and at the same time secure about his lessons. He departs from the dialogues, makes us re-enact them, picks out difficult bits and goes over them again with a different twist to them. He makes me surprised about myself: about how much Chinese comes out of me. Occasionally he talks about our difficulties. He asks whether we take in what others say in class (which is exactly what I find difficult). Are we able, if it is someone else's turn to do an oral exercise, to keep one step ahead? His interest in our answers seems genuine. It makes me want to tell him my story. He says we should, at least occasionally, say something that is true and not only make up answers the content of which does not matter to us. Don't say something just for the sake of having spoken the language. Everybody gets their turn. He knows when to call on someone. He answers questions, but also knows when to stop before his answers get too long. When I give my talk the next morning he says it is too short. This won't do. Something I haven't been told in a long time (ibid., 68–69).

4 April: Waiting for the Break
As a teacher I often dread the sound of the bell which puts a premature end to my lesson plans. As a student I'm craving for the end of the lesson, when regimentation ends and I can speak to the others in the group. I am reminded of how important the interaction taking place during break time must be for my students back at school. At the moment I, too, am waiting for the break, pretending to take notes but actually looking at my watch or out of the window at two house fronts (ibid., 69).

NONNATIVE SPEAKING TEACHERS

A huge number of language teachers around the world are not native speakers (NSs) of the language they teach. Nonnative speaking (NNS) professionals face different challenges than do those teachers whose subject matter is their own first language.

We three authors hold the position that NNS teachers can be just as effective as—in some instances, more effective than—native speakers, and especially when compared to native speakers of the target language who have no professional preparation. The following statement was written by George Braine, Jun Liu, and Lia Kamhi-Stein (1998, 1), three experienced NNS teachers of English, in starting a caucus of nonnative speaking professionals in TESOL (Teachers of English to Speakers of Other Languages, Inc.):

> Despite the TESOL organization's opposition to discrimination in hiring practices, nonnative speaker English teachers continue to face discrimination in obtaining employment. Although most native speaker colleagues are supportive, some administrators and colleagues appear to view English language teaching as the sole domain of native speakers. This attitude is highly ironic, considering our profession's strident championing of multiculturalism, diversity, and other worthy sociopolitical causes, often on behalf of ESL students and immigrants. Although ESL students are praised and admired for the multiculturalism and diversity they bring into language classes, nonnative English teachers, who can also contribute their rich multicultural, multilingual experiences, are often barred from the same classes. As a result, many nonnative speaker English teachers feel the pressure of low morale and self-esteem, lack of recognition, and marginalization. As professionals involved in teaching English, we need to address these and other issues related to the role of nonnative speakers in the profession.

In this Teachers' Voices section we hear George Braine's account as a nonnative speaking teacher of English. George is a teacher and teacher educator from Sri Lanka.

George Braine

In a delightful article in *The New Yorker* (1998, 14), the Indian-born doctor Abraham Verghese recalls an incident that occurred soon after his arrival in the United States. Emboldened by his medical abilities and high scores in the required examinations, Verghese is confident of obtaining an internship at a "Plymouth Rock" hospital affiliated to a prestigious medical school. However, a more experienced compatriot warns him that these hospitals "have never taken a foreign medical graduate" and advises Verghese "not even to bother with that kind of place." Instead, he is told to apply to more humble "Ellis Island" hospitals, those situated in inner cities and rural areas, which American doctors avoid. "We are," Verghese's compatriot continues, "like a transplanted organ—lifesaving and desperately needed, but rejected because we are foreign tissue. But, as they say in America, tough...."

Although many foreign medical graduates eventually get internships, filling positions that Americans refuse to accept, NNS English teachers are less fortunate in finding employment. What chances do foreigners have in a market glutted with American teachers willing to accept even low-paying adjunct jobs with heavy workloads? Further,... for many NNS English teachers, qualifications, ability, and experience are of little help in the job market.

Especially at the Masters degree level, where most English Language Teaching (ELT) jobs are restricted to intensive English programs, few NNS have succeeded in breaking the unwritten rule "No NNS need apply." [M]ost intensive program administrators (with some notable exceptions) do not hire NNS. In fact, some administrators have openly stated so at professional conferences and job interviews.

The most frequent excuse for this discrimination is that ESL students prefer being taught by NSs. About 10 years ago, despite resistance from NS colleagues, I was hired to teach part-time in an intensive English program. About two weeks after classes began, two students complained about my accent and requested transfers to classes taught by NS. Some ESL students naively subscribe to the native-speaker fallacy—that the ideal English teacher is a NS. This belief stems mainly from their frustration with incompetent, barely proficient English teachers in their own countries, and is especially evident in intensive English programs, in which these newly arrived students enroll. When I later taught at a United States university, ESL students flocked to my first year and advanced writing classes, relishing the support of fellow ESL students and a NNS teacher, who they said would better understand their language problems....

Perhaps the main reason is never explicitly stated but nevertheless apparent. A fairly recent phenomenon in Western academia is the increasing presence of foreigners, as teachers, researchers, and scholars, in almost every discipline, including ELT. Although this is only to be expected—there are at least four NNS to every native speaker of English—it is naturally resented when scarce jobs are threatened....

A further irony is that NNS English teachers who return to their countries after qualifying in the West are not always able to find work. Some language program administrators, notably in Japan, Korea, and Hong Kong, prefer to hire unqualified NS instead of qualified locals. The classified pages of newspapers in these countries are strewn with advertisements for "native English speakers." Exposed to such propaganda day after day, the minds of parents and students are brainwashed and the native-speaker fallacy is perpetuated. Indeed, we in ELT inhabit a weird landscape. A colleague in Hong Kong was once asked how she could teach English, since she is American. Another American friend, being interviewed for a private tutor position over the phone, was turned down because she did not have a "British" accent....

6.9 PROS AND CONS

Investigations

What are the pros and cons of teaching your native language? What are the pros and cons of teaching a language you have had to learn? Please compare and contrast these contexts, using a grid like the following to frame your thinking:

	Native Speaking Teachers	Nonnative Speaking Teachers
Pros		
Cons		

A SURPRISING AWARENESS

Paul Kei Matsuda had a surprising awareness related to this task. He was one of four people who were teaching ESL students in an introductory composition course at Purdue University. The four teachers were all taking university courses in TESOL theory and pedagogy, and they had all taught introductory college composition to native speaking students in the past. In the following Teachers' Voices narrative, we hear Paul's ideas about NS and NNS teachers.

> As part of [a] self-initiated collaborative effort, the four of us kept and shared teacher reflection journals through e-mail.... We used this forum to discuss issues, concerns, and questions and to share ideas, suggestions, and solutions related to our teaching practices. It started out simply as a mechanism for sharing our journal entries, but it began to grow more interactive as we found ourselves responding to each other on a regular basis....
>
> The issue of NS and NNS teachers became a topic of discussion early in the semester, when the four of us got together to rate writing samples. During the rating session, one of the NS teachers mentioned that she felt disadvantaged because she did not have the

Teachers' Voices

Paul Kei Matsuda

kind of insights and experiences that a nonnative speaker would have regarding the process of language learning. As a nonnative speaker of English, I was rather surprised by her comment because at the time that was how I felt about my not being a native speaker. After talking about this issue for awhile, we came to realize that our views of native and nonnative speakers had been based on what may be call a *deficit model* of teacher development....

In... sharing our reflective journals, we realized that the deficit view of teacher development was supported only by myths and unexamined assumptions; we were merely looking at the glass as being half empty. As the group discussed the different strengths that each of us brought to the group, we came to a different understanding of the NS/NNS distinction: that both NS and NNS teachers possess particular strengths. We began to see each other as resources. That is, our view shifted toward a collaborative model of teacher qualification....

In this model, teachers see themselves as members of a collaborative community in which they share their special strengths to help each other out. Listening to other teachers' ways of dealing with classroom issues helped us recognize our own strengths and preferences and... encouraged us to adopt, adapt, and learn from other teachers' approaches and strategies that are informed by differing linguistic, cultural, and educational backgrounds (1999, 1 and 10).

6.10 *Tasks for Development*

The remaining investigations in this chapter are designed to help you utilize a wide variety of language learning opportunities for your own professional development purposes, whether you are a native or a nonnative speaker of the language you teach. Some of these activities are doable by yourself, while others are better suited for a group or class environment.

1. A *think-aloud protocol* is a record of what a person says while engaged in another process. For instance, if you were to talk (typically in your first language) about the process of reading a text in your second language as you were reading, the transcript of what you said would be a think-aloud protocol. (See Nunan, 1992b, 117, for further information.) Try to generate a think-aloud protocol in a second or foreign language context that is not too challenging for your proficiency level. What does the record reveal to you about your efforts? Did the act of creating the think-aloud protocol impede your L2 processing? If so, how and how much?

2. Put yourself in a context in which you are trying to do a solitary task in a non-L1 language that is definitely too difficult for you (e.g., doing a grammar or vocabulary exercise in an advanced textbook). As you attempt the task, think aloud, talk about your mental processes and your affective state(s), preferably with a tape recorder, to create a think-aloud protocol. What do you notice about your own efforts? In

what areas do you feel successful? In what areas do you feel confused or overwhelmed? What do the data suggest for you as a teacher?

If you are working with classmates or a study group, you may find it useful to compare your think-aloud protocol with those of your colleagues. Are there commonalities and/or differences across the records of the various persons' experiences? With your colleagues, look for possible teaching implications in your data. Are there both commonalities and differences if you compare the responses of NS and NNS teachers?

3. Try reading a text in your second language that is too difficult for you. (We suggest reading for this activity since the written text is there for you to return to and examine as you need to.) If you are an experienced teacher, before starting to read, list three bits of advice you have given your students about reading in a second or foreign language. If you are a new teacher, imagine the kind of advice you might give your students about reading. Now try reading the difficult L2 text. As you read, record the processing strategies you use to deal with problems that arise. (Again, it will be useful to have a tape recorder running so you can simply "think aloud" instead of having to stop reading to write down your awarenesses.)

To what extent do you follow your own advice to your students? To what extent do you sidestep your advice? What did you find yourself doing instead? Why?

4. This chapter reports the comments from language teachers who put themselves in language learning (or use) situations. Look back and see which of these situations seem(s) similar to an experience you have had. Which seem(s) unlikely or unfamiliar? Why?

5. Think of an experience you have had learning either a foreign or a second language. Please tell that story to a classmate or colleague. Or if you prefer, write your story as a *case report*. Based on that experience, what advice would you give your own language students? What advice would you give a new teacher?

6. If you are a native speaker of the language you teach, find a nonnative speaking teacher (of any language) and interview that person about his or her strengths as a NNS teacher. If you are a nonnative speaker of your target language, interview a NS teacher about his or her strengths as a NS teacher. Also ask the person you are interviewing about the problems that may arise as a result of being either a native or a nonnative teacher of the target language. How do your data compare with Paul Kei Matsuda's ideas?

Suggested Readings

John Flowerdew (1998) has described the language course component of the BA in TESL Program at the City University of Hong Kong. The paper includes many interesting quotations from journals kept by the participants (native speakers of Cantonese in training to be EFL teachers), who were taking an introductory German course.

Some diary studies have been published by teachers who put themselves in a language learning context. These include Cherry Campbell's (1996) account of a Spanish immersion experience in Mexico, Schmidt and Frota's (1986) study of Dick Schmidt learning Portuguese in Brazil, and Kathi Bailey's (1981, 1983) analysis of her initial attempts to learn French. Joan Rubin and Rosemary Henze (1981) co-authored a paper about the learning strategies Rosemary used in studying Arabic while she was also a teacher-in-training.

Tim Lowe (1987) has described the interesting professional development activity mentioned at the beginning of this chapter. A group of English teachers with varying amounts of teaching experience enrolled in a 12-week, 30-hour course in Mandarin Chinese. The teachers kept diaries about their language learning experiences during the course. This article provides convincing first-person testimony that learning a new language offers excellent awareness-raising opportunities for language teachers.

Four language teacher educators at the University of Lancaster have discussed language learning experiences in teacher training (Waters, Sunderland, Bray, and Allwright, 1990).

George Braine (1999) has edited a volume called *Non-Native Educators in English Language Teaching*, which we recommend for anyone who is interested in the topic.

7

VIDEO: SEEING OURSELVES AS OTHERS SEE US

I am a control freak. I am impatient. I was a successful student in the teacher-centered model, so I am comfortable with it, although I recognize that a student-centered classroom is a better alternative. I have now seen two of my videotapes and I don't shut up for a second. OK this is obviously something of an exaggeration—but I talk excessively and I don't give enough wait-time (Numrich, 1996, 136).

For teachers who have viewed videotapes of themselves teaching, the comment above (made by a preservice teacher quoted in Carol Numrich's research) will probably have a familiar ring. When we teachers see ourselves on videotape we are often surprised (and not necessarily pleasantly so). Whether the footage provides good news or causes for concern, we are of the opinion that viewing videotapes of our own teaching can provide us with valuable information for our own professional development.

In this chapter we explore the use of video in professional development. Capturing samples of teaching on video from time to time is a salutary and often humbling experience. It serves to throw weaknesses into relief, but it also reveals teaching strengths, and highlights the ongoing struggle we have to define ourselves professionally. We have come to realize that the idealized images of ourselves as teachers are just that—images and ideals that may never be fully actualized.

Videotape recordings also remind us that much of what goes on in teaching is invisible. Video does not capture the planning, the meetings with co-teachers, the materials development, the hours spent grading papers, the countless meetings and consultation sessions with students. It doesn't show the splitting headache that makes a particular class a nightmare, nor the acrimonious meeting with a dean, headmaster, principal, or department head that colors the whole day. Nor does video usually reveal the split-second decision making that characterizes interactive teaching.

VIEWING VIDEO RECORDINGS OF OURSELVES TEACHING

Video recording has been used in teacher education for nearly 30 years, with teachers watching themselves (Paulston, 1974) and other teachers on video (Borg, Kelley, Langer, and Ball, 1970). However, apart from some more recent examples (e.g., Tsui, 1996), videotaping is still often used as a preservice assignment (e.g., in a practicum setting), rather than in self-initiated professional development contexts. When video is used in this way, the results can be quite dramatic. In this chapter we will focus on the use of video to record our own teaching, rather than for watching demonstration lessons.

Leo van Lier's idea of the "estrangement device" as it is used in ethnography is important here. He says that more and more these days,

> recording is used as a tool for description and analysis, not just as a mnemonic device, but more importantly as an *estrangement device*, which enables the ethnographer to look at phenomena (such as conversations, rituals, transactions, etc.) with detachment (van Lier, 1988, 37).

As an estrangement device, video enables us as teachers to create more distance between ourselves and our teaching than perhaps any of the other approaches we consider in this book. This may be partly because many of us have spent our whole lives in television cultures, so that anyone on the small screen can be thought of as a character playing a role, even if it's us. Also, video enables us to see ourselves the way others see us. The idea of *seeing* is stressed because most of us communicate a great deal of information nonverbally—information about our message, our attitudes, our affective state at the time. For this reason, video works as a powerful prompt for stimulated recall. Whatever the cause of this video-enhanced distancing, the separation between our teaching selves and our viewing selves usually creates enough space for us to watch ourselves teaching with the kind of objectivity that is usually possible only when we are viewing someone else. We can, in a sense, see more by being further away.

The theoretical and conceptual bases for using video have been discussed for some time. Wallace points out that video "provides some kind of objective record of what actually took place" (1981, 8) and describes it as "individualized training *par excellence*" (ibid., 11). In an earlier study, Wallace found that 87 percent of the inservice and preservice EFL teachers he studied said that "seeing themselves on videotape had made them aware of habits and mannerisms which they were now trying to change" (1979, 13). He concluded that the main advantage of video is that it serves as "a means of objectifying the teaching process and converting what is subjective and ephemeral into something that is experienced in common and capable of analysis" (ibid., 17).

Video offers a partial solution to the problem of loss of face, which has long been regarded as especially important in Asia (e.g.; Lin, 1935; Bond, 1991; Curtis, 1997). Since viewing a video does not require another teacher or a supervisor, the potential loss of face is minimized. If we are satisfied with what we see on tape, we may show it to others for comment, but if not, the contents can remain private.

Another concern relates to the fact that teaching-related data are often collected for evaluative rather than developmental purposes. This tendency has led to worries about any kind of data gathering. However, with video, as long as the video-recorded teacher decides who views the tape, these kinds of worries can be considerably reduced.

We can also take notes while viewing videos of our own teaching. The notes might be similar to those a peer observer would make, but with the important difference that they document self-generated awareness. The nonselective recording of all that happens in front of the lens, used as a visual record to stimulate recall, means that viewing our videos can yield a great deal of understanding. This is particularly true if we can compare a number of extracts of our teaching, recorded over time.

Because a video camera can record so much of what occurs in classrooms, looking for long-term development can be a little overwhelming. One possibility is to focus on a particular aspect of our teaching, such as our responses to students' comments, their turn-taking behavior, or the use of questions in our lessons. Such a focus can help us to see more sharply what kinds of developments have occurred (or are needed).

In this chapter we will work with activities that are based on video self-viewing. Of course, it is possible to learn much from viewing video recordings of others teaching. We can make notes based on these video-based peer observations as well. This practice is especially useful if you can talk with the teachers whose teaching you are watching. For complete reciprocity, you can watch recordings of one another's teaching, with and without each other present, which can also lead to useful discussion.

7.1 *GETTING YOURSELF VIDEOTAPED*

If you are teaching now, or if you are enrolled in a preservice training program, find out if your school or program has videotaping capabilities. If so, what is involved in the process of getting videotaped? How do you feel about the possibility of being videotaped while you are teaching or doing your practice teaching?

ANDY'S FILM DEBUT AND LATER

The first time I saw myself on video, I didn't.

Andy Curtis

It was around 10 years ago, on my first teaching practicum. I was in a school in the Northeast of England, in a grim, bleak place, parts of which were suffering from nearly 50 percent unemployment, having had the heart of its shipping industry torn out by a government bent on making an example of the town's defiance of its plans for national privatization. Not surprisingly, such an environment did not do much to engender in the local children a positive disposition toward learning in schools (or being in schools at all).

I was "power dressing," which meant wearing dark colors. So there I was, dressed head to toe in black, standing in front of a floor-to-ceiling black chalkboard. The video camera was the only one in the school, and did not work very well, especially in the lowlight conditions of the dark room where I was teaching. Much has changed since then. But one thing that has not changed is my dark skin coloring, the product of North Indian great-grandparents, and South American (Guyanese) parents and grandparents.

When we sat down to watch the video of my teaching, there was an embarrassed silence, until I started to laugh uncontrollably, breaking the tension and giving permission to the other (light-skinned) teachers to do the same.

There I was. Not. All of the various darknesses had combined to produce a shadowing effect, in which all that could be seen on the video recording was a piece of white chalk, dancing in the darkness, a dazzling white smile, and almost nothing else.

I still have the tape, and show it occasionally, when talking with teachers about the potential pitfalls of using videotapes to record our teaching.

This episode taught me many things, not least about technology's limitations when it comes to capturing teaching and learning on tape. A decade after this unpromising television debut, I have realized that there is a useful analogy here for the way a video camera actually masks what goes on in classrooms, as well as, paradoxically, at the same time shamelessly and unflinchingly recording everything that passes before it. The idea that "the camera never lies" is itself a great lie, as anyone knows who's ever seen how cinematic special effects are created.

However, this technological weakness can also be a strength. In my case, the camera didn't record what was going on in my head and my heart, that is, it couldn't record what I was thinking and feeling. To record these things, I look to my journal entries or the audiotape recordings of discussions with other teachers. But the very fact that the camera did *not* record these internal workings was of value, as it helped to show the difference between what I was feeling and thinking inside, versus the professional teaching persona I was projecting to the outside world, most immediately to the students sitting in front of me, and then to my teaching peers.

When Kathi and I video recorded ourselves co-teaching an MBA (Masters of Business Administration) course on Running Effective Meetings at the Chinese University of Hong Kong, we were, frankly, both in over our heads. An interesting difference between our situations was the fact that I had already spent some hours with the MBA students and had established my credibility and some rapport with the group, whereas the video-recorded lesson was Kathi's first meeting with them. On the other hand, Kathi had had around 25 years' teaching experience, more than twice mine. I have a clear memory of the first few seconds after the end of the lesson:

Andy: "Great stuff! That went really well!"

Kathi (with a disbelieving tone): "You think so?"

We reviewed the tape six months later, at which point another strength of video emerged. Just before viewing the tape, Kathi and I were talking about how little we would remember after that long and intense semester. But as soon as the tape started, memories came flooding back—not just memories of what we had done, but vivid memories of what we had been thinking and feeling during the lesson.

Kathi's very first comment when viewing the tape reminded me of the reactions of many teachers I've sat with as they watched themselves on video for the first time. "Oh, no! I'm so glad I've had my hair cut since then," said Kathi. Very often the first reaction in this self-viewing is to the way we look on screen.

At around the same time, another teacher working in my department came to work with a new hairstyle the day after I'd video recorded his lesson. I asked about the new hairstyle, and he explained that he'd seen a balding patch emerging when he watched himself on tape, and rearranged his hair accordingly. In both instances (i.e., Kathi and myself and then the other teacher and myself), we went on to talk about more pedagogical aspects of the lesson on tape, but only after each of them had been able to get over seeing themselves. Both teachers had been videotaped many times over the years, and yet they were still initially focused on how they looked. Some teachers note in particular how different they thought they looked and sounded on screen versus in real life.

Another thing that occurred to me as I watched the video is the need for an acclimatization period. Recently I traveled from Hong Kong, where people were complaining about the terrible cold as the temperature had plunged to (plus) 15 degrees C (i.e., 59°F), to England, where people were complaining about the terrible cold as the temperature had plunged to minus 2 degrees C (35.6°F). A few days later, I arrived in Edmonton, where people were excitedly welcoming the unseasonally warm weather, as the temperature had gone all the way up to minus 15 degrees C (5°F). Apart from demonstrating the human body's hopeless inability to assess absolute states, but its extreme sensitivity to relative changes, this phenomenon also relates to the need for acclimatization. In terms of self-viewing, just as we need climatic adjustment periods, we need to allow ourselves time to go beyond our first, appearance-oriented reactions to seeing ourselves before we can really benefit from viewing videotapes of ourselves teaching.

When we watched the video of two of us (Kathi and Andy) co-teaching, David facilitated the discussion, observing, taking notes, and making an audio recording of the conversation while we were viewing the video. This process enabled us to set up a highly collaborative form of triangulation, with three different people interpreting the data. David's questions paralleled the use of the stimulated recall technique in research (see Nunan, 1992b, 94–96), applied in this case to professional development.

As noted above, one of the unique strengths of video relates both to what it does and does not record. Even though we viewed ourselves on tape six months after the original recording was made, the detail captured by the camera led to vivid recollections of what we had done and even of how we had felt during that particular lesson. Of special interest was what the camera did *not* record; in our case, the difference between the way Kathi felt during and after the lesson—stressed and not confident—and the fact that she presented herself to the class (and to the camera) as confident and calm.

7.2 VIDEO VERSUS AUDIO

What are the differences between making videotapes and making audiotapes of your teaching? What are the pros and cons of each approach to data collection?

ACQUIRING EFFECTIVE TEACHING SKILLS

Nancy Stenson, Jan Smith, and William Perry worked extensively with videotape as a source of feedback to language teachers at the University of Minnesota. In this Frameworks section we will use some ideas from a workshop they did on the use of video in teacher development. These teachers start with the assumption that "acquiring effective teaching skills is a developmental process" (Stenson, Smith, and Perry, 1979, 2). In their work they identified five necessary components of this process:

Obtaining Feedback. In order to determine how effective their teaching is, teachers first need to have information about their performance in the classroom. Obtaining feedback is thus the first component of the developmental process.... [A] crucial aspect of feedback is the extent to which the teacher feels able to accept it and work with it. Videotape, *when properly used*, can be an invaluable tool for providing a teacher with objective information....

Becoming Introspective. Given a source of feedback, the teacher needs to be able to analyze the information in a productive way.... [T]he most important factor of this component is the ability to be introspective about one's own teaching. The teacher must... develop the ability for self-evaluation rather than continue to rely on external judgment.

Accepting Responsibility. The ability to be introspective and to evaluate one's own teaching is a prerequisite to the third component, the teacher's acceptance of responsibility for his/her further growth as a teacher. Only from this point of view is it possible to recognize and accept both positive and negative aspects of one's own teaching as a preparation for bringing about appropriate change.

Choosing What to Change. The fourth developmental component involves the teacher's decision to devote the time and energy necessary to effect change. A major part of this decision will be the teacher's choice of which aspects of teaching s/he is ready to work on. It is... only when teachers themselves decide when and what to change that any real change occurs.

Effecting Change. The final component of the growth process addresses the need of teachers who have chosen to change some aspect of their teaching and are looking for information on ways of bringing about the desired changes (ibid., 2–5).

These authors emphasize that "the developmental components involving the teacher's ability for introspection, acceptance of responsibility, and internal motivation for change are all aspects of teacher behavior that no trainer/supervisor can control" (ibid., 4).

Stenson, Smith, and Perry (ibid., 6) also discuss several advantages of videotape for professional development:

> ...[V]ideotape is a valuable source of feedback because it allows teachers to see themselves from the students' point of view and to obtain an accurate record of what happens in the classroom. By viewing tapes of their classes, teachers can profit from the information videotape provides on teacher performance, student participation, and the lesson itself.

Videos provide impartial records (Wallace 1981, 8). Stenson et al. put it like this:

> The value of videotape lies in its objectivity. The tape can show specific aspects of a teacher's performance, such as rate and intensity of speech, nonverbal behavior, techniques of presentation and practice, sequencing of materials, and methods of providing feedback to students. It can show the verbal and nonverbal performance of students, their degree of participation in the class and level of attention, as well as individual student behavior. Finally, the tape can provide information on the content and organization of the lesson, variety and pacing of classroom activities, use of teaching aids, and ratio of teacher talk to student talk (1979, 6).

The key here is that, unlike most human observers, "videotape provides the facts without itself making any judgments" (ibid.).

Because teaching is very demanding work, we cannot always fully observe ourselves while we are teaching. This is another benefit of videotape:

> By viewing a tape of his/her class the teacher can relive the experience from a different point of view. Teachers may become aware of aspects of their own performance, the lesson, or student behavior that they did not notice during the class session because they were too involved in the actual teaching process (ibid., 6–7).

Stenson et al. also talk about the value of emotional distance in improving our teaching:

> Videotape also allows a teacher to gain emotional distance from the class by viewing the tape at a later time. For example, a teacher may wish that a particular classroom incident had been handled differently. Upon viewing the tape of the class, the teacher can dissociate him/herself from the image on the screen, and with this new perspective, may be able to determine how to handle the situation the next time it arises (ibid., 7).

This point is related to van Lier's (1988) idea of the *estrangement device*: The video record separates us from our teaching and lets us view it more dispassionately.

Stenson, Smith, and Perry also note the potential for collaborative uses of video when they comment on the value of watching videos of our teaching with someone else:

It is our contention that all teachers, no matter how experienced or inexperienced, can benefit from discussion generated by viewing themselves on tape. The presence of a second person, a facilitator who can focus the attention of the teacher on particular issues, is crucial in motivating teachers to become introspective about their role in the classroom. The role of the facilitator can be taken on by anyone who works with teachers, whether as a colleague and peer or as a trainer or supervisor (Stenson et al., 1979, 8).

They note that a facilitator should be open to different viewpoints, and take the role of a "concerned colleague rather than expert or authority figure," because such a stance is much less threatening to the teacher engaged in self-evaluation (ibid., 10).

7.3 WATCHING YOURSELF ON TAPE

Imagine videotaping a class that you think you taught quite well. Think of a person you would ask to watch the video of your class with you. Why did you choose this person? What personal qualities, professional skills, or expertise does this person possess that make him or her your preferred viewing partner in this context?

Now imagine videotaping yourself teaching a class that did not go well—in fact, one in which you had some problems. Consider the same questions again: Whom would you ask to watch the video of your class with you? Why did you choose this person? What qualities, skills, or expertise does this person possess that make him or her your preferred viewing partner in this context?

Watching yourself and having some else watch your teaching on tape can be a useful exercise, though this practice requires trust and a mutually supportive professional relationship. A useful three-part, collaborative viewing-feedback technique is to first watch recordings of your teaching privately, without anyone else around. Keep notes or have an audiotape recorder running to capture your think-aloud responses. Then ask a colleague to look at the same tape without you there and also to make notes of some kind. Finally, both of you can view the tape together and compare your notes. There will be many things that you both noticed, but the most interesting points for discussion may occur when the two of you have noted different issues.

KATHI WATCHES A VIDEO OF HER WORKSHOP

Kathi Bailey

Okay. We've made a lot of claims about what teachers can learn by watching videos of themselves teaching. Andy shared his experience of seeing himself (or rather *not* seeing himself) on video as a teacher-in-training. He also wrote about the experience he and I had while watching a video of ourselves team teaching for the first time. In that instance, David watched the tape with us and facilitated the discussion. But we've also claimed that just viewing videos of our teaching alone can be helpful. Is this true?

I decided to watch a videotape of me leading a workshop, but to watch it all by myself, to see what I could learn. It was a video of a workshop I do on using pictures in language lessons. I have probably presented this workshop a dozen times over the past 20 years. I think I've got it just about right, but I wondered if there was anything I could learn by looking at a video of this familiar event. So I watched the video alone and made a few pages of notes for myself. Here is a list of the things I realized while watching the tape. Some items on my list are quite predictable while others are rather surprising.

1. I say "Okay?" quite often. It is used as a comprehension check to give the workshop participants a chance to express confusion or ask questions. It's also a sort of discoursal punctuation mark which signals the end of one episode and the beginning of another. As the workshop went on, I began to feel as if I say it too much and that it feels empty as an invitation to the participants to speak. I want to develop some alternatives.

2. I need to remember to erase the blackboard before moving on to another activity. I noticed that I had left notes on the board related to something we'd finished already, and when I saw the video all that writing seemed like a distraction to me—in spite of the fact that when I had put it up for the earlier activity, I was pleased that my handwriting was neat and legible.

3. I also realized that as I was bringing one activity to a close and getting ready to start another, I often looked down at my lesson plan on the table. In doing so I would lose eye contact with the group, my voice wouldn't project as well, and I appeared to be a little confused, or at least detached from the group. I still need to check my lesson plan every now and then, but I'm going to try to finish talking first and allow a moment of silence while I check the plan, instead of potentially giving the impression that I'm lost or uninterested in the participants or the activity by looking down while speaking.

4. I noticed that each time I put the students into groups I gave instructions and signaled a clear start to the group work but I didn't set any time parameters (e.g., "You will have three minutes for group work and then you'll report to the entire class"). A couple of times I had to check on the groups to see if they were done, or nearly done. This checking seemed like an intrusion, but I wanted to let the participants know that time was pressing. Maybe it would be better to set clear time parameters at the outset of the group activities. I will experiment with this idea and see how it works.

5. For some of the more involved picture-based activities I had handouts about the procedures, but for other, simpler activities I just explained the steps orally. This seemed to work pretty well, but it was clear on the video that there was one activity where

I really need to develop a worksheet. The participants were writing furiously to copy down the steps as I explained them. And even though I already know how to do the activity, I don't think I could have replicated the procedures myself based solely on that quick oral description.

6. I also noticed a lot of confusion in one of the pairwork activities. I need to rethink that task and figure out a clear way for the partners to know when they have achieved closure and actually accomplished the task. While I watched the tape I was thinking, "Hmm. This isn't working the way I thought it would. How do they know when they have successfully completed the task?" Then, at the end of the activity, one of the participants asked the same question! Clearly I need to revisit this task and come up with a better set of procedures.

This list of six items relates to issues I want to improve in my workshop, but the video also showed me some good things. My voice was clear and pleasant, I smiled a lot and mostly maintained eye contact, and my hair looked great! I also looked confident and well-organized (except for the points noted above), and the workshop seemed fun, interesting, and practical. All the participants were actively engaged, and each person in the room contributed his or her own ideas in the discussion. One surprising result of viewing the video was that in the videotaped session I had included two components of the workshop that I had forgotten about in recent years. I now want to reintroduce those segments as regular parts of the workshop, and I have the notes to remind me to do so.

7.4 *ANALYZING A REPORT*

In the Frameworks section above (starting on page 122) we summarized work by Smith, Stenson, and Perry (1979), who said that there are five necessary components involved in the developmental process of acquiring effective teaching skills: (1) obtaining feedback; (2) becoming introspective; (3) accepting responsibility; (4) choosing what to change; and (5) effecting change. Reread the Teachers' Voices segment above, in which Kathi reports on the experience of watching the video of a workshop she led. Try to find evidence of as many of these five components as possible. Keep notes and discuss these with a colleague or classmate.

MORE PROBLEMS AND MORE BENEFITS

So far in this chapter we have encountered some of the advantages and disadvantages of using videotapes for professional development purposes. We will now consider more problems with video and some possible solutions.

Unfortunately, not all technological weaknesses can be viewed as strengths. Some are just weaknesses. But it is possible to limit their potentially negative impact. One of the main weaknesses is the tunnel-vision effect of most cameras:

All you can see is what is directly in front of the camera, with almost everything to the sides being off-camera. This means that if you're focusing on the teacher at the front of the class, if the teacher moves, you're left with an off-camera voice that is hard to follow when viewing the tape. The easiest way to remedy this problem is to have someone operating the camera. One problem with this idea, of course, is that the video camera itself can be enough of an intrusion even without the extra person (who is not normally in the room) to operate a piece of equipment (which is not normally there either).

Labov's (1972) concept of "the observer's paradox"—the idea that the act of observation influences what is being observed—may be technologically exacerbated by the presence of the recording equipment and the camera operator in the classroom. (The video recording of a natural event is almost a contradiction in terms.) In this sense, video recording can be an intrusive form of data collection.

Fortunately, in our experience, teachers and learners who are really involved in teaching and learning forget about the camera surprisingly quickly. This adjustment relates to the acclimatization period we referred to earlier, but here this period is time for the participants to get used to the presence of the camera in the classroom.

Even if the class does become accustomed to both the camera and the operator, there is still the problem of the limited vision of the camera. If the camera is at the back of the room, focused on a teacher at the front, most of the nonverbal interaction between students and teacher and among the students will not be recorded. What will be seen are the backs of the students' heads. Conversely, if the camera is at the front of the room, focused on the students, the teacher will be lost. Even if the students are working in small groups, the camera would have to be constantly moved all around the classroom in order for it to capture more than either just the students or just the teacher. Having tried this tactic, we can confirm that the roving camera can be very distracting. One possible solution is to have two cameras, one at the front and one at the back, but this is often not feasible due to limited resources. And in many parts of the world school classrooms simply do not have enough space in which to fit one camera, let alone two.

The other main problem with video, in addition to the tunnel vision, is sound quality. One of the most common complaints we hear after showing videotapes of classrooms is that the viewers could not hear what was being said by the teacher and the students. The built-in microphones of most cameras are not very sensitive, but it is possible to have a small microphone clipped to the teacher's clothing. Also, omnidirectional microphones, which can pick up sound from all directions, are now widely available. These are typically more sensitive than the built-in camera microphones. However, if the teacher is talking with a particular student or circulating around the room and talking to smaller groups of students, the teacher's voice may be fairly clear, but the students' voices may be lost. Technological advances and increased user-friendliness mean that it is now possible to simply "point and press" in creating a video record. However, special care still needs to be taken with recording sound and selecting camera positions.

Despite its shortcomings, video has a tremendous amount to offer. It is first and foremost an estrangement device, a distancing mechanism from the moment-by-moment reality of the class itself (van Lier, 1988). Teachers who see themselves on video are sometimes amazed at how different the class looks from their recollection of what went on during the class itself. The video can document the teacher's interactional style, *action zones* within the classroom (areas of a classroom that are privileged by the teacher in terms of questions to students, frequent eye contact, etc.), the affective climate, and so on. It can also reveal a great deal about the students that may not be apparent during the lesson (for example, which students are on-task and which are not).

If you want to try videotaping your teaching, which lessons should you record? It might sound a little masochistic, but taping lessons that you do not expect to go especially well can lead to more developmentally useful material than taping lessons that go well. Recordings of good lessons can be instructive too, as we are generally more confident in such lessons, and so are more likely to take risks and to be more creative.

Of course, videotaping lessons which you are in some way unsure of, or even a little anxious about, such as when you're starting to teach a new course, means that your weaknesses are more likely to show. For example, a common weakness Andy noticed by watching a video of himself teaching a new course is the tendency to go too fast, in the same way that some nervous presenters rush through their material. As Andy relaxes into the course and gets to know the students and the material better, he becomes more open to letting the students take the lesson into areas that he had not planned on, rather than staying more rigidly with the lesson plan, as he does in the early days.

This issue leads us to another point—the frequency of recording. How often should you videotape your classes? As with observation, a single recording will tell you things about what is going on in your classroom that you perhaps did not know beforehand. However, these single recordings can give only an animated snapshot of you and your learners. For a more complete picture you need more pieces of the puzzle. Recording every lesson is not normally feasible, but recordings made at the start, halfway through, and toward the end of a course, can reveal even small changes.

Videotapes are useful because the medium has such rich potential for analysis. The tapes can simply be watched, or you can turn the sound off and concentrate on the visual. You can also darken the picture and attend to just the sound. Or you can use the video as primary data that can be analyzed through transcriptions or coding procedures if you want to go into more detail than simply viewing the tapes will allow.

7.5 *WHAT CAN A TRANSCRIPT TELL YOU?*

Study the transcript in Appendix A in this book. How much can you tell about the class from which the transcript is taken? Try to answer the following questions:

Appendix A starts on p. 249.

1. Is the extract taken from the beginning, middle, or end of the lesson? What are the objectives (grammatical, functional, etc.) of the lesson? Does the lesson occur at the beginning, middle, or end of the course? Is it an ESL or an EFL class?

2. Are the students children or adults? How old do you think they are? What is their level of proficiency?

3. How many students are there? How are they arranged—in rows, small groups, pairs? What does the classroom look like? How long does the lesson take?

4. Based on the transcript alone, how much can you say about the teacher? Is it a woman or a man? Is he/she relatively experienced or inexperienced?

Now, go back over the transcript and make a list of questions or issues that could be revealed by the video clip of this same lesson. Finally, think about the questions that would NOT be revealed by the video. What questions would you like to ask the teacher?

WHAT VIDEOS CAN AND CAN'T REVEAL

The teacher in this transcript sometimes uses the following procedure in teacher training work to dramatize what videos can and what they can't reveal about what goes on in teaching. First, the teacher distributes copies of the transcript reprinted in Appendix A and asks the participants, who are working in groups of three or four to reconstruct the lesson, to consider a number of questions like those printed above. After answering these questions on the basis of the transcript alone, the participants then listen to an audiotape of the interaction, and note how their impressions change from those they formed on the basis of the transcript only. Next, they watch a videoclip of the interaction and note what seeing the video adds to their impressions of the interaction. Finally, they complete a grid, documenting the strengths and weaknesses of the three different methods of recording classroom interaction (i.e., transcripts only, the audiotape, and the sound and vision combined in the videotape). Having taken part in this process, one of the teacher's MA students (who preferred to remain anonymous) had the following reaction.

THREE KINDS OF DATA

Student teacher

When we were given the transcript [Appendix A] to study, I had a very strong negative reaction to the teacher [in the transcript]. I was sure it was a man, although I couldn't say why. I was also sure that the person was relatively untrained—probably doing initial training. I thought he was arrogant and overbearing, and I was sure that he'd make a bad teacher. I got the impression he was just standing at the front of the class and pontificating.

When I heard the audiotape, I had a much more positive impression. What appeared on the transcript as arrogance came through on the tape as really humorous. The humor and the laughter and interaction and sense of fun on the part of the students didn't come through at all on the transcript—not to me anyway.

Of course, the video revealed lots more. You know, the number of students in the class, and their age, and so on. I was surprised to find that they were older than I'd thought. The other thing that the video revealed was just how much the teacher moved around, and how dynamic the lesson was. From that point of view, the video reinforced the audiotape. It showed lots of other things as well, of course, like the totally bored student in one corner of the room who didn't take part in the lesson at all.

Investigations

7.6 *TASKS FOR DEVELOPMENT*

Although there are problems with videotaping, it can be very helpful in professional development. The following tasks are designed to help you explore this tool.

1. Imagine yourself being videotaped in a non-teaching context where you are not performing—for example, at a family gathering or a party. Now picture yourself being videotaped in a non-teaching performance context—perhaps playing a musical instrument, singing, dancing, or participating in your favorite sport. Finally, imagine yourself being videotaped while teaching (or practice teaching). How are the three contexts different? How are they similar? What are the factors that distinguish the three contexts? Set up a worksheet with the following headings to record your ideas: [– performance – teaching]; [+ performance – teaching]; and [+ performance + teaching].

2. It has been estimated that as much as 60 percent of information in interactions is communicated nonverbally. This suggestion can be illustrated by viewing a video of ourselves teaching with the sound turned down. For instance, in a video of your teaching, you could look for recurring movements you make, and pay particular attention to where you position yourself relative to your students. Do you, for example, move toward students, make eye contact, or in some other nonverbal way shift the focus of the group from you to particular students when they are contributing verbally to the lesson? Do you favor students on one side of the classroom over the other, or those in the front over those in the back?

3. A somewhat comical variation on the theme—and this is one of those that you may well want to try first in private—is to run the videotape on fast-forward with the sound muted. This process can be amusing or even painful to watch, but it can also be a great way of getting some very interesting insights into aspects of your nonverbal behavior in the classroom that you may not have been fully aware of before seeing yourself on video.

4. We referred above to the limits of single recordings and the benefits of viewing recordings made over time. If you do not have video recordings of your teaching made over time, now is a good time to start. Building a video library of yourself teaching may sound somewhat

narcissistic, but such a collection can be a rich source of information about how you grow, change, and develop professionally over time.

If you are an experienced teacher, think of three lessons you've taught in the past that you would have liked to videorecord. Why did you select these particular lessons?

If you are a new teacher, think of three lessons you would like to videotape for your own professional development purposes. What are the characteristics of the lessons you've chosen (or imagined)?

5. You may wish to try the procedures that David (yes, he is the teacher in Appendix A) sometimes uses to dramatize what videos can and can't reveal about teaching. Here again are the steps: examining a transcript; listening to the sound only; and watching the videotape with sound. Finally, the participants can complete a grid, documenting the strengths and weaknesses of the three different methods of recording classroom interaction:

	Strengths	Weaknesses
Transcripts		
Audio Recordings		
Video Recordings		

6. Tony Lynch (1989, 126) suggested a "cooperative peer group approach" in using videotape for professional development. His suggestion is reprinted here as an investigative task:

Colleagues might agree to meet weekly to view a videotaped lesson by each of them in turn—perhaps on the same skill areas. (Here I would suggest the use of video because a sound recording would convey insufficient information for those who had not been present at the lesson to get an idea of what was going on in the classroom.) The viewers would be able to stop the tape at any point and explore the motivation behind specific procedures; equally, the recorded teacher would have the chance to ask his or her colleagues what decision they would have made—or believe they do make—in situations such as that depicted (ibid.)

Lynch acknowledges that this idea has its risks. He says, "My experience is that we can be oversensitive and overprotective about what we do in the classroom; but it would be an opportunity to see our own actions through others' eyes" (ibid.).

8. Stenson, Smith, and Perry (1979) wrote about using videorecordings for professional development long before "reflective teaching" became popular. Yet much of the reflective teaching literature refers to the five components of professional development they identified: obtaining feedback; becoming introspective; accepting responsibility; choosing what to change; and effecting change. Turn back to Chapter 3, Reflective Teaching, and make some connections between that literature and the ideas from Stenson et al. (1979). Make a note about the same (or a similar) concept and the author(s) who used it in discussing reflective teaching.

Suggested Readings

Susan Stempleski and Barry Tomalin (1990) have written a book called *Video in Action*. Although it is about using video with language students rather than for professional development purposes, the appendices contain information useful in both contexts. Appendix 1 is about "Logistics" (including information about tape counters, memory, remote controls, TV monitors, etc.). Appendix 2 is about global TV standards.

Michael Wallace's (1981) article, "The Use of Video in EFL Teacher Training," raised issues that are still discussed today (e.g., the difference between developmental and evaluative uses of such recordings).

An article by Bailey, Curtis, and Nunan (1998) discusses three procedures for teacher development, one of which is video. It highlights some benefits of collaborative viewing.

"Video as a Source of Data in Classroom Observation" (1998), by Andy Curtis and Liying Cheng, discusses the practical applications of video for helping teachers to become more aware of the myriad interactions occurring in language lessons.

Other useful articles about the use of videotaping in teacher development are by Cullen (1991), and by Laycock and Bunnag (1991).

James B. Rowley and Patricia M. Hart (1996) have written an interesting article about combining video technology with the case study approach and reflective teaching to promote professional development. An article by Barry Hutchinson and Peter Bryson (1997) discusses the use of the video and reflection combined in action research.

8

ACTION RESEARCH: IN-CLASS INVESTIGATIONS

Slowly, the profession as a whole is realizing that, no matter how much intellectual energy is put into the invention of new methods (or of new approaches to syllabus design, and so on), what really matters is what happens when teachers and learners get together in the classroom.... Being a good classroom teacher means being alive to what goes on in the classroom, alive to the problems of sorting out what matters, moment by moment, from what does not. And that is what classroom research is all about: gaining a better understanding of what good teachers (and learners) do instinctively as a matter of course, so that ultimately all can benefit (Allwright and Bailey, 1991, xv–xvi).

This chapter is about conducting action research as a way of pursuing professional development. It draws on David's and Andy's experiences in conducting action research in their own classes, in training teachers to do action research, and in setting up action research networks. We begin with an example that arose in David's university EFL classes in Hong Kong, which will be woven through the chapter.

DAVID'S CLASSROOM-BASED ACTION RESEARCH

It was my second semester at my new school, and I realized that things weren't working out the way I wanted. It was a speaking skills class, but my students just wouldn't open their mouths. The first semester had been the same. At that time, I had thought it was just a matter of my adjusting to a new situation. Now I knew it was something more serious. I decided to audiorecord my classes over several days. The recordings confirmed my observations. The tape was filled with the sound of my voice, punctuated by prolonged silences, and the occasional monosyllabic student response. I consulted colleagues who said it was a "cultural thing."

"So why have they enrolled in the class?" I asked.

"Well, they have no choice. Anyhow, it isn't as if they don't want to be able to speak—it's a cultural thing. They want the magic language pill," said one colleague.

"Hmm—don't we all!" I thought.

David Nunan

So there was my challenge—and my dilemma: how to get my Cantonese-speaking Hong Kong students to speak English. After further thought and discussion, I decided to change the dynamics of the classroom, focusing more overtly on group work, and encouraging students to speak through split information tasks [information gap tasks] in which students *had* to speak English if the tasks were to be completed successfully.

I also tried to encourage students to redefine their own concept of what a classroom was (heretofore a place where the student sat silently while the teacher talked) by encouraging them to "break the rules." On one desperate occasion, I asked a group of reluctant speakers to stand up and move about the classroom as they completed their task. Amazingly, once they had been liberated from their seats, they began to talk.

I made audio and video recordings of my class, which I reviewed from time to time, and was gratified to find a dramatic increase in the amount of student speech. However, I also noticed that the distribution of turns was uneven. Not all students were taking advantage of the opportunities to talk.

This new awareness led me into a second investigative cycle, focusing this time on the reluctant speakers in the class. I decided that these students were having difficulty redefining their roles, and concluded that if I added a learning strategy dimension with a focus on learner roles and responsibilities, it might help sensitize them to this very different kind of classroom.

WHAT IS ACTION RESEARCH?

The story presented above is a summarized example of a teacher using the action research cycle to address a problem. As you can see from David's ideas in the Teachers' Voices section above, action research involves systematically changing some aspect of our own professional practice (in response to some issue, problem, or puzzle), collecting relevant data about the changed practice, and interpreting and analyzing the data. Typically, action research consists of a series of small-scale investigations, so the next step is usually to plan another intervention and begin the process again.

Action research is defined as self-reflective inquiry which people in social situations undertake so that they can improve the "rationality and justice of their own social or educational practices, as well as their understanding of these practices and the situations in which these practices are carried out" (Kemmis and McTaggart, 1989, 2). Elsewhere, action research has been characterized as "... a form of self-reflective inquiry carried out by practitioners, aimed at solving problems, improving practice, or enhancing understanding" (Nunan, 1992b, 229).

The action research process warrants the label of *research* because it contains the essential ingredients of (1) questions, problems, or puzzles; (2) data that have a direct bearing on the question, problem, or puzzle; and (3) some form of analysis or interpretation of the data. One key difference between action research and other kinds of research is that action research is carried out by those who are best placed to solve problems, improve practice, and enhance understanding—that is, the participants in the situation under investigation. This stance contrasts with the experimental tradition of viewing people in research studies as subjects. Cheryl Mattingly explains:

> In action research the "subjects" are no longer subjects but rather find a way to become researchers of their own practice. More than many research traditions, action research represents a kind of ideal practice. Those studied must come to see something at stake in examining their own practice, they must be willing to risk a certain exposure to themselves and to colleagues, they must even be willing to chance the possibility of changing and taking new actions. If the research subjects remain just subjects, then there is no action research (1991, 255).

As a genre, action research has been around for over 50 years. It was first developed in the social sciences (the sociologist Kurt Lewin coined the term *action research*), and has been deployed in many diverse situations. "Notable instances of the use of action research may be found in such starkly contrasting worlds as insurance, prisons, social administration, ships, hospitals, community projects, education, industry, coal-mining, and business management" (Cohen and Manion, 1980, 210).

Although action research was imported into education in the 1940s, it received a boost in the 1960s and 1970s when it was embraced by influential educators such as Lou Smith and William Geoffrey (1968) in the United States and Lawrence Stenhouse (1975) in the United Kingdom. In his work, Stenhouse pointed out that although action research is intended to solve problems, it is capable not just of improving practice, but also of contributing to theory building in a way that is accessible to classroom teachers.

Numerous reasons have been advanced for the use of action research in professional development. Wallace, for example, argues (1991, 56–57) that action research can be attractive for two particular reasons:

1. It can have a specific and immediate outcome that can be directly related to practice in the teacher's own context.

2. The findings of such research might be primarily specific, i.e., it is not claimed that they are necessarily of general application, and therefore the methods might be more free-ranging than those of conventional research.

Wallace continues, "'Research' of this kind is simply an extension of the normal reflective practice of many teachers, but it is slightly more rigorous and might conceivably lead to more effective outcomes" (ibid., 57). However, there is some disagreement on this point. For instance, one challenge described by Monica Mingucci (1999, 16) is "informing teachers about what constitutes research and the difference between action research and applying known techniques or implementing strategies that teachers are convinced will work." She notes that action research is "systematic and entails gathering evidence on which to base rigorous reflection" (ibid.).

Action research is also described by Leo van Lier (1992, 3), who argues that it can bridge the gap between theory and practice. Teacher educators know that one of the most difficult things to balance in a professional preparation course is the tension between theoretical and practical aspects of the profession. Usually,

> ...theory and practice are not perceived as integral parts of a teacher's practical professional life.... This situation is the result of communication gaps caused by an increasingly opaque research technocracy, restrictive practices in educational institutions and bureaucracies (e.g., not validating research time, or not granting sabbaticals to teachers for professional renovation), and overburdening teachers who cannot conceive of ways of theorizing and researching that come out of daily work and facilitate that daily work (ibid.).

Like David in the example above, van Lier also conducted research in his own classroom. This experience led him to depict the action research process in the following diagram (reprinted from van Lier, 1994, 34):

Figure 8.1: Cycles of Action Research

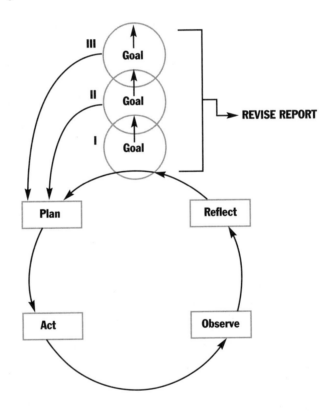

Notice that van Lier's model allows for the fact that the original goals of an action research project often evolve over time.

The Teachers' Voices section above illustrates how action research typically evolves through a series of cycles, as depicted in Figure 8.1. More specifically, these include (1) the identification of a puzzle or problem, (2) some sort of preliminary investigation to obtain baseline data on the issue in question, (3) the formulation of an intervention strategy, (4) activation of the strategy and documentation of the results, (5) reporting on the outcome, and (6) planning the next cycle in the process.

8.1 *STEPS IN THE ACTION RESEARCH CYCLE*

At this point please check your understanding of the action research cycle, using the illustration from David's experience. Fill in the boxes below with details from David's situation. The first one is done for you as an example.

INITIAL CYCLE	
1. Problem	*David's students were reluctant to speak up in class.*
2. Preliminary investigation	
3. Reflect/Form hypothesis	
4. Plan intervention and act	
5. Monitor/Collect data	
6. Observe the outcome	
SECOND CYCLE BEGINS	
7. Reflect	
8. Plan intervention and act	

Now think about the steps in the action research process and relate them to a situation that puzzles you. The idea here is to begin to craft an action research project based on your own work. Make notes on the following points as you think about your situation:

1. The problem: What is puzzling, intriguing, or worrisome to you?

2. The hypothesis: What do you think is the source of this problem or puzzle?

3. The intervention: What action would you like to take first?

4. The data: What records would help you determine the results of your action?

It will be helpful if you save these notes for further investigations that will emerge as we pursue the professional development opportunities afforded by action research.

The steps of the first part of this investigation are completed for you in Table 8.1 below, which summarizes David's views about the study he undertook when he was grappling with his Hong Kong students' reticence to talk in their English class:

Table 8.1: **Steps in the Action Research Cycle**

INITIAL CYCLE	
1. Problem	My students were reluctant to speak up in class.
2. Preliminary investigation	I obtained baseline data by recording and observing class over several days, and by interviewing students.
3 Reflect/Form hypothesis	Because of their cultural and educational background, the students were inhibited about speaking up in front of the whole class.
4. Plan intervention and act	I changed the dynamics by focusing on group work, split information tasks, and more physical movement in class.
5. Monitor/Collect data	I made audio and video recordings of my classes.
6. Observe the outcome	The amount of speaking by students increased. Most were ready to speak up in front of the whole class.
SECOND CYCLE BEGINS	
7. Reflect	I noticed a continuing reluctance on the part of some students to redefine their own roles and to take greater responsibility for their own learning.
8. Plan intervention and act	I incorporated a learning strategies and reflective learning dimension into the course.

David's experience maps neatly onto van Lier's model: As David's project evolved, his goals shifted slightly, so he started a new cycle to address the new goals.

GETTING STARTED

Action research works as a professional development strategy because it focuses on genuine issues and difficulties that we confront as teachers. It is therefore directly connected to our practice, and offers us the opportunity to generate contextualized theories of language learning and teaching based on and immediately connected to our own reality. Since it is the teacher who decides what to investigate in action research, the issues and, to a certain extent, the procedures are under the teacher's control.

However, the action research process need not always begin with a problem. It may emerge from simple curiosity. Your springboard may be that you wish to know more about some aspect of your teaching or your students' learning processes. In this approach, the action research cycle often begins with a period of observation and reflection. The observation (which may take the form of self- or peer-observation) will raise issues or questions that lead into the cycle of question, preliminary investigation, hypothesis formation, data collection, and data analysis and interpretation, as described above.

8.2 *WHAT WOULD YOU LIKE TO KNOW?*

In order to identify some issues or areas for possible action research in your situation, write down three things you would like to know about your own teaching. Next write down three things you would like to find out about your learners. Please save these lists as they will be useful if you choose to develop an action research plan of your own.

THE IMPORTANCE OF DATA

Whether you begin your action research project by identifying a problem or simply by reflecting on your teaching situation, the process should always involve some form of data collection. Later, when the action research project becomes more formalized, the systematic collection, analysis, and interpretation of data will be central to the process. Indeed, it is the posing of questions and this systematic collection and analysis of data that allow us to characterize the process as "research." In the initial stages, however, it is also highly beneficial to have some data that can serve as a sort of reality check. Allwright and Bailey (1991, 74) say that *baseline data* consist of "information that documents the normal state of affairs. It provides the basis against which we make comparative claims about how different or unusual the phenomena we have seen may be." Baseline data are collected before an intervention is attempted.

Both baseline data and data collected after an intervention can be of many different sorts—video or audio recordings, transcripts, observation checklists, and diagrams showing patterns of interaction (between teachers and students or among students). The data can also be learner-generated. For instance, David once used the reflective journals that were kept by his students about learning strategies as the point of departure for an action research project.

8.3 TYPES OF DATA

A question posed in Investigation 8.1 asked about the sorts of records that would help you determine the results of your action, if you were to undertake an action research project. In experimental research, data are often quantitative in nature, with students' test scores being one very familiar example.

However, the term *data* has been broadly defined as "records or descriptions or memories of events or objects" (Bateson, 1972, xviii). Action research permits a wide variety of data to be used in investigating classroom puzzles or problems. Listed below are several types of data that have been used in action research on language teaching and learning. Thinking about the action research project that you began to formulate above, put a "+," "?," or "−" next to each type of data in the following list depending on whether or not it might be very useful, possibly valuable, or not useful in your project:

_____ interviews with students	_____ audio recordings
_____ interviews with parents	_____ video recordings
_____ student questionnaires	_____ test scores
_____ parent questionnaires	_____ grades
_____ school records (e.g., attendance)	_____ students' work
_____ teachers' journal entries	_____ classroom maps
_____ students' journal entries	_____ observer's notes
_____ think-aloud protocols	_____ photographs

If you are working with a group of classmates or colleagues, it may be helpful to compare your responses. Remember though that appropriate types of data will vary from one action research project to another, depending on the goals and the participants involved.

Teachers' Voices

David Nunan

DAVID'S CLASSROOM EXPERIENCE CONTINUES

As I struggled to find ways of encouraging my Cantonese-speaking students to talk more in our English class, I realized that what had seemed, on the surface, to be a pretty straightforward and practical matter was underscored with a tangled mass of issues related to the cultural context in which the learning was taking place, and the educational context that had created conditioned reflexes in my learners. I also realized that the solution lay, not in simply identifying and adopting different classroom techniques, but in developing a long-term strategy for bringing about change in my students.

I was then confronted with another dilemma: To what extent did these learners have the right to reject a communicatively oriented approach, and to opt out of the tasks that flowed from that approach? If I were to go along with the transmission view of learning that had been inculcated, then it could be said that I was adhering to a principle of learner-centeredness by allowing them to remain largely silent. However, in doing so, I would have been violating another principle—that of relying on professional knowledge and practice. In this situation, faced with potentially competing principles when it came to the learners' stated goal (that of improving their oral proficiency), I was confident that I did indeed know best.

Eventually, the dilemma resolved itself through the inherent instability that characterizes any classroom. Gradually the intervention about learning strategies began to have an effect. Given structured opportunities to extend the range of learning strategies available to them, and to reflect on and articulate their attitudes toward the learning process, the students did begin to change. By the end of the course, most of them had become active learners who were invested in their own learning to the extent that they began to take control of the class, often in small but telling ways, such as by bringing their own language data to work on in our class.

POTENTIAL PROBLEMS

While action research brings numerous benefits, including the potential professional development of the teachers involved, it also entails dangers and difficulties. With all of the action research projects in which we have been involved, and with all of the action research networks we have helped to establish, problems have arisen. These can be traced to one or more of the following causes.

1. Teachers are typically not given recognition or time for doing research.

The time required to do even the most limited research project can be immense. The teachers concerned need to conceptualize their research projects, discuss them, formulate action plans, gather or create materials, seek advice, collect data, transcribe interactions, analyze the data, and write up the projects. Failure to provide adequate (or even any) time carries more than a resource implication. It also carries the message that the administration does not value the efforts that teachers themselves are making to change, in a critical and informed way, what is happening in their classrooms.

Even in those projects in which limited time is provided by the administration, the lack of recognition given to the additional efforts that teachers put into their action research projects can lead to a feeling of demoralization. If you wish to embark upon an action research project, think about your time constraints and your own need for support and/or recognition. How will those needs be met?

2. The agenda can be hijacked by the administration.

Action research is frequently associated with curricular innovations. As a result, there is often either the concern or the perception that action research will be used to determine whether the intended innovation is leading to improved learning outcomes.

A factor that can and, in our experience, has frequently worked against the success of action research projects is the interference of an administrative agenda in one way or another. In one large-scale, systemic action research network, the government funding agency, which had hitherto adopted a hands-off approach, insisted that the results of the research be used to evaluate the effectiveness of change. In response, the teachers backed off, and the action research network was seriously weakened.

Why should administrators want to hijack an action research agenda? We believe there are two main reasons. First, bodies funding an innovation think that they can get evaluative feedback "on the cheap," regardless of the fact that having an action research project designed by someone other than the researcher is inimical to the philosophy and practice of action research. Secondly, those who feel threatened by the research activity may see their involvement as a way of exercising control.

Even in cases where the administration has not attempted to hijack the action research agenda, the perception that it might do so can be an inhibiting factor. In one project where there was no intention to interfere, some teachers were still suspicious that the process was either controlled by the administration or likely to become so. This perception was fueled by comments from inside and outside the administration that were sometimes misinterpreted or taken out of context. Nonetheless, these remarks had the effect of creating a climate of suspicion that helped to destroy the project or at least seriously weaken it.

3. The agenda can be subverted from within by teachers who feel threatened or who want to bolster their own position within the political context of their work.

For reasons that are partly explicable and partly inexplicable, action research seems to be a lightning rod that attracts controversy and contention. In some contexts, especially those in which teachers are engaged in political or industrial dispute with the school administration, teachers wanting to research their own professional contexts have sometimes drawn criticism from their peers.

Several years ago, David was working as a facilitator to an action research network in a large secondary school. At the beginning of the project, the teachers who had volunteered to become involved were excited and enthused. Gradually the enthusiasm waned, despite the fact that some participants were generating important insights into teaching and learning in their situation. At a round-table discussion, several teachers admitted that they had come under attack from colleagues who argued that the action research project was an exercise in self-aggrandizement, and that "teachers were not paid to do research."

4. Teachers may lack the technical skills and knowledge to conceptualize and put into operation the research that interests them.

Teachers who are new to research sometimes find that they lack the conceptual and technical skills needed for planning and implementing their chosen research agenda. Very often, they bite off more than they can chew, framing a research question so large that it would be more appropriate as doctoral research. In addition, many university-based advocates of action research seriously underestimate the skills needed to conceptualize and carry out action research in on-going instructional programs.

Another problem is the perception of some teachers who are eminently capable of doing action research that the process is "too difficult." However, action research is becoming more familiar as an approach to classroom investigation, and a number of helpful guides are available (e.g., Kemmis and McTaggart, 1988; Nunan, 1989) for those who wish to undertake action research projects.

5. Doing action research can get in the way of teaching.

Almost inevitably, adding a data collection dimension to our work increases the burden of our teaching. In some instances, a deterioration in teaching can be caused by the need to set up recording equipment and ensure that it is working, by the problems associated with collecting data from students in pair and group work situations, and by the students' potential worry that the data being collected could be related to the evaluation of their projects. And, as noted in Chapter 7 about videotaping, sometimes intrusive recording devices (like video cameras) can trigger the observer's paradox. Other forms of data collection and analysis are time-consuming to manage, and can interfere with our time for lesson planning, materials development, marking students' papers, and so on. In our experience, however, the results have justified the time investment in terms of increased confidence, clearer planning, and ultimately better teaching.

While there are certainly drawbacks, we want to encourage you to consider action research as an avenue for professional development. For this reason, we have been quite candid in discussing potential problems associated with this approach. Some of the pitfalls described in this Frameworks section will be illustrated in the continued account of David's action research in his EFL class in Hong Kong.

DAVID'S CLASSROOM JOURNAL ENTRY

David Nunan

As I reflected on the last class I had today, I became more and more despondent. The lesson, which had begun well enough, ended in confusion, if not chaos. And it was to have been significant, for it was the first day of collecting data for my new research project. I was looking at the different patterns of interaction that were stimulated by different kinds of communicative tasks. I put the students into small groups, and then placed a portable cassette recorder in the center of each group. However, I had underestimated the time it would take to set up the recorders and make sure they were working correctly. During the lesson, I constantly had to go around the class, checking that the recorders were still working, so I didn't pay sufficient attention to classroom management. My instructions were unclear and some students became confused. Finally, they rebelled. I noticed in several groups that the students were switching off their recorders. Later, after the class, one of them admitted to me that, despite my disclaimer to the contrary, they thought I would be using the data on the tape to evaluate them.

8.4 AUDIORECORDING: WAYS AND MEANS

Think of a situation in which you might wish to audiorecord some classroom interaction. Which type(s) of interaction would you want to record: (1) teacher and students (whole class); (2) teacher and student (individual); or (3) student and student (in pairs or small groups)? And once you have an audiorecording of an interaction, how will you analyze the data? Here are some possibilities:

1. You could transcribe (portions of) the data, for subsequent coding or counting.

2. You could code the interactions (in the transcripts or the audiotapes).

3. You could summarize the interaction, based on the audiotapes.

4. You could use the audiotapes and/or the transcripts as the basis of a stimulated recall experience (e.g., have particular students listen to the tapes and explain what they were thinking about at key points in the lesson).

5. You could listen to tapes of several different lessons and then write a composite description of a "typical" lesson (as described in Chapter 5).

Can you think of other ways to analyze audiotaped data from your classroom? If you are working with a group it may be helpful to brainstorm about your ideas.

David's journal entry above documents the problems he encountered while trying to audiorecord small group interaction in his EFL class. Using David's students' reactions as a springboard, write down three things you could do to prepare students for the experience of being audiorecorded. Again, if you are working with a group it will be helpful to pool your ideas before you actually begin to video- or audiorecord classroom interaction in an action research project.

In the following Teachers' Voices segment you will read about David's experience in trying to set up an action research project with a group of teachers. As you read this section, try to be mindful of the sorts of pitfalls you might encounter if you and a group of colleagues were to undertake such a project.

DAVID SETS UP A TEAM PROJECT

Teachers' Voices

David Nunan

In the 1980s, I was approached by the coordinator of a program for providing professional support to foreign language teachers in Australia. The coordinator, whom we will call Phil, had heard me give a talk on ways of empowering classroom teachers by giving them power and responsibility for critical aspects of their work, such as curriculum development, through school-based curriculum design, and professional development through classroom observation and action research. Phil wanted to know whether I was interested in working with him to plan, implement, and evaluate a program of professional renewal for a group of secondary school teachers of foreign languages, including Indonesian, French, German, Chinese, Italian, and Vietnamese.

I was excited at the prospect of systematically implementing my ideas with a different group of teachers, so I agreed on two conditions: First, that the project must extend over a reasonable span of time, that is, two to three years, and second, that the Ministry of Education should provide the teachers taking part in the project with eight full days of paid release time during the course of the project. The first condition was readily agreed to. The second involved considerable negotiation. The final compromise was that the Ministry would pay for eight half-days, on condition that teachers contributed some of their own time. This compromise was less than ideal, but it did result in the project getting under way.

What was the stimulus for change? Apart from Phil's enthusiasm, as the project coordinator, and mine as the project consultant, what was the spark that ignited what had been merely a good idea? The most important stimulus was the imminent appearance of a controversial set of curriculum guidelines for teaching languages other than English in Australian schools. These proposals were called, appropriately enough, the "ALL Guidelines" [Australian Language Levels Guidelines]. To be properly implemented, they would have required a major shift in the way many foreign language teachers conducted their daily professional lives. The project was designed as a consciousness-raising exercise to encourage teachers to reflect on their teaching, to collect data on what went on in their classrooms, and to identify areas where they wanted to improve.

What happened? The project succeeded with some teachers who felt that, despite the anxiety and amount of work involved, they had developed a more reflective attitude toward their teaching. In addition, they had identified and solved some of the problems with which they were confronted in their daily lives, and they had gained a greater sense of control over their own professional destiny. For other teachers, the result was not quite so happy. They felt that they needed support on a day-to-day basis, rather than the infrequent half-day consultations that the project provided for. Some felt devalued and alienated within their schools (although others reported that their status had been enhanced by involvement in the project). Many were unable to conceptualize and focus their investigation, and this led to feelings of frustration and even anger. Finally, and perhaps inevitably, there were those who were fearful of being observed.

Nevertheless, emboldened by the general success of our initial efforts, Phil and I decided to expand the project in the second year. This time the results were not quite so happy. The government, as a condition of funding, insisted that the action research projects had to be explicitly tied to the implementation of a new set of curriculum guidelines. In effect, the government officials were saying that they would fund the research only if it gave them answers to questions arising from their curricular innovation. They also reduced the amount of time made available to teachers outside of the classroom to obtain expert help, to collaborate with colleagues, and to report on their work. Several teachers, believing that they were to become pawns of the bureaucracy, refused to continue their association with the project. The stricture that teachers could only research an issue or area of direct interest to the funding authority violates one of the fundamental principles of action research—the freedom of the individuals concerned to determine what to investigate, how to investigate, and how to report.

8.5 *ACTION RESEARCH: PLANS AND PROBLEMS*

In reflecting on the ideas you have developed about action research so far, try to anticipate the potential problems that might arise if you were to implement your own project. What are some of the solutions that could help you to overcome these problems? You may find a grid like the following helpful as you organize these concerns.

STEP	POTENTIAL PROBLEM(S)	POSSIBLE SOLUTION(S)
1. Identifying the general area for investigation		
2. Conducting the preliminary investigation		
3. Forming the hypothesis		
4. Planning an intervention		
5. Collecting data		
6. Observing the outcome		
7. Repeating steps 1–6 as needed		
8. Reporting on the project		

The potential for the success of any action research project can be greatly enhanced if you reflect critically on your plan before taking action. Such critical reflection can help to identify shortcomings, gaps, and inconsistencies in your plan. Remedying the shortcomings before initiating action is much easier than attempting to do so once the project has started.

Evaluate the action research plan that you have developed so far, using the following questions to guide your evaluation:

1. Is the project logical and coherent? If not, where are the gaps?

2. Is there harmony between the teaching and the research? (Does the research flow out of and back into the teaching?) Why or why not?

3. Is the research question worth asking? Why do you think so?

4. Are there alternative ways of investigating the question? If so, what are they?

5. Can you predict a follow-up question (or questions)?

6. Are the students participants in or objects of the research? If the latter, how could their role be enhanced?

7. Is the proposed data collection method consistent with the research question? If not, what additional or alternative methods could be used?

8. How will the data be analyzed?

9. Is there someone you could work with, or at least consult occasionally, in conducting this research?

Practicing collaborative action research, working together with other teachers who share your interests, can stave off many of the difficulties we have identified. Simply discussing your action research plan with a trusted colleague can also provide you with very useful insights about your ideas.

PLANNING FOR SUCCESS

The problems described above underline the importance of adhering to fundamental principles. In our experience, in order to be effective, action research must be tied into the following principles: It is connected directly to practice, and assists the teacher to do his or her job better; it enables teachers to build on strengths and to identify weaknesses; it allows for the emergence of multiple perspectives on teaching; it is under the direct control of the teacher; and at its best, it is collaborative in nature.

In this section, we briefly outline a number of practical steps that can be taken to maximize the chances of your success in undertaking an action research project. While these strategies won't guarantee success, they will, at least, minimize the risk of failure.

1. Start small.

People who are just beginning to make action research part of their professional lives may underestimate the social and psychological pressures of taking part in such projects, the practical complexities of collecting and making sense of data during the course of teaching, and the difficulties involved in conceptualizing research. Looking back at projects that we have been involved in over the years, we see that the most successful of these were ones in which the teachers either started small, or managed to reduce the scope of their original idea to manageable proportions.

Even projects that do not succeed (because their initial size and scope are too ambitious) can have practical spin-offs. In one project, the teachers backed off from action research because they felt overwhelmed by its demands. However, they became enthusiastically involved in a program of peer teaching, which shares several key characteristics with action research. Perhaps, in time, involvement in the peer teaching program will lead beyond observation and analysis to intervention and experimentation, and thus take these teachers forward into action research.

2. Collaborate with colleagues.

Doing action research can be time-consuming. Administrators are often understandably reluctant to grant teachers release time in order to conduct research, since ongoing classes must be taught. It is sometimes possible to work collaboratively with a colleague, however, in order to accomplish professional development goals via action research. For instance, when Leo van Lier was conducting an action research project that focused on his teaching of a low-level ESL class as well as his graduate courses in applied linguistics, he asked Kathi to observe his ESL class. She benefited from seeing Leo teach, and his research project benefited from her observational notes.

Another interesting example of collaboration comes from Lee Enright's (1981) report on an action research project conducted in a middle-school science classroom. In that case the deputy head of the school agreed to run the class from time to time so the teacher could participate in the lessons and see them from the learners' point of view.

While many administrators are reluctant to provide release time, particularly in periods of economic stringency, it is often possible to arrange some kind of responsibility sharing with a colleague. The teamwork is usually positive, and positive results can help teachers to achieve at least a modest degree of recognition. This acknowledgment and camaraderie pay off in terms of teacher enthusiasm and involvement.

3. Get someone in from the outside to legitimate the exercise.

Anecdotal evidence suggests that the involvement of an external consultant or adviser assists those engaged in the action research process. This assistance might entail technical help in selecting appropriate methods for data collection and analysis, or in conceptualizing the research project.

However, a key value seems to be a psychological one. The fact that someone beyond the institution itself feels the project has value and is prepared to invest time and expertise can provide a huge mental boost. In addition, involvement of a credible external agent can help to legitimize the project to colleagues and to the local administration.

4. Have someone on the inside who "owns" the process.

When it comes to collaborative projects involving networks of teachers, it is important to have someone on the inside of the project who is prepared to take responsibility for it. Without such a person, the action research project may sputter, fizzle, and ultimately die.

We are not aware of any instances of action research that have gone beyond the initial discussion stage without an active leadership role being played by someone inside the organization who was prepared to take ownership of the project. The nature of the ownership might vary, from negotiating with the administration to convening discussion groups to contacting external consultants. Regardless of their roles, and regardless of their status within the organization, the individuals who take this responsibility are crucial to the success (limited or otherwise) of action research projects.

Unfortunately, outsiders cannot create this sense of ownership any more than teachers can do the learning for their learners. It is something that must happen within the group. For teachers who are interested in developing an action research project it is important to discuss the issue of ownership, and to see whether there is at least one person in the group who is prepared to embrace this role.

5. Turn your research into a narrative account.

Another idea that is gaining currency is the use of narrative accounts through which teachers tell their own stories in their own ways, as we saw in Chapter 5. The notion of narratives as a justifiable form of documentation has been powerfully described by Freeman (1998a). He argues that teacher-research as storytelling has three tangible benefits: It allows for the articulation of personal theories, it highlights the social nature of teaching, and it results in the emergence of naturally occurring texts.

Freeman makes the point that storytelling is often devalued by those who see it as less compelling than more traditional, experimental research. He seeks support for his views from the Nobel laureate Toni Morrison who, in her Nobel lecture, states that "Narrative has never been merely entertainment for me. It is, I believe, one of the principal ways in which we absorb knowledge" (Morrison, 1994, 7). Further support comes from Freema Elbaz, who says,

> Initially, a "story" seems to be a personal matter: There is concern for the individual narrative of a teacher and what the teacher herself, and what a colleague or researcher, as privileged eavesdroppers, might learn from it. In the course of engaging with stories, however, we are beginning to discover that the process is a social one: The story may be told for personal reasons but it has an impact on its audience which reverberates out in many directions at once (Elbaz, 1992, 5).

This is one reason why collaborative action research can have such positive professional development results: We benefit from listening to other teachers' stories.

Casting classroom problems or puzzles as stories can help us clearly define the issues. One way to both begin and end an action research project is to articulate the issues as a story. Whether you write a journal entry to yourself or actually talk aloud about your teaching with a trusted colleague, casting the puzzle as a story can help you identify the problem you wish to address and begin to tease out possible resolutions.

6. Consider less conceptually challenging or less time-consuming alternatives.
Making entries in a teaching journal can be a valuable source of data for an action research project. If you don't feel compelled or you aren't ready to embark on action research, simply keeping a journal for a time can help you discover regularities and anomalies in your teaching that you might wish to investigate at some future date. In fact, making journal entries and then letting them sit for a time and reading them later can be a very fruitful source of ideas for research. Such journal entries, made before you undertake action research, are also a valuable source of baseline data. There are numerous other possibilities in this volume that might be more manageable than action research if you are a less experienced teacher, or if you don't have the time to devote to action research.

EXPLORATORY PRACTICE

Dick Allwright and his colleagues (e.g., Allwright and Bailey, 1991; Allwright and Lenzuen, 1997) have written about *exploratory practice*. It is

> a sustainable way of carrying out classroom investigations which provides language teachers (and potentially learners also) with a systematic framework within which to define the areas of language teaching and learning that they wish to explore, to refine their thinking about them, and to investigate them further using familiar classroom activities, rather than "academic" research techniques, as the investigation tools (ibid., 73).

How is exploratory practice different from action research? In our field, both are classroom-based. However, exploratory practice

> differs importantly from Action Research not only in its reliance on existing pedagogical practices as fundamental research tools but also in its use of teacher and learner "puzzles" about classroom events as its starting-point for the pursuit of **understanding** *what happens in classrooms*, as opposed to Action Research's use of standard academic research techniques and innovative pedagogical practices in an attempt at **directly solving** *practical classroom problems*. Exploratory Practice emphasizes the logically prior stage of attempting to reach understanding before trying out potential solutions to practical problems (ibid.).

There are two fundamental principles in exploratory practice. They are (1) promoting understanding, while also (2) promoting language teaching and learning. Allwright and Lenzuen insist upon a close relationship between these two principles:

> They must be honoured together, in harmony, and not be allowed to come into conflict with each other, competing for the teacher's attention. Exploratory Practice is not a way of getting "research" done, but a way of getting teaching (and learning) done in a way that is informed by an exploratory perspective intent on developing a rich understanding of what happens in the language classroom (ibid., 75).

Four additional principles are used to guide the steps in exploratory practice:

First, the practice of starting with whatever puzzles teachers (and/or their learners) is designed to guarantee that the content of all investigations has relevance to both teachers and learners. Secondly, the use of familiar classroom activities as investigative tools, rather than elaborate academic research techniques with all their potential for adding to teachers' burdens, is intended to ensure that exploratory practice has indefinite *sustainability*—that it is not allowed to become something that is so time-consuming and difficult that it can only be done for a special limited-term project for which release time and other forms of logistical support can be given. Thirdly, working with teachers' (and/or learners') puzzles is expected to encourage *collegiality*—bringing teachers and learners, and even academic researchers, together in a common enterprise of developing practically useful understandings.... Fourthly, and finally, all of the above are intended to foster *professional development*—helping all participants (learners and teachers) to achieve productive progress through their developing understanding of language teaching and learning (ibid., 75–76).

Thus exploratory practice can be a viable alternative to action research as an avenue to professional development.

WHAT FOUR TEACHERS FOUND

Printed below are brief comments from four teachers who engaged in action research projects in their own classrooms. They were part of a group of Hong Kong secondary school teachers attending an inservice course that Andy taught. One of the aims of the course was to introduce the participants to action research for discovering more about what was happening in their classrooms (Curtis, 1999b). The teachers investigated why their students were using little or no spoken English during their English classes (i.e., the same problem that David wrote about in the first two Teachers' Voices sections of this chapter).

Lawrence, Ling, Richard, Carrie

Of the four teachers, Lawrence and Richard are native speakers of English from England. Ling and Carrie are native speakers of Cantonese. Here's what they found.

1. **Lawrence:** Reviewing the questionnaire results did give me an opportunity to try to reach the lower ability boys via a sporting interest—football. They are more interested, motivated, and animated when discussing the chances of [soccer teams like] Ajax, Porto, Manchester United, etc., than when discussing the future perfect continuous tense. (Who isn't?) But as to improving pupil-pupil interaction in English, I have to report a general lack of success. The products of pupil-pupil interaction (e.g., group answers on a worksheet or teacher-pupil interaction via feedback) are acceptable and improving but the process of achieving the product is conducted in a mixture of Cantonese and English.

2. **Ling:** As a teacher, I play the role of a helper rather than a dictator in the class. I move around the class to listen and help individuals. The designed activities allow the focus to shift from the teacher to the task and to the whole class, group, or pair cooperation. I find this project very useful and successful because my passive students are willing to speak English afterwards.

3. **Richard:** This project has generally encouraged me as a teacher to put myself in my students' shoes, to look at oral participation from their point of view. The project has given me clearer insight into why some students do not (or do not want to) speak out in class by asking me to identify reasons for lack of oral participation and to find adequate strategies to counteract these problems. I have also developed my observational skills as a teacher, noting errors for later use in feedback sessions.

4. **Carrie:** The results of the project further consolidate my teaching strategy. I have always thought that children learn most effectively through play, because of its enjoyable, self-initiated, and low-risk nature. Teachers, therefore, have to achieve a balance between coping with the tightly packed curriculum and making the students learn enjoyably.

8.6 *WHAT DO YOU WANT TO KNOW?*

Imagine that you have the opportunity to interview or correspond with one of the four Hong Kong secondary school teachers whose comments are quoted above. The purpose is to learn more about conducting action research. Choose the teacher you would most like to talk with and answer the following questions:

1. Why did you select this particular teacher?

2. What questions would you want to ask about the data collection and analysis procedures used?

3. What questions would you want to ask about the outcomes of the action research project?

RESTRUCTURING OUR TEACHING

Monica Mingucci has written a brief article on "Action Research in ESL Staff Development." In her conclusion she makes the following claim:

> [For] teachers to fully embrace the principles and philosophy of action research they need to begin by reinventing themselves. Practitioners must look at themselves and their practices, as if for the first time, and try to see themselves as the central object of their research if true change is to occur. We can only address the outside world after we have addressed our individual internal ones. We can only create alternatives to the existing methods and structures after we have restructured ourselves (1999, 16).

As teachers who have done action research, we agree with this statement. In fact, we believe that it is the constant restructuring of our teaching selves that leads to professional development.

Following this line of thought, Kathi and Andy asked David to explain what he had learned, as a teacher, by doing action research. His reply (which is printed here as the last Teachers' Voices section of this chapter) leads the discussion back to Donald Freeman's (1989a) framework about awareness, attitudes, knowledge, and skills (see Figure 2.1 on page 23).

WHAT DAVID LEARNED

Teachers'
Voices

David Nunan

Doing action research has had a significant impact on my professional development as a teacher. I have felt this impact at two different levels. At a general level, it has affected my attitudes and awareness. At a more localized level, it has had an impact on my knowledge, and skills as a teacher.

In terms of attitude and awareness, I appreciate the value of data, particularly student data. Whether or not I am doing action research, I regularly collect samples of student speech, small group interactions, student journal entries, essay drafts, and data on my learners' needs and interests. This practice has reinforced my belief in the centrality of the learner to the learning process. It has also encouraged me to believe in the possibility of achieving harmony between teaching and research. (In his book on teacher-research, Freeman [1998a] talks about working at the "hyphen" in the phrase *teacher-research*. Through my work as an action researcher, I have come to see what he means.)

The knowledge and skills arising from doing action research seem to function at a local, contextualized level. In other words, they are situated knowledge and skills. This point specifically reflects the fact that such knowledge and skills arise out of and in response to a puzzle or problem in a particular context. So while they work in that situation, they may not necessarily be relevant in another situation. For example, the action research that I carried out at the University of Hong Kong (reported in the early Teachers' Voices segments of this chapter) arose out of the reluctance of my students to speak up in class. Through that action research project, I developed strategies for changing the dynamics of the class in ways that facilitated communication. I am not at all sure that these skills would be relevant, or even necessary, in another context.

8.7 *TASKS FOR DEVELOPMENT*

Investigations

We hope this chapter has stimulated your interest in action research. The following Tasks are intended to deepen your understanding of action research as an approach to professional development. The Suggested Readings have been selected to provide both examples of action research projects done by teachers and sources for methodological guidance.

1. Interview a teacher who has conducted action research about language teaching and learning. Try to discover the following:

   A. How did he/she choose the focus of the research project?

   B. What problems arose during the course of the study?

C. How were the learners involved in the project, if at all?

D. What would the teacher do differently if he/she were to repeat the study?

E. What advice would this teacher offer to novice action researchers?

2. If you can, in fact, conduct the interview described in Task 1 above, it will be useful to tape-record the conversation, or to make notes on the teacher's ideas. We suggest two possible comparisons that might be helpful to you and your colleagues:

A. Compare the list of problems identified by the teacher you interviewed with the potential problems described in the Frameworks in this chapter. Were the two lists similar, or did different problems arise?

B. Compare the advice this teacher offered you with the suggestions we've made in this chapter. Look for new guidance about conducting action research.

3. We believe that effective action research is based on five principles, which are printed below. Write a brief comment about how each principle would (or could) be realized in your own action research project.

A. The action research is connected directly to practice, and assists the teacher to do his or her job better.

B. It enables teachers to build on strengths as well as to identify weaknesses.

C. It allows for the emergence of multiple perspectives on teaching.

D. It is under the direct control of the teacher.

E. It is collaborative in nature.

Appendix A starts on p. 249.

4. Appendix A of this book is the transcript of an EFL lesson David taught. Imagine that a colleague taught the lesson and has transcribed the video in order to gather baseline data about his teaching. Now he is trying to find a likely focus for an action research project. If he were to ask you for your advice, what aspects of his teaching would you suggest he investigate? List three possible foci for investigation, as suggested by the transcript.

Next choose the topic that most appeals to you out of these three areas. What question(s) would you like to investigate about this topic? What are some likely interventions that you could use? What sorts of data would be most helpful?

Suggested Readings

Amy Tsui (1996) worked with 38 EFL teachers in Hong Kong, who investigated their EFL students' reticence to speak in class. The most fascinating comments from Tsui's account are the surprising things that the teachers learned about their own behavior—in other words, the professional awareness they gained and the resulting changes they made by conducting action research.

Another resource is found in the British Council publication *Action Research in the Lower Silesia Cluster Colleges*. This collection of 10 articles documents action research by Polish teachers who formed an action research group. The participants felt that the group was successful because "it gave teachers an opportunity to reflect on their own teaching and on some aspects of the curriculum" and because "teachers of different subject areas could exchange ideas" (Michon'ska-Stadnik, 1997, 9).

David Nunan's (1989) book, *Understanding Language Classrooms*, is a manual for teachers interested in investigating teaching and learning in their own classrooms. It takes the reader through the process of collecting, interpreting, and presenting data. Andy and David have also written articles about action research (Curtis, 1998; Nunan, 1990; 1993).

Ann Snow, John Hyland, Lia Kamhi-Stein, and Janet Harclerode Yu (1996) conducted action research in Los Angeles using both students' and teachers' input.

Leo van Lier's short paper on action research was printed in the Spanish journal, *Sintagma*, in 1994. Although the journal may be hard to access outside Europe, we recommend this article as a clear introduction to action research.

A very helpful document for getting started on your own action research project is *The Action Research Planner*, by Steven Kemmis and Robin McTaggart (1988). It contains a number of clear diagrams and frameworks that can be used in making decisions about your project and interpreting the data.

The concept of getting "someone from the outside to legitimate the exercise" is very nicely illustrated in an article by Ruiz de Guana, Díaz, Gonzales, and Garaizar (1995). They discuss an action research project conducted in a Basque preschool context.

Geoff Brindley (1991) has described his work with six teachers in Australia (three ESL teachers and three who'd been working in EFL contexts) as they were learning about action research. The article contains many useful quotations from the teachers themselves about the learning process and the results.

Mary Ann Christison and Sharon Bassano (1995) have written a practical article about the uses of questionnaires and interviews to gather data in action research. The paper contains several clear examples.

Angela Mok (1997) undertook an action research project that looked at four components of an English enrichment program for secondary school students in Hong Kong: (1) networking activities, (2) inter-class activities, (3) class activities, and (4) small group activities. The article provides examples of questionnaires used for data collection and gives numerous comments from both students and teachers.

The notion of research as storytelling has been around for a long time. In the 1970s and 1980s, members of the Cambridge Action Research Network and the Centre for Applied Research in Education, including Denny (1978, 1982),

Goodson and Walker (1982), and Walker (1982), advocated the use of narrative accounts. See also Clandinin and Connelly (1991).

Two recently published books on action research are designed specifically for people in our field: *Collaborative Action Research for English Language Teachers* by Anne Burns (1998) and *Action Research for Language Teachers* by Michael J. Wallace (1998). See also Burns (1997). In addition, Anna Uhl Chamot (1995) published a three-page introduction entitled "The Teacher's Voice: Action Research in Your Classroom." We also recommend the conference series entitled *Teachers Develop Teachers Research: Papers on Classroom Research and Teacher Development* (see, e.g., Edge and Richards, 1993).

There is also a journal called *Educational Action Research*. Although it is not devoted exclusively to language teaching and learning, it contains many articles of relevance to language teachers.

9

PEER OBSERVATION: SOMEONE ELSE'S SHOES

To be open to questioning long-held beliefs, to be willing to exam-
ine the consequences of our actions, and to be engaged fully in the
teaching endeavor is certainly a rewarding but also very demanding
effort. To be engaged in this sort of examination with others
requires that trust becomes a prominent feature of these conversa-
tions among and dialogues between practitioners. Without those
companions, and without that trust, our reflection on our teaching
will be severely limited (Zeichner and Liston, 1996, 19).

The main purpose of this chapter is to provide our readers with frameworks for observing language teachers, language learners, and the interaction among them. We also hope it will indirectly help you develop your skills in observing and in recording data generated during observations.

PROBLEMS WITH OBSERVATIONS

We have found that peer observation is an excellent way to break down bar-riers and begin conversations that lead to professional development. By *peer observation*, we mean the act of being openly and attentively present in another teacher's classroom, watching and listening to the classroom interaction primarily for reasons of professional growth (rather than supervision or evalu-ation). Of course, as teachers we can also participate in peer observation for professional development purposes by inviting our colleagues into our class-rooms to watch us work with our learners.

We are not talking about the traditional practice of novice teachers being observed by an expert, with the purpose of the experienced teacher providing the novice with feedback and teaching tips. While that practice can be useful in certain contexts, there are problems with it, as outlined by Marion Williams (1989, 86):

> Classroom observations have traditionally entailed the familiar sce-
> nario of a nervous teacher, trying to perform correctly, while the
> trainer sits at the back ticking items on a checklist and making
> decisions as to what is "good teaching" and "bad teaching." The
> teacher reads a report on his or her performance, and tries harder
> to get it right next time.

Williams explains why this approach to observation was unsatisfactory:

- The teachers didn't like it. It was threatening, frightening, and regarded as an ordeal.

- The teachers had no responsibility for the assessment. It was trainer-centered. Meanwhile, we were promoting child-centered teaching.

- It was prescriptive.

- The checklist focused on too much at once.

- There was no continuity from the first to the third visit, and the visits were therefore not linked to the course.

- There was no provision for individual pace or wishes (ibid., 86).

Similar problems have been noted by Peter Sheal:

1. Most classroom observations are conducted by administrators rather than by practicing teachers. Peer observations are not very common. Consequently observation tends to be seen as judgmental, and one more aspect of administrator "power."

2. Much of the observation that goes on is unsystematic and subjective. Administrators and teachers generally have not been trained in observation or the use of systematic observation tools. Consequently they tend to use themselves as a standard, and they observe impressionistically.

3. Most observation is for teacher-evaluation purposes, with the result that teachers generally regard observation as a threat. This leads to tension in the classroom, and tension between teacher and observer at any pre- or post-observation meetings.

4. Post-observation meetings tend to focus on the teacher's behavior—what he/she did well, what he/she might do better—rather than on developing the teacher's skills. As feedback from observers is often subjective, impressionistic, and evaluative, teachers tend to react in defensive ways, and given this atmosphere, even useful feedback is often "not heard" (Sheal, 1989, 93).

We wish to overcome these problems while still promoting the benefits of classroom observation for both the observer and the observed.

When we think of all the feedback conversations we've had—both as observers and as teachers who have been observed—we realize that we weren't just talking about what we remember doing. In those conversations we were actually being assisted in the recall process.

Our recollections and ideas were being probed with questions, in a kind of collaborative think-aloud between the observer and the observed. This lateral disclosure and seeking of feedback led to the co-construction of meaning.

As mentioned in Chapter 1, Dan Lortie (1975, 223) has called teaching the "egg carton profession" because once the classroom doors are closed, teachers are insulated from the outside world. This separation reduces the risk of criticism: If no one sees us, no one can question what we do. But it can also breed isolation, a distancing of professionals from one another. Engaging in teacher development in such isolation can lead to what Wells (1994) has called "the loneliness of the long-distance reflector" (11). Such habitual isolation may also lead teachers to feel territorial in response to the anxiety caused by having observers in their classrooms (Williams, 1989). This situation is described in the following Teachers' Voices section, in which Mark Clarke recalls an event in his early years of teaching (Clarke, 1982, 442).

PEER OBSERVATION IN CAIRO

Mark Clarke

I was one of 20 or so teaching assistants [TAs] at the American University of Cairo. We were all teaching in the preacademic intensive English program and working on our masters degrees in TEFL. For one of the methods classes two of the TAs conducted an experiment which required them to observe all of our classes. They didn't say what they were looking for, but it was quite clear that they knew what they were looking for, that it was bad, and that they were confident of finding it in our classes. The effect of having these observers in our classes was electric, in spite (or perhaps because) of the fact that they were our peers: We all became nervous, irritable, jumpy. We knew we should probably be doing something different, but we had no idea what we should change or how. As it turned out, they were measuring language use in the classroom, comparing the proportion of teacher-talk to student-talk, guided by the assumption that the latter should exceed the former. Now, I have no quarrel with the assertion that greater use of the language in class by students is desirable. What bothered me about this project was the aura of moral judgment with which it was conducted, the imperfectly disguised assumption that all of us were probably doing something that we should not be doing, the Gestapo-like presupposition of human frailty. And the galling thing is that we all shared these assumptions, observers and observees alike, so that when we discussed the results of the study, we did not focus on the legitimacy of the assumptions, nor on the inquisitional nature of the observations. No, we meekly and somewhat guiltily explored means by which we could increase student participation, or, more to the point, means by which we could purge our classes of teacher-talk.

EVALUATION AND DESCRIPTION

One way to decrease this feeling of territoriality and isolation is to take part in peer observation for developmental purposes—to gain insight about our own and our peers' teaching. As Fanselow puts it, "seeing you allows me to see myself differently and to explore variables we both use" (1988, 115). This purpose for teacher observation results in a dynamic that is quite different from the "hidden agenda" situation described above.

Our position in this chapter is that peer observation is more than simply an equal-power alternative to supervisory observation, since it can be as beneficial to the classroom observer as it is to the teacher, if not more so. However, a clear distinction between *evaluative* and *descriptive* observation is crucial (van Lier, 1988, 69). The typically negative response to supervisorial observation (which is usually evaluative in nature) has been recognized for some time (Freeman,

1982; Sheal, 1989), along with the developmental benefits of peer observation. Some key points on these issues have been listed by Jill Burton (1987, 164–165):

- Observation as a means of staff development must be kept separate from administrative supervisory requirements.

- Observation could beneficially be built into staff development programs as a regular ongoing activity.

- Observation is effective when it is teacher-initiated.

- Observation is most usefully conducted by teachers (who might also sometimes be middle managers because middle managers do often teach).

- Team-teaching incorporating team staff development could be more strongly encouraged.

- Teachers and observers (one and the same person on different occasions) need training to use the observation process constructively and analytically.

- Classroom research and observation (a method of classroom research) enable individualized teacher development.

- Self-administered classroom research encourages teacher change.

- Teacher development programs have to be seen to be helpful; self-initiated development programs (such as peer observations and conferencing) are felt to be helpful.

The concepts discussed below will help illustrate the differences between evaluative and descriptive observation practices.

BREAKING THE PRIVACY RULE

Joachim Appel, the EFL teacher in Germany whose diary has been cited in previous chapters, made some entries in his teaching journal regarding his desire to observe his colleagues and to be able to talk with them more openly about teaching concerns. We have reprinted three of those entries here.

Joachim Appel

16 March: Closed Doors

One good thing during training was that I could sit in on other teachers' classes. Today I would benefit from an occasional visit to a colleague. It would help to put into perspective what the others in the staffroom say. But teachers work behind closed doors. The privacy of the classroom is sacred (Appel, 1995, 6).

18 March: Breaking the Privacy Rule

K (we started at the school together) is breaking the privacy rule. He comes back into the staffroom after a lesson telling the others how difficult it has been to calm down the class. One of my colleagues tells me he thinks K is a fool to do this. It would destroy his reputation, if he had any left to destroy. None of those K was opening up to would try to help him (ibid.).

22 July: Fun to Watch

I went north to visit Peter, who has been a teacher for about 20 years.... Because I was a friend from far away rather than a colleague at the same school, he took me with him into his classroom. He was great fun to watch. There is nothing more stimulating than seeing someone who teaches well. What I learn is not so much method but behavior. What I see are reactions, like when he wakes up a pupil who is about to doze off by putting his hand on his shoulder—quite lightly and matter-of-fact. What I see are gestures: how he invites someone to speak. It is such little things ... that make all the difference. It is an annoying thought that good lessons are, in a way, "wasted" on those who do not need them, i.e., inspectors, supervisors, etc., and, for reasons of time and unwritten rules of the profession, not accessible to those who do need them (ibid., 27–28).

FOUR QUADRANTS

Observations are conducted for many reasons, including supervision, research, and professional development (see Murphy, 1992). In some situations, the observer becomes actively engaged in the event he or she is observing. In this case, he or she is practicing *participant observation*. In other contexts, an observer may not interact in the situation. This would be an instance of *nonparticipant observation*. These two possibilities are not clearcut categories but rather form the two ends of a continuum.

Likewise, observations may be conducted *covertly* (without the knowledge of those being observed) or *overtly* (with their full knowledge, and typically with their permission). Again, these two constructs mark the ends of a continuum. By overlaying these two continua, we produce the grid depicted in Figure 9.1:

Figure 9.1: Overtness and Participation in Conducting Peer Observations

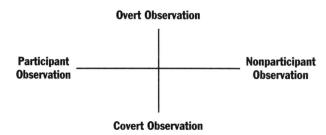

There may be many reasons to conduct covert observations, either as a participant or nonparticipant observer. For instance, rooms with one-way mirrors have been used in "lab schools" in preservice teacher education contexts in order to collect data without alerting the teachers and pupils to the observers' presence. This strategy is an attempt to overcome the *observer's paradox*, the fact that the very presence of an observer can distort the dynamics of the event being observed (Labov, 1972).

Garry Powell has suggested three advantages of what he calls "unseen observations." In this process, no visitor is present in the classroom. Instead, the teacher fills out a questionnaire, after a typical lesson, which can then be discussed with the "unseen observer." The advantages of this procedure are that "it is very time-effective for a busy trainer/director of studies; some issues—for example, how lessons are planned—are actually more susceptible to honest introspection than to observation; and above all, it tends to be less judgmental; as a rule, description rather than prescription occurs, and this tends to generate more alternatives" (Powell 1999, 3). Powell's ideas about "unseen observations" are interesting. However, we believe that collegial peer observations are most conducive to our professional development as teachers when we are observing. Therefore observing for developmental purposes in an overt, agreed-upon manner is worth the effort and the potential risks involved.

There are various permutations possible with peer observation, which increase the flexibility and usefulness of this approach. The nonparticipant observer may be in a stationary mode at the back of the classroom, or the participant observer can circulate and interact during small group work activities. The observer can use an observation checklist, take detailed shorthand notes, make video or audio recordings, use a combination of these methods, or just sit and watch without formally collecting data. The Teachers' Voices sections of this chapter will illustrate some of these possibilities.

In terms of the focus, what is observed should be negotiated by the observer and the teacher. The observer can be asked to carry out a global observation, noting as much as possible about the lesson, or a more focused observation, for example, watching specifically for the teacher's wait time, error treatment, or elicitation of student input. Whatever focus is chosen, time should be set aside for pre- and post-lesson discussions between the observer and teacher in order to tap into both parties' goals.

Working with other teachers in Hong Kong schools, we have found that one of the main advantages of peer observation relates to class size. In this situation (and elsewhere) it is common to have 40 or more learners in one room for a lesson that lasts less than 40 minutes. Under these conditions, without the extra pair of eyes that a peer observer provides, it is very difficult for the teacher to observe much of what is happening. In such circumstances, a second viewpoint is very helpful in co-constructing an account of what happened in the lesson (Curtis, 1997).

But with the kind of self-disclosure required and the potential loss of face, a good deal of trust is also needed in peer observation. The importance of establishing trust is emphasized by Batey and Westgate (1994, 84). They say that having a discussion with a colleague can promote the development of trust "which often pays dividends at later stages when potentially awkward questions about each other's teaching may have to be faced. If such a framework of trust is developed, those questions can be asked and considered in dialogue." Such trust is required in both *reciprocal peer observation*, in which the observer and the teacher observe each other's lessons, and *coaching* (see Chapter 12), which involves several such observations with the objective of the coaching partners achieving specific changes in their teaching.

Practicing reciprocal peer observation allows us as teachers to put our professional selves in someone else's shoes, and to have someone else try ours on as well. This process can help to build an atmosphere of mutual respect and understanding. These factors are especially important if teacher development is to be promoted in institutions or educational systems undergoing rapid change, as well as in those in which attitudes and teaching behavior may have become entrenched or static.

9.1 OBSERVER AND OBSERVEE

Please turn back to Figure 9.1 (p. 161), the overlapping continua of overtness and participation possible in peer observations. Imagine (or recall, if you have experience) a situation that fits in each quadrant of the figure. For instance, an example of a covert participant observation would be one in which an observer viewing a language class through a one-way mirror, unbeknownst to the teacher or pupils, takes part in the activities vicariously (by answering questions, repeating new vocabulary, etc.).

Now imagine yourself in the role of the teacher being observed. Which of the four quadrants would you prefer to work in? Does your opinion change if you picture yourself in the observer's role? Why, or why not?

COMMANDMENTS FOR OBSERVING AND BEING OBSERVED

In order to surface concerns about classroom observations, we asked a group of language teachers to write two sets of guidelines for peer observation. One set was intended for observers coming into the writer's class. The other set was meant for teachers whom the writer would be observing. These guidelines were written in the style of the Ten Commandments of the Old Testament. Each began with "Thou shalt…" or "Thou shalt not.…" Here are the issues these teachers raised:

Various
teachers

When I am observing thee thou shalt:

- let me know your needs of me as an observer and tell me the rules, if there are any.

- explain any extraordinary circumstances that may be affecting you or your students.

- introduce me; mention who I am, but thou shalt not keep alluding to "our guest."

- offer suggestions on how I can best collect my data without making your students feel uncomfortable or insecure; tell your students that they are not being evaluated.

- refrain from calling on me to participate unless you ask or tell me before class.

- not alter your behavior on my behalf; behave as usual; thou shalt act naturally.

- try not to get flustered about being observed.

- *not* ask my opinion or feedback of your teaching in front of the class.

When thou art observing me thou shalt:

- arrive early for class and introduce yourself to everyone at the beginning.

- not tell me what you are looking for until you are done, if you have a preset agenda.

- sit behind the students, out of their direct view.

- observe and obey the same rules the students follow, and thou shalt respect the opinions and ideas of the students.

- interact with the students only when requested to do so; thou shalt not disrupt the class or detract from the students' learning.

- not use my materials without permission and not take up my break time.

- observe with an open mind; thou shalt not get hung up on petty mistakes or gaps.

- share feedback with me in response to specific questions I ask, but thou shalt not talk to me about what I should or should not have done (unless I ask).

You can see that these teachers had a wide range of opinions as to what constitutes desirable and undesirable behavior on the part of observers and observees. If you are about to attempt peer observing, it will be helpful for you and your colleague(s) to make explicit any concerns like these before the actual observations begin.

9.2 *Your Own "Do's and Don'ts"*

Write your own list of "Ten Commandments" (1) for someone you would observe, and (2) for someone coming to observe you teaching. If you are working with a group of classmates or colleagues, compare your lists of "do's" and "don't's." (If you don't feel you can write ten, write as many as you can, then turn back to the list above and put a star next to those that are important to you.)

With a partner, role-play the preobservation conference between two teachers who are about to engage in reciprocal peer observations. In planning the observation, imagine that the two of you have written the "Commandments" quoted above (i.e., one person as the observer and one as the observee). Negotiate the observational focus while also clarifying your attitudes about observing (or being observed) to your partner. What issues, if any, does the role-play experience bring to light?

Observers' Behavior

The question of how to behave during peer observations has been addressed in the professional language teaching literature. For example, John Murphy (1992) has written about the "etiquette" of nonsupervisory observations. He notes that:

Common sense might lead one to assume that a visitor who observes in an official, administrative role is potentially more threatening to a classroom teacher than a colleague or novice teacher who is not a supervisor. Given the complexity of human relationships and classroom settings, however, this premise is difficult to maintain (217).

This comment underscores Clarke's point about him and his classmates being observed by two of their peers. Murphy continues:

In comparison with nonsupervisors, supervisors are more likely to have been trained to observe in a nonthreatening and non-anxiety provoking manner.... Although there are exceptions, many supervisors complete course work or in-service workshops centered upon this topic. In contrast, peers or teachers in training who are not supervisors are less likely to have formally examined these issues. In this respect a nonsupervisor presents even more serious problems for a classroom teacher because s/he is less likely to be aware of, and more likely to be insensitive to, issues of classroom observation etiquette (ibid., 218).

We will return to issues of how to behave when visiting classrooms in the Investigations throughout the rest of this chapter.

Much of the discomfort teachers feel about being observed has to do with being evaluated. Fanselow (1977, 1978, 1980, and 1987) has argued that the profession needs a shared vocabulary for describing teaching rather than evaluating it. Over the past two decades the field has made some progress in this area. For example, in addition to Fanselow's *FOCUS* system, there are now many other observation instruments designed for analyzing classroom data as opposed to evaluating teaching (see, e.g., Allen, Fröhlich, and Spada, 1984; Allwright, 1988; Day, 1990; Long, Adams, McLean, and Castaños, 1976; Sinclair and Coulthard, 1975). In addition, the role of language teacher supervisors is now better understood (see, e.g., Lewis, 1998; Wajnryb, 1994).

When conducting classroom observations, it is useful to distinguish among three related concepts: *observations, inferences,* and *opinions.* Please stop reading for a moment and think how you would define these terms. Imagine a case where your language students asked you to explain the vocabulary items *observations, inferences,* and *opinions.* What would you emphasize? Definitions of these three terms include the following points:

1. *Observations:* noting and recording facts and events (e.g., in a scientific study); the data resulting from the observational act; comments or remarks based on something observed.

2. *Inferences:* decisions or conclusions based on something known; ideas derived by reasoning; decisions based on facts or evidence; conclusions or deductions.

3. *Opinions:* beliefs not necessarily based on absolute certainty or factual knowledge, but on what seems true, valid, or probable to one's own mind; evaluations, or impressions of the value of a person, practice, idea, etc.

In conducting peer observations it is particularly important to distinguish among these three concepts. Observations are essentially factual in nature. Two or more observers in the same classroom could agree, for example, on the number of times a particular pupil raised his hand in a 20-minute period (provided they were paying attention to the same student and counting carefully). Inferences, on the other hand, are more interpretive in nature. For instance, one observer might conclude that a learner raised her hand 12 times in 20 minutes because she was knowledgeable about the topic and was eager to contribute to the discussion. Another observer might infer that this learner was confused and had many questions. Unless the teacher calls on the learner and the student verbalizes his or her needs, the observers cannot know for certain what the student's motivation is without asking him or her. Opinions often include an evaluative attitude, and may be held independent of (and sometimes even contrary to!) available data. In the scenario described above one observer might believe that the teacher was ignoring this learner and should call on her or him more often, while the other might believe that the teacher did a good job in distributing the turns evenly among all the pupils.

9.3 *Observations, Inferences, and Opinions*

Decide whether each item in the examples below illustrates an observation, an inference, or an opinion:

Example 1:

    A. There was a great social climate in this classroom.

    B. The students seemed comfortable raising questions and making comments.

    C. During the first 20 minutes of class, each student took at least one self-initiated turn.

Example 2:

    A. The teacher was probably trained in the audiolingual method.

    B. The teacher treated every oral error by modeling the correct form.

    C. The teacher's treatment of the students' oral errors was very heavy-handed.

As a follow-up activity, it may be helpful to identify several important classroom-related issues (such as participation and error treatment in the examples above) and write an observation, an inference, and an opinion about each issue. If you are working with a group, you could exchange the items you wrote with your colleagues, so each member of your group could get more practice in identifying observations, inferences, and opinions.

CONTRACT, DURATION, AND RESOLUTION

Donald Freeman (1998b) has suggested that arrangements for observing a peer should include three components: (1) the *contract* (the specific purpose of the observation, or what the observer will be watching for); (2) the *duration* (when the observation will begin and end); and (3) the *resolution* (what the next step will be between the observer and the observee). It is important to note that the resolution does not refer to the resolution of a teaching problem; it is simply the follow-up to the observation. The resolution can range from meeting for five minutes to chat about the lesson, to the observer giving a copy of his/her notes to the teacher with or without an in-depth discussion, or even to writing a formal report about the observation experience.

Peer observation is a very valuable professional development tool, particularly if it is designed to benefit the observer. In many programs, however, peer observation is used as pseudo-supervision to evaluate the teacher being observed. This sort of feedback can provide useful information, but the real educational power of peer observation is found in the sheer luxury of watching someone else teach for a time and discussing the teaching afterwards. If this process is entered into willingly by both parties—the observee and the observer—and the contract, the focus, and the duration agreed upon by the two, the experience can be very rich indeed. In the following Teachers' Voices sections, we will see three different sorts of contracts, durations, and resolutions.

The next Teachers' Voices section shows what Kathi learned by observing her colleague, Bob Oprandy, as he taught the students in her class, who were teachers-in-training. In this instance Kathi watched a one-hour class (the duration) without taking notes and with no specific purpose or contract, but wrote up a retrospective account, which was given to Bob for administrative evaluation purposes (the resolution). Although the motivation for the peer observation experience began with an administrative decree that the members of the department would observe one another, Kathi felt she benefited nonetheless from carefully attending to Bob's teaching. Because this write-up was intended for evaluative purposes, it contains several opinions, as well as more factual observational data and the observer's inferences. (The report is reprinted here with the teacher's permission.)

WATCHING WITHOUT NOTES

Kathi Bailey

Observer's Name: Kathi Bailey

Date of Observation: 22 September 1998

Name of Teacher: Bob Oprandy (guest presentation in Kathi's class)

Description of the Course: This was the next to last meeting of the one-unit introduction to classroom observation course. Bob did a guest presentation on *FOCUS*, both to inform the students about that particular observation system, and as an example of such instruments in general.

Description of the Students: There were 42 students present. Some had read about *FOCUS* in the Allwright and Bailey (1991) book, but others had not.

Method(s) of Data Collection: I observed passively and did not take notes. After the lesson I jotted down some ideas and later wrote this account. In this report, "OC" stands for "observer's comment."

Descriptive Summary of the Lesson: I watched Bob teach when he gave a one-hour guest presentation to two combined sections of my class. The two sections met together, as depicted in the following chart, from 4 to 5 PM:

3–4 PM	4–5 PM	5–6 PM
Section A n = 21 students (Kathi teaching)	Sections A and B n = 42 students (Bob teaching)	Section B n = 21 students (Kathi teaching)

Bob gave an excellent introduction to the seminal observational framework of Bellack, Kliebard, Hyman, and Smith (1966) and then moved into the development and use of Fanselow's (1977) observation schedule, *FOCUS (Foci for Observing Communication Used in Settings)*. He began with a succinct historical overview of classroom research in general education, which predated the work of Bellack et al. [OC: I learned some things about early L1 classroom research which I had never known before.]

Bob's preparation for the session was apparent: He had made a handout with many examples of classroom talk, and had set up our meeting room as well. A framework was written on the blackboard, a flipchart drawing was prepared, and the overhead transparencies were sequentially ordered for the presentation.

Bob moved easily between lecturing, eliciting input from the students, and having them do brief pairwork (e.g., to analyze a bit of classroom data). He has phenomenal wait-time and comports himself with pleasant, positive affect in the classroom. He often gave the students helpful hints (both about observing and about teaching).

One of the things that struck me about Bob's teaching was that he really demonstrated the idea that the "medium is the message." [OC: This teaching adaptation of Marshall McLuhan's truism is something I began thinking about years ago: So many teacher educators in our field go around lecturing about communicative language teaching that it gives teachers a very mixed message. Bob, in contrast, consistently practices what he preaches.] For instance, he demonstrated the simple technique of kneeling down and backing up to groups of students during group work, to minimize the disruption of the group's equal-power discourse by his presence. Another example was when he *changed medium* (one of the categories in the *FOCUS* system) by beginning to hum and then to gesture while singing an African rowing song.

Observer's Commentary: I will start my commentary with this particular point—the rowing song. Two things surprised me about this simple change (singing instead of talking): (1) that it is such a powerful but quick demonstration of the *change medium* category, and (2) that I have often used it myself for memorable effect, without realizing what I was doing in terms of the *FOCUS* categories. For example, when I am teaching about t-tests in the statistics course, to get students to remember that the use of t-tests is restricted to comparing only two means, I always sing "Tea for Two" and do a few steps of a soft-shoe [a dance commonly associated with this song]. After seeing Bob use his African rowing song to illustrate *change medium*, I realized that what makes this moment (and therefore the concept) memorable for my students is the fact that the change of medium is so surprising: We seldom sing as part of lessons in graduate classes.

To summarize my reaction to the presentation, I would return to the consistency with which Bob does what he says. His teaching was a model of clear exemplification. Not only did my students learn about *FOCUS*, but they also saw a model of fine teaching.

After the hour Bob spent with us, I taught the second section from 5 to 6 PM based on the same lesson plan I'd used with the first section from 3 to 4 PM. But my treatment of the topic had changed. Because of Bob's presentation I had come to see new possibilities in the material I was covering, and so I worked with it differently. In fact, as a result of Bob's presentation, I wrote up a new assignment option for the students, utilizing *FOCUS* to analyze a transcript they had studied. So observing Bob's presentation directly influenced my teaching, both in the subsequent class hour and in long-term course development.

9.4 *MORE ABOUT OBSERVATIONS, INFERENCES, AND OPINIONS*

Read through Kathi's report of Bob Oprandy's teaching. Identify each instance of an observation, an inference, or an opinion. Do the available observational data justify the inferences and opinions stated? As an administrator reading Kathi's report, what would you conclude she had gained from the experience of watching Bob teach for an hour? If you were Bob, how would you feel about this report? What questions or comments would you have for Kathi?

USING FIELDNOTES

In the following record, we see the elaborated fieldnotes from a brief peer observation. In this case the resulting document was not negotiated with the teacher, although the focus of the observation was (i.e., there was a clear preset contract).

Donald Freeman discussed a model of training and development (see Freeman, 1989a) at a workshop he and Kathi were conducting. He asked her to observe his teaching for two things: (1) the clarity of his instructions in the setup, and (2) making sure the activity didn't overwhelm the content of the explanation. (These two foci constitute the contract.) The teaching Kathi observed lasted 20 minutes (the duration). The resolution consisted simply of giving Donald a copy of the elaborated fieldnotes.

The following report illustrates both having predetermined observational foci (set in the contract) and using intensive note-taking for data collection. Brackets indicate the observer's comments, inferences, and questions. This write-up contains few opinions because Kathi tried to concentrate on the data related to the contract Donald had set. The Teachers' Voices section here presents Kathi's voice as she takes the role of peer observer.

Notes from a Peer Observation

Kathi Bailey

Donald begins by referring to the framework [a printed workshop handout] called *Training and Development*, which the group has already been working with for two days. The seven participants in the workshop are supervisors and teacher educators. Donald tells the group that we'll spend maybe 15 minutes on this topic today, and tomorrow the application will follow. He then instructs the group members to draw a circle divided in half with a vertical line.

Maurice asks, "How big?" [I think Donald said it didn't matter.]

Donald tells the participants to draw a second diagram, a line with two arrows.

Donna asks, "Pointing which way?"

Donald replies, "Out."

Donald says, "For the third one, draw two circles inside one another."

Donna asks, "Looks like an O, right?"

Donald says, "It looks like a cheerio." [I wonder if Donald said a "cheerio" rather than "Yes" or "concentric circles" or whatever because he was trying to give a three-dimensional character to Figure 3. (A cheerio is a small, round type of breakfast cereal with a hole in the middle.)]

The participants have now drawn three different figures based on verbal instructions alone. Donald has not drawn anything or revealed any previously drawn models of training and development.

Donald tells the participants to label Figure 1, the circle with a vertical line through it, with *Training* on the left side and *Development* on the right. He asks, "What does this suggest about the possible relationship between training and development? What does this <u>diagram</u> suggest?" [I infer that Donald noticed the use of *this* as the subject without a head noun and restated his question, using *diagram* as the noun, in order to clarify.] The participants note that the divided circle could represent a division between training and development. *Bifurcation* and *yin/yang* are among the words they use.

Regarding Figure 2 (the one with the arrow pointing both ways), Donald tells the group to put *Training* at one end of the arrow and

Development at the other. The participants then discuss the question, "What does this suggest about the relationship?" for about a minute. While the participants talk, Donald positions the overhead projector in front of the screen. He watches the table of three women for a moment. Then Donald says, "OK—Let's go on. What are some of the things you see in the second diagram?"

Rich talks about tension as an issue in the second diagram. The three women at the table together also commented. After this discussion, Donald asks, "Is that what you mean, Rich?" There was some light banter among the group members. [My impression is that the participants are really focusing on the idea here: How do the different visual models depict the relationship of training and development differently?]

Referring to Figure 2, Donald asks, "What do the arrows suggest about the relationship...?" After some discussion, Donald asks the group, "What else did you see about the relationship?" Maurice responds and Donald restates Maurice's comment with rising intonation. Jackie says, "I see movement...." Donald restates her point and contrasts Figure 2 and Figure 1. He invites other input and then moves on to Figure 3. [I'm confused about Figure 3. I don't understand what Donald means and my confusion causes a lag in my note-taking.] Donna says, "You totally lost me," and seeks clarification. Donald reiterates. While he is talking, I overhear part of Jackie's and Maurice's conversation. [They seem to be clarifying.] Donald speaks to them about the task and then leaves their table.

Maurice asks, "Did she do it right?"

Jackie asks, "Did I do it right?"

Donna and Susan speak together. One of them says, "I'm confused with this one." [It was Donna, I think.] Susan says that they put *Training* as the nucleus, and adds, "But you said it shouldn't matter." [I infer that there is an implied question in Susan's comment.] Donald explains his point. Donna says, "I'm totally confused now." Donald says, "Yeah, the third one is confusing."

Jackie says, "We put *Development* in the middle..." and explains her idea further.

Maurice says, "The circle we considered to be a person."

Donald says, "OK—This is very fertile ground for interpretation" and smiles. Some of the participants laugh. Donald comments [about Figure 3], "There isn't the order. Is it fair to say maybe there's a more relativist view." This comment has the syntactic structure of a question but it's uttered with falling intonation. [This is very interesting. Why does it have the syntactic structure of a question but without rising intonation? My interpretation is that Donald sometimes uses this discourse strategy in his teaching to restate his view of an issue by using the students' comments and building on them. I realize that I have heard him use this combination of falling intonation with the syntactic structure of a question on previous occasions.]

Donald restates his earlier point about *Training* and *Development* shading into one another in this diagram. Maurice said he feels constrained about or by the diagrams and Donald explains that he's "trying to get the ideas out there."

Sabine said [I think primarily to Maurice], "They're Don's inkblots."

Donald puts up another overhead projector transparency and says, "The third picture is a Möbius strip." [I infer students *realize* something at this point. Someone says, "Oh!"] Rich apparently recognizes the three-dimensional figure, which Donald has made from a torn strip of paper. [A Möbius strip is defined as "a one-sided surface that is constructed from a rectangle by holding one end fixed, rotating the opposite end through 180 degrees, and applying it to the first end" (*Webster's Collegiate Dictionary*, 1990, 762). In effect, it is a closed loop with one twist in it, which results in a three-dimensional figure having one continuous side and one continuous edge.]

Donald asks, "Is it fair to say..." and then restates the implications of Rich's recognition of the Möbius strip. Some participants get engaged with the physical model. They are touching it and tracing the edge. Donald says, "It's a continual relationship" as he builds on the Möbius strip as an image of *Training* and *Development*. He says it has two sides but they're connected. He adds, "This third one makes a couple of points. The relationship of *Training* and *Development* can be seen as separate"—(he points to Figure 1 on the screen)—"a separable kind of 'function'." He gestures to Figure 2 and refers to the chronology of the three questions teachers ask at different phases of their development: "What am I doing? How am I doing it? Why am I doing it?" Donald maintains sweeping eye contact as he talks, gesturing with his left hand to the arrow (Figure 2) on the screen.

Sabine bids for a turn. [I infer that she is bidding from her in-breath and her half-raised pen.] Donald says, "Yeah" and thereby nominates her. Sabine talks about the questions of *what* vs. *why* (when she was a young teacher). Donna also comments. Donald says, "Yeah, and in fact..." and then builds on her comments by referring to research conducted in the last seven or eight years regarding teacher development.

As an observer rereading the notes on this lesson, I find Donald's strategies fascinating: In the first place, why did he choose to describe the three figures verbally, instead of just displaying them on the overhead projector? And secondly, why did he run the risk of confusing the participants with Figure 3? Why didn't he just tell them that Figure 3 is a Möbius strip? Upon reflection, I think Donald purposefully chose to withhold the visual images and the label, "Möbius strip" (even to the point of referring to Figure 3 as a "cheerio"), in order to force the participants to focus carefully on the three descriptions and really grapple with the question of what each model conveys about training and development. I believe that he delayed saying "Möbius strip" so the participants would have to confront the ambiguity inherent in Figure 3. It seems to me these strategies helped to make the content memorable. I am going to try this idea with some visual models next time I teach research design in the statistics class.

9.5 *Discussing Fieldnotes*

Examine the fieldnotes based on Kathi's observation of Donald. Identify any instances of the two foci he set: (1) the clarity of his instructions during the set-up, and (2) making sure the activity didn't overwhelm the content. If you were Donald reading these fieldnotes alone, what questions or comments would you have for Kathi?

Next, with a colleague or a classmate, role-play the conversation that might have taken place between Kathi and Donald based on the fieldnotes as a record of the observation. The "observer" should read and/or discuss the fieldnotes with the "teacher," pausing to ask questions, or to allow for the teacher's questions and comments. Note the sort of discourse that emerges and how you feel during and after the role-play.

COOPERATIVE DEVELOPMENT

In the third situation we will see excerpts from a transcript based on the collaborative conversation of two colleagues (the resolution) after one had observed the other teaching for one-and-a-half hours (the duration). In this case again the dual focus of the observation was set in a negotiated contract prior to the lesson. At Bob Oprandy's request, Kathi gave a workshop in his practicum class. Bob took observational fieldnotes during the workshop, which was about the use of mounted pictures (e.g., from magazines or wall calendars) in language classes.

In Chapter 1 we introduced Julian Edge's ideas about cooperative development, an approach that has influenced Bob as an observer. Edge espouses a non-judgmental approach to talking about teaching that involves one person in the role of the Speaker and the other in the role of Understander. The key to the relationship is that "the Understander accepts the Speaker's decision on what should be talked about and worked on" (Edge, 1992, 11). Also "the Understander accepts what the Speaker has to say and accepts the Speaker's evaluations, opinions and intentions without judging them according to the Understander's knowledge or values" (ibid.). The point is that:

For Edge's ideas, see p. 11–12.

> We are working for the development of the Speaker's ideas. The Speaker needs to feel that these ideas can be pursued safely as they start to flow, without their being attacked if they show some weakness to someone else, or because someone else has other views (ibid.).

In Edge's view it is an essential attitude for the Understander to respect the Speaker's ideas:

Colleagues have every right to their views on teaching and students; they come out of their own experience and understanding. Development can only take place when Speakers recognize their own real views, and then see something in there which they wish to investigate, or to take further, or to change. Mutual, non-evaluative respect is fundamental to Cooperative Development (ibid.).

The following conversation occurred after Bob observed Kathi leading a workshop. You will see that Bob takes the role of the Understander in this discussion.

TALKING ABOUT TEACHING

The presentation occurred in the evening, after a very long day. In negotiating the peer observation contract, Kathi asked Bob to watch specifically for two things: (1) whether she was able to appear energetic and enthusiastic even though she was quite tired, and (2) how well her attempts to cover the material in a limited amount of time would work. (This second focus was based on Kathi's ongoing struggle with time management and on her attempt to document some activities clearly in her handouts, rather than to work through all of the activities in live demonstrations.) Bob addressed these concerns, but a number of other issues also arose during their conversation.

Note how the equal-power discourse encourages the exploration of teaching alternatives. The first excerpt relates to a part of the workshop in which there was no clearly defined task to accompany a particular set of photographs. In the first excerpt, both teachers acknowledge new ideas that they might use in the future.

Kathi Bailey
Bob Oprandy

Kathi: This section of the workshop is one that I sometimes drop out if I'm pressed for time. I love those pictures of the ocean, and they illustrate the fact that calendars are a powerful, thematically tied or unified device. But I worry about that section of the workshop because I have no activity that goes with it. I just show the pictures and then ask people "What could we do with these?"

Bob: Aha, right.

Kathi: In the past, I've asked my English students to use the pictures as prompts, either to talk about or write about. I ask, "How does this picture make you feel?" which is kind of a superficial level prompt, although it can lead to some deep writing. But I worry about that piece of the workshop because I don't feel like I have a gimmick with it, you know?

Bob: Hmm, without a task to go with it. Huh, yeah. I wonder, since you mentioned that thing about vocabulary, maybe they could sit for a minute and just generate how much vocabulary, say in pairs or small groups, they would come up with looking at that particular theme in the pictures that you exhibited.

Kathi: That'd be fun.

Bob: You know, it's something. I don't know what I would do.

Kathi: So, you didn't see that as a hole in the workshop?

Bob: Uh, no, I think people were so engaged by the photos. I mean the photos are so great, that you're enjoying the visual feast in a way, and to me it didn't matter. I didn't notice that as a hole at all. To me. Because I thought "Gee, yeah, calendars are great for getting these themes" and I hadn't really thought about that before.

Kathi: Good. Well then, I'll keep doing it. And I may try your idea. It could open up a vocabulary brainstorm—asking what vocabulary does this picture generate.

Bob: Maybe, yeah, I mean, you know it's a little task, but maybe it would work.

Later Bob commented on the fact that Kathi had gotten his practicum students to focus on the specific language used during the picture-based activity. The second excerpt documents an idea that arose during this part of the conversation.

Kathi: You know what? It occurs to me that there is a connection here that I don't think I made during the workshop. Did anybody in the workshop comment that it ties into the language awareness movement? Do you remember hearing that?

Bob: I don't remember having anything in the notes on that.

Kathi: I'm going to try to remember to pull that out next time because of course I've been doing this workshop since before language awareness became a buzz phrase.

Bob: Right, right, but that would be perfect to lead in to the concept.

Kathi: There's a connection there that I hadn't made before.

Bob: Yes, yes. Good. Hm, and then.... (His voice trails off.)

Kathi: Now, isn't this funny. If we weren't having this conversation, I wouldn't have made that connection, because it was something that you said that made me think of it.

Bob: Mhm, yeah.... I think it's so important, especially with something that's sort of a tried-and-true presentation, to go back and be able to explore that with somebody to see what might be new and put a new twist on it. You know, not that I've come up with anything, but I think just the talking got you thinking about language awareness.

The third excerpt is taken from near the end of the 90-minute conversation about the workshop. In rereading his fieldnotes to Kathi, Bob had commented that she sometimes audibly reminded herself to slow down and not get confused when she was looking for the pictures for the next activity. It is this datum that he refers to where he says (below), "Here's a teacher thinking about this thing in front of the class."

Kathi: You didn't end up giving me any negative feedback or making any suggestions.

Bob: No, I'm sorry, I don't know...(his voice trails off).

Kathi: It's okay, you don't have to apologize for not criticizing (she laughs).

Bob: I couldn't think—I mean, I really can't think of what I would have done differently, because even where you felt things weren't as smooth as you would like, to me, it was like a moment of reality. Here's a teacher thinking about this thing in front of the class, but for teachers-in-training I think it's all good stuff, you know. And it made me realize I want to be a little more transparent sometimes when these things happen.

Kathi: We should have a conversation again someday when we've been with a lesson that basically didn't work or that had some problems with it.

Bob: Yeah.

A few days later, Bob stopped by and suggested bringing materials to the workshop for the students to make their own mounted pictures, which for some (perhaps most) would be the start of their own picture files. Shortly after that, Kathi was replaying the audiotape of the post-observation conference and got an idea for a completely different picture-based activity just by listening to Bob's comments again. (Coincidentally, about two months later Kathi watched a videotape of herself leading this same workshop, but on a previous occasion—about two years earlier. The list of what she learned by viewing the tape is printed in Chapter 7.)

See pp. 124–126.

9.6 *TASKS FOR DEVELOPMENT*

We hope the Teachers' Voices in these three data sets have illustrated some of the possible data collecting procedures and follow-up actions for peer observation. The following Tasks should help you personalize the issues related to peer observation and get started on some peer observing with trusted colleagues.

1. Imagine being one of Bob's and Kathi's colleagues. Make a list of the questions and comments you would like to put to them about their experiences of observing one another. Does your list change if you are very eager to participate in peer observation as a professional develop-

ment process? What if you are hostile to the administrative expectation that you will do peer observations?

2. Interview at least three teachers. Find out how they feel about peer observation as a professional development practice (in the abstract). Then ask them to expand on those ideas when they think of themselves (A) as actually doing the observing, and (B) as actually being observed by another teacher. Do the answers of novice teachers differ from those of more experienced teachers? If so, how?

3. The following statements are taken from John Murphy's article about the etiquette of nonsupervisory observation (1992, 223–224). After each statement, circle the letter(s) that best represent your response to that item: SD = strongly disagree; D = disagree; A = agree; and SA = strongly agree.

A. The observation/visitation of classroom teachers is serious business; it should not be approached casually.   **SD D A SA**

B. Classroom observations are not easy for the classroom teachers involved.   **SD D A SA**

C. Knowing how to teach a second language (L2) and knowing how to observe L2 classroom dynamics competently are two very different abilities. An experienced L2 teacher is not necessarily an effective or well-informed observer.   **SD D A SA**

D. Learning how to observe in a manner acceptable to all parties involved is a slowly developing ability. It takes time, careful reflection, personal tact, and creativity. Visiting and visited teachers should expect that this ability will develop, change, and improve over time.   **SD D A SA**

E. An observer is a guest in the teacher's and the students' classroom. A guest in the classroom should not attempt to take away even a modest degree of classroom responsibility, control, or authority from the classroom teacher or L2 students.   **SD D A SA**

F. A guest's purpose for visiting is not to judge, evaluate, or criticize the classroom teacher; it is not necessarily even to offer constructive advice.   **SD D A SA**

G. One option is for the guest to envision his/her role as that of an interested visitor, someone who has entered into a long-term process of learning to observe.   **SD D A SA**

H. Observing others as they teach provides invaluable opportunities for "visiting" teachers to learn to see more clearly in order to increase awareness of their own classroom practices.   **SD D A SA**

I. Reflecting upon what we see other teachers do in classroom settings sometimes helps us to become more aware of our own classroom behaviors.

SD D A SA

If you are working with a group of classmates or colleagues, comparing your responses to these statements may provoke an interesting conversation.

4. Some authors cited in this chapter feel that peer observers can be more threatening than supervisors. What is your opinion? What experience is it based on?

Appendix A starts on p. 249.

5. Appendix A contains a transcript of an English lesson that David taught. Read the transcript and jot down three to five questions or comments you would have for David if you had been an observer during this lesson. Next imagine yourself in David's role as teacher and write three to five questions or comments you would like to share with your peer observer. How do your questions or comments vary when you switch roles?

6. Find a teacher who is willing to let you observe his or her class. Before the class, negotiate the contract, the duration, and the resolution. Make a commitment to engage in the observation and the follow-up. What do you learn in the process? (Try to be clear about the differences among observations, inferences, and opinions.)

7. If you are currently teaching, make arrangements for someone to watch you teach. Before the lesson, negotiate the contract, the duration, and the resolution. What do you learn from the process? (Again, try to be clear about the differences among observations, inferences, and opinions.)

8. Imagine that you are a member of a teaching staff that has been told that new procedures of teacher evaluation will be implemented in your program. These new procedures include the requirement that each term every teacher will either (A) be observed by a peer while teaching, or (B) be videotaped while teaching. In the latter case, the video will be reviewed by one of your peers, and in both instances your peer will be required to discuss the teaching with you and write an evaluation for the administration. Which of these scenarios would you prefer? Why? How is your thinking influenced if you choose your partner rather than having a colleague assigned by the administration to be your peer reviewer? Do your ideas change if the observations and videorecordings are done for professional development purposes rather than for evaluation (that is, if you and your colleagues could choose to discuss the lesson, but no written evaluation would be filed)?

Suggested Readings

Dick Allwright has written a book called *Observation in the Language Classroom* (1988), which traces the history of observation in both language teacher education and language classroom research through the 1980s. The chapters focus on the main observation instruments used in language teaching, and each contains portions of work by the instruments' originators, interspersed with Allwright's commentary.

Elizabeth Rorschach and Robert Whitney (1986) are two college composition teachers who observed one another's classes over the course of a semester. Their paper documents what they learned through peer observation.

Ruth Wajnryb's (1993) book of classroom observation tasks provides a good rationale for observing in classrooms, no matter what the observer's stage of professional development might be. This little volume contains 35 tasks to do while observing, as well as several simple procedures for collecting observational data.

John Murphy's (1992) article is a useful starting point for people seeking guidance on how to behave while observing other teachers. He builds on work by Peter Masters (1983), whose article about the "etiquette of observing" triggered a particularly interesting response from Joyce Zuck (1984).

In case you would like to learn more about *FOCUS*, John Fanselow (1977, 1978, 1980, and 1987) has written several items that will introduce you to this coding system.

Jill Burton (1987) has written an interesting paper about observation in the context of the Adult Migrant Education Program in Australia. The paper uses the framework of the Johari Window, which we discussed in Chapter 2.

For the Johari Window, see p. 25.

Jack Richards and Charles Lockhart (1991–92) have described a peer-observation program undertaken by EFL teachers in Hong Kong. The article contains examples of questionnaires and data collection procedures, as well as comments from the teachers.

Richard Day (1990) describes the use of observation in teacher education programs (i.e., the context in which experienced teacher educators observe novice teachers). His article discusses a number of data collection procedures that could be useful in a peer-observation context as well.

Peter Sheal has written an article about a workshop for training observers. The goals were for participants to identify classroom observation problems, develop ways to cope with such problems, and assess their own reliability as observers (1989, 94).

Two chapters in Gebhard and Oprandy (1999) are pertinent to the issues raised here. Chapter 3, "Seeing Teaching Differently Through Observation" (by Jerry G. Gebhard), contains many practical suggestions for how peers and individual teachers can collect and interpret descriptions of teaching. Chapter 8 is called "Teachers Talking About Teaching: Collaborative Conversations About an Elementary ESL Class" (by Robert Oprandy with Laura Golden and Kayoko Shiami). It reports on "collaborative conversations" among an elementary ESL teacher and two other teachers who observed her classes over a 10-week period.

10

TEAM TEACHING:
LEARNING TO DANCE

*When I read over my journal, I can sense the growth that has
taken place in me as a partner. I feel that Margaret and I reached
a point in which we were working well together. We were able to
team teach quite well, which is much different than that first night.
Some of my best memories were the times that Margaret and I
taught together with the class. I think that we both learned a lot
by working together (Numrich 1996, 137).*

This comment was made by a novice teacher about a practice teaching situation.
But we believe that even veteran teachers can learn "a lot by working together" (ibid.). In this chapter we will define team teaching, examine the advantages
and disadvantages of this instructional format, and discuss the professional development opportunities that can be found in a positive team teaching environment.

ORGANIZATIONAL PATTERNS IN TEAM TEACHING

We will start by defining team teaching: "A teaching team is a group of two or
more persons assigned to the same students at the same time for instructional
purposes in a particular subject or combination of subjects" (Johnson and Lobb,
1959, 59). Team teaching can actually be realized through several different organizational patterns. Here are descriptions, which we have paraphrased from
Cunningham (1960, 2–3), of four traditional types of team teaching arrangements:

1. **Team Leader Type:** In this arrangement one team member has a
   higher status than the others. He or she may well have a special
   title ("team leader," "head instructor," etc.).

2. **Associate Type:** Here there is no designated leader. Leadership
   emerges as a result of interactions among the members of the
   team in given situations.

3. **Master Teacher/Beginning Teacher Type:** In this arrangement,
   team teaching is used to foster the acculturation of new teachers
   into the school (or the profession).

4. **Coordinated Team Type:** In this format there is no joint responsibility for a common group of learners, but there is joint planning
   by two or more teachers teaching the same curriculum to separate groups.

These types of team teaching arrangements are actually more fluid than the categories would suggest. For example, as described in Chapter 1, Kathi and Andy first worked together in a team leader situation, in which Andy was the coordinator of the program. As the lessons began, however, an equal partnership (more like the associate type) evolved in the classroom.

Only a small part of team teaching actually happens with teachers working together in classrooms. A great deal occurs *before* lessons, and might more properly be called "team planning." Such planning can entail the macro levels of an entire curriculum or the syllabus for a course, or it can be the preparation for a specific lesson plan. In terms of the framework introduced in Chapter 3, these tasks are examples of pre-active decision making. Likewise, a great deal of the responsibility in team teaching relates to what happens *after* our lessons. This area includes marking students' papers and/or exams, meeting with students, evaluating our lessons, and beginning the planning and teaching cycle again. So team teaching really consists of three (reiterated) phases: (1) preinstructional planning, (2) instructional in-class teamwork, and (3) postinstructional follow-up work. Cunningham's fourth category (the coordinated team type) consists of only the preinstructional and postinstructional phases.

See p. 37.

10.1 *WHAT DO YOU THINK SO FAR?*

Before reading further, we suggest you take an inventory of your current ideas about team teaching. Try to think of at least three advantages and three disadvantages of team teaching. Write these down. If you do not have any personal experience with team teaching (either as a teacher or a learner), you can draw on your existing opinions, you can speculate, or you can talk to someone who has had firsthand experience with team teaching.

ADVANTAGES AND DISADVANTAGES OF TEAM TEACHING

There are many advantages to teaching with a partner. According to David Armstrong (1977, 66), team teaching:

1. permits team members to take advantage of the individuals' strengths, in planning and in teaching;

2. spurs creativity—we teach for our colleagues as well as for our students;

3. facilitates individualized instruction by providing situations of close personal contact with teachers for individual learners;

4. provides for better decisions (e.g., re: pacing, sequencing, etc.) because the ideas of an individual team member are verified by at least one other; and

5. builds program continuity over time.

However, Armstrong was not writing about language teaching, and his article is over 20 years old. There are even more advantages to team teaching in language programs.

One obvious advantage of team teaching in language classrooms is that the teaching partners can demonstrate interactive activities, such as role-plays, with one another. Another benefit is that, depending on their characteristics as speakers (country or region of origin, gender, age, etc.), the two teachers can provide different linguistic models for the learners. For example, when Andy and Kathi team taught in Hong Kong, the students were interested in the lexical and phonological contrasts between his British Midlands (male) speech and the North American (female) variety Kathi used. In addition, if partners prepare together and actually share the teaching space, team teaching entails a built-in peer observation component, which allows us to see another person implementing a lesson plan with which we are very familiar. And finally, debriefing after a lesson with another person who has a personal stake in the lesson's success (as opposed to someone in the more detached role of a visitor to your classroom) allows for in-depth exploration of what worked, what didn't, and why.

Another advantage to team teaching in language teaching curricula is associated with *content-based instruction*. In this approach, students learn foreign or second languages by studying a particular topic or content in the target language (see Snow and Brinton, 1997, for an overview). In some content-based approaches, team teaching is employed by definition. For instance, in sheltered and adjunct programs, the language teacher plays a supporting role and "the content is taught by a content expert rather than the language teacher" (Turner, 1992, 43; see also Turner, 1997; Chapple and Curtis, 2000).

Peter Shaw's description (1997, 263–264) of five types of curricular models used in content-based instruction is paraphrased below. All but the first of these entail some form of team teaching.

Type 1: Direct Content Model: In this approach the subject matter is provided in the students' target language, including all the readings, classroom discussions, and assignments. The instructor may be a native or a nonnative speaker of the target language. Either way, he or she delivers all the teaching in the learners' target language. (There is no team teaching involved.)

Type 2: Team Content Model: Once again the subject is taught in the students' target language, but there are two teachers: one who is a subject-matter specialist and one who teaches the language of instruction. They use a team-teaching format that draws upon the combined knowledge of the teaching team.

Type 3: Subsidiary Content Model: In this model a subject-matter teacher delivers the content in the students' first language. A related subset of the subject matter is taught in one or more of the students' target languages by teachers in the language faculty. So in one class meeting, a new topic is introduced in the students' first language. At the next class meeting the topic is then studied with greater specificity in the target language session. The members of the teaching team thus interact with the students in alternate class meetings.

Type 4: Supplementary Content Model: In this model both instructors are present in class sessions. The content is taught by a subject matter specialist. Then the same topic is covered by a language teacher in the students' target language. In this model the subject-matter teacher must have some fluency in the foreign language, and the language teacher must also be familiar with the course content.

Type 5: Adjunct Model: In this model the members of the team are less closely associated. The content is presented in the students' target language in one course and a separate but related language class provides the target language skills for the students to be successful in the subject-matter course. In the adjunct class, reading and writing assignments on the topic may be provided as the basis for language practice, but the language teacher does not teach the content per se.

As you can imagine, a great deal of coordination and communication is needed for such cross-disciplinary teaching teams to be successful. Using models such as these, "[l]anguage teachers have forged common ground with subject-area educators in implementing content-based syllabi" (Short, 1993, 627).

Team teaching is a natural format for content-based instruction, but it is not for everyone and it's not ideal under all circumstances. There are some potential problems, which cannot be discounted. These include the likelihood of confusing or upsetting the learners if the teaching is not well planned, as well as possible power struggles if the teaching partners do not agree on goals or teaching philosophy. However, such problems can often be overcome, particularly if people (a) self-select into a team teaching situation, and (b) get to choose their teaching partners.

The following Teachers' Voices account is from an article by Ruth Johnson (1999, 16). This excerpt candidly portrays a situation in which team teaching was not successful.

RUTH'S RETROSPECTIVE ACCOUNT

Something was very wrong. My team teacher and I, strangers to each other when the semester started, were losing control of our phonetics class, a big required class consisting of graduate and undergraduate students. [T]he department chair, met with [my team teaching partner] one morning, and with me in the afternoon because three graduate students had complained, declaring neither of us was competent to teach the course. They demanded that [the teacher], who had taught phonetics before, be brought back. [My partner], they charged, did not know the material, and I acted like a drill sergeant.

Ruth Johnson

Something had to be done, but what? I mistrusted [my partner], and I felt myself digging into my position. I wondered if I disliked [my partner] or her teaching style. It did not occur to me that there might be a cross-cultural misunderstanding between us.

When [my teaching partner] arrived on campus in mid-August, she, [the department chair], and I met to discuss the phonetics course we were going to team teach. [The department chair] asked what type of course project we were planning. [She] replied too quickly, presenting a course project she had done as a graduate student. I replied enthusiastically, but I was irritated that she had not had the courtesy to ask if I had a suggestion.

During the first week of classes, I observed that [my partner] went to [the department chair's] office with my class handout and seemed to be discussing it with him. She never brought any content questions to me regarding phonetics. She addressed [others as Dr. So-and-So] but called me "Ruth." Yet I had a Ph.D., I had several years' experience, and I was a generation older. She was not showing me respect.

The crisis of the third week abated. Then, [my partner] introduced the course project. Within days, students came grumbling to my office. I was not surprised. The project was not pedagogically oriented, yet the bulk of the students were master's-level TESOL majors. Also, it appeared difficult and time-consuming. I felt little desire to defend it, because it was [her] idea, so I told the students I would design an alternate project. [She] was furious. She said we needed to show loyalty to each other; I disagreed. I wanted the students to feel they were learning something relevant in the class. Finally, we agreed that the course project would remain, but with adjustments to make it less difficult.

Our midterm test was a disaster. We did not consult each other beforehand. I gave my half of the test to [my partner] 10 days in advance, but I did not see her half until the day of the test. The exam was much too long, repetitive, and irrelevant in places. Scores were very low, and students were furious.

[My teaching partner] and I discussed the matter on the phone. She wanted to stick by the test scores. She felt the students had demonstrated that they did not know the material and that this was not our fault. I disagreed. I felt that results so dismal spoke to incomplete or incoherent teaching, to a bad instrument or both. I said as much in class, without [her] agreement. The students were up in arms. Yes, we were incompetent, they said. Yes, we were incapable of writing a valid test. They wanted us removed immediately and [the previous teacher] brought in.

[My teaching partner] and I were not speaking to each other. We limped along during the second half of the semester, until I began to think about student evaluations and my chances for tenure. I wanted us to make up enough that the students would see us as a united team and would evaluate me as average or above.

Finally, [my partner], [the department chair], and I met with the associate dean for academic affairs. She was shocked at the manner in which our team-teaching assignment had been set up. No wonder, she said, that it had failed so badly. Usually, team teachers have known each other for years and are familiar with each other's teaching styles. Team teachers work out a common syllabus; they share the same philosophy towards learning, testing, and other classroom issues. I felt vindicated.

Before continuing with Ruth Johnson's report, we are going ask you to do some thinking, as if what you've read so far of Ruth's situation was an example of Shulman's unfinished A case (1992, 11; see Chapter 5 about using cases).

For information about *A cases*, see p. 80.

Either alone or with a colleague, think of four or five things that Ruth could have done differently, either before or during the team teaching experience. What steps might she have taken to forestall or solve these problems? Please write your ideas in a brief list and save the list for our next Investigation. Now we will return to Ruth Johnson's story, the conclusion of which provides a *B case*, in Shulman's terms (ibid.).

RUTH'S ACCOUNT CONTINUES

Teachers' Voices

Ruth Johnson

But soon I began to feel guilty. I had expected courtesy and respect from [my partner], yet I had never bothered to define these for her. I had never been explicit about my expectations of our relationship. I questioned my own behaviors in the team-teaching experience with [her]. Several times I had felt irritation, a sure sign of culture adjustment. But I was not the one undergoing culture adjustment—or was I?

Cross-cultural communication never occurs across cultures. It occurs between people, each of whom is from a different culture. I had not taken advantage of my own knowledge in cross-cultural understanding and applied it to my situation with [my teaching partner].

Given the same situation again, I would do things very differently:

1. I would offer my own suggestion for a course project and discuss it with my team teacher. Once we agreed, I would be loyal to that decision.

2. If bothered by my team teacher discussing my handout with a colleague, I would discuss the issue.

3. If bothered by my team teacher calling me by my first name, I would ask to be called "Dr. Johnson."

4. I would play down the differences in teaching styles and adjust my own so that we matched better.

5. I would delay a decision about the midterm exam until my team teacher and I had agreed on a course of action.

The teaching of this course suffered because of the cross-cultural misunderstanding that existed between [my partner] and me. We did not team teach the following semester, and I had the most successful teaching experience I have ever had that term. I heard that her courses went very well, too. We are both good teachers; we were not good team teachers. Much of that was attributable to our differing expectations arising from our cultural backgrounds (R. Johnson, 1999, 16).

10.3 QUESTIONS ABOUT TEAM TEACHING

Please compare the list of ideas you wrote in the preceding Investigation to the five points Ruth Johnson made about what she could have done differently. Were there any parallel suggestions on the two lists? If not, why were the two lists so different?

Before proceeding with the rest of this chapter, we suggest that you take a few minutes to respond to the following questionnaire (which is reprinted from Bailey, Dale, and Squire, 1992). If you are planning to team teach, you and your partner could benefit from responding to this questionnaire and discussing the results. In particular, it would be worthwhile to explore any wide discrepancies. In Appendix B (pp. 262–263) we provide the responses of experienced team teachers to these same statements.

Questionnaire on Team Teaching

Please respond to the following statements by circling the number that represents your opinion: 5 = strongly agree, 4 = agree, 3 = neutral, 2 = disagree, and 1 = strongly disagree; NA = not applicable in your case.

1. Only teachers themselves should decide whether or not to enter into a team teaching arrangement.   **5 4 3 2 1 NA**

2. Planning together is the most valuable part of team teaching.   **5 4 3 2 1 NA**

3. Team teaching works best if the partners' teaching styles match.   **5 4 3 2 1 NA**

4. Working in class together is the most valuable part of team teaching.   **5 4 3 2 1 NA**

5. My students seem to appreciate team teaching.   **5 4 3 2 1 NA**

6. Team teaching is an effective way to teach languages.   **5 4 3 2 1 NA**

7. Sometimes situations of shared responsibility result in no one taking full responsibility.   **5 4 3 2 1 NA**

8. Serious problems could arise in situations in which the collaborating teachers have widely divergent teaching styles.   **5 4 3 2 1 NA**

9. It is helpful to agree to disagree in advance of entering into a team teaching arrangement.   **5 4 3 2 1 NA**

10. Having a partner helps to give me a new perspective on my teaching.   **5 4 3 2 1 NA**

11. Having a partner is helpful in evaluating students.   **5 4 3 2 1 NA**

12. Team teaching doesn't seem to work for my students.   **5 4 3 2 1 NA**

13. Having a partner gives me someone to appeal to for examples or clarification of explanations in class.   **5 4 3 2 1 NA**

14. Our students seem to like having a choice of which teacher to seek out for help.   **5 4 3 2 1 NA**

15. Working collaboratively provides two perspectives for self-evaluation of our team teaching.   **5 4 3 2 1 NA**

16. Working collaboratively provides two perspectives for evaluation of my individual work.   **5 4 3 2 1 NA**

17. I have learned things about myself from working with a partner.   **5 4 3 2 1 NA**

18. The amount of time necessary to collaborate on goal setting, syllabus design, and lesson planning is more trouble than it's worth.   **5 4 3 2 1 NA**

19. Team teaching is an effective means for teacher development.   **5 4 3 2 1 NA**

20. Serious problems could arise in situations in which the collaborating teachers have different goals.   **5 4 3 2 1 NA**

21. Team teaching is more trouble than it's worth.   **5 4 3 2 1 NA**

22. Only teachers themselves should decide who their teaching partners will be.   **5 4 3 2 1 NA**

23. It is only in an atmosphere of trust and mutual respect that teacher partnerships can achieve their full potential.   **5 4 3 2 1 NA**

24. In team teaching it is useful to focus on goals rather than personalities in order to lessen power struggles.   **5 4 3 2 1 NA**

25. My partner's feedback after our lessons was not helpful.   **5 4 3 2 1 NA**

26. Recognizing that alternative solutions exist makes planning and follow-up easier and smoother.   **5 4 3 2 1 NA**

27. The benefits of team teaching far outweigh the effort involved.   **5 4 3 2 1 NA**

LEVELS OF RISK

Michael Wallace (1991, 90) has ranked a number of teacher education procedures in terms of the amount of risk or cost they entail. Team teaching is included in his table, which is reprinted below:

Figure 10.1: Sample of Training and Teaching Activities Categorized According to Putative Risk/Cost

DEGREE OF RISK/COST	ACTIVITY	GENERAL CATEGORY
Minimum	Observation/analysis of lessons on film	1. Data collection/ analysis activities
	Observation/analysis of live taught lessons	
	Analysis of lesson transcripts	
	Draft exercises Draft lesson plans	2. Planning activities
	Microlessons (nonrecorded)	3. Microteaching activities
	Microteaching (group preparation)	
	Microteaching (individual preparation)	
	Microteaching (peer group)	
	Microteaching (real pupils)	
	Extended microteaching	
	Supervised teaching	4. Supervised professional action
	Auxiliary teaching	5. Shared professional action
	Team teaching	
Maximum	Individual teaching (NB varying degrees of autonomy)	6. Individual autonomous professional action

According to Wallace, the category of *shared professional action* includes auxiliary teaching and team teaching. For Wallace, "In *auxiliary teaching*, an experienced teacher has overall responsibility for the class, while an auxiliary teacher (perhaps a trainee) has some limited responsibility" (ibid., 91). In contrast, in a team teaching context, "the responsibility for the class is equally shared between two teachers (who may both be experienced, both trainees, or one experienced and one trainee)" (ibid.). Wallace also notes that, although it is not common, more than two teachers can be involved in both auxiliary teaching and team teaching.

10.4 MORE QUESTIONS ABOUT TEAM TEACHING

Look at Figure 10.1 (p. 188). Wallace places team teaching closer to the risky or costly end of the continuum than microteaching or supervised teaching. The only format he considers riskier is individual teaching. What are the situational or personal variables that make different teaching contexts "risky"? List three situational factors and three personal factors that create risk in teaching.

Given the variables you identified, which would be *improved* by working with a team teacher? Which would be *exacerbated* by working with a teaching partner? Why?

Imagine working in the following situations:

1. an equal-power team (the *associate type*, in Cunningham's terms [1960]);

2. the *team leader type* with you as the team leader (ibid.);

3. the *team leader type* in which you were *not* the team leader (ibid.);

4. a *master teacher-beginning teacher* arrangement (ibid.), with you as the beginning teacher; or

5. a *master teacher-beginning teacher* arrangement (ibid.), with you as the master teacher.

How would your replies to the questions above differ across these five contexts? In the Teachers' Voices section that follows, we will hear the perspective of a beginning teacher working in a team arrangement with a more experienced teacher (situation 4 above).

BENJAMIN'S DIARY ENTRIES

When Benjamin Squire was completing his ESL practicum, he and Kathi decided to team teach together. While preparing for team teaching, Benjamin recalled a positive experience he had as a student in a team-taught history course. The following retrospective entry from his teaching journal gives us a learner's point of view:

> These two teachers had decided to combine their classes, so the number of students was large, but they also had different views in the study of history. It was nice not to just hear the official or remembered version of historical events, but also to hear the other side of the story. By taking different viewpoints, and even creating a sense of competition between themselves in the classroom, the teachers made the course interesting and fun (Benjamin Squire, in Bailey, Dale, and Squire, 1992, 168).

Teachers' Voices

Benjamin Squire

Benjamin's recollections are underscored by Nora Shannon and Bonnie Meath-Lang, who conducted research with experienced team teachers. They noted that when such teaching teams hold different points of view "such disagreement could help students see that: (1) one teacher is not always right; [and] (2) there are various perspectives on issues and within fields of study" (1992, 125).

Benjamin and Kathi taught a mixed-level ESL course for young adults in California. The course was about learning styles and strategies, with an emphasis on speaking and listening. The original format was what Cunningham would call the "master teacher-beginning teacher" arrangement (1960, 3), or what Wallace would term "auxiliary teaching" (1991, 91), but this relationship soon evolved into more of an "associate type" (Cunningham, 1960, 3). In the following journal entry, Benjamin describes a lesson in which he took over more responsibility for conducting the class:

> Today it seemed like the sharing of the leadership role in the class was a lot more evenly delegated than it has been in the past. Even though we had planned it so that Kathi would be leading most of the activities, and I would just be her resource (e.g., when I went over my typical day's listening activities), I felt like I was in charge of more of the activities. When I was doing my listening spiel, she was working on their dictations, so rather than feeling like the "resource," I felt like I was leading the class at that time. I think that was because she was focused on something else, and though she had introduced the task, she relinquished the leadership role... (Bailey et al., 1992, 165).

This entry illustrates the fact that sometimes when team teaching partners share the classroom space, they may be working independently. At other times they may be interacting as part of the lesson.

As Ruth Johnson pointed out, some people are not well suited for team teaching. For Benjamin, as a novice, team teaching was a good match with his style:

> For me personally, team teaching fits in very well with my working style. I'm not much of an idea person, but once given an idea, I feel that I have the ability to really take it and develop it into something good. I have trouble working from scratch, so the teamwork of team teaching gives me the feedback that I need to get ideas, and to bounce my own development of ideas off someone else (ibid., 167).

Advocates of team teaching often comment on the synergy that develops in effective teaching teams in which the partners are able to capitalize on one another's strengths. Shannon and Meath-Lang point out, based on their research, that "respect for the competencies of the other person did not in any way dilute [the respondents'] sense of competence" (1992, 131). In their data from successful team teachers, the "team members recognized the gifts, skills and expertise of the partner without feeling denigrated, or in any way less skillful" (ibid.).

We claim that one of the benefits of team teaching in language classrooms is that the teaching partners can demonstrate interactive tasks to the learners. The next entry from Benjamin's diary describes a demonstration he and Kathi provided before an information gap task in which pairs of students built a structure of plastic building blocks:

> While we were demonstrating the [building block] exercise, I noticed that Kathi made a couple of her instructions deliberately ambiguous so that I would have to ask for clarification. I had

already asked for clarification on a couple that I had really understood, in order to demonstrate the idea to the students, and I could
tell that she was doing the same thing. It really felt good that we
hadn't planned to do this beforehand, but just sort of automatically
did it without having to discuss it. I felt like we were really working
as the most highly effective team possible at that point because we
were working together and following and understanding each
other's cues without having to pre-plan it (Bailey et al., 1992, 168).

Another benefit of team teaching is that if one partner is not present, the
other can take over the teaching (albeit with a large class). This fact ensures that
there is no need for a substitute teacher who does not know the students. Our
point is illustrated by the following excerpt from Benjamin's diary, about a class
he taught alone when Kathi was not present. The lesson involved a listening
comprehension activity based on a class party, which would be held at Kathi's
house. She had made an audiotape with directions to the house from the school,
which Benjamin played for the students in her absence. This was a demanding
and authentic exercise, since the house was way out in the country, on a wind-
ing dirt road, about a 30-minute drive from the area the students knew well.
Benjamin's journal entry describes the lesson he taught alone:

The first activity, when I played the directions and they took notes,
was the hardest....I let the students compare notes and listen again.
After the second time around, one student said that he would probably find the house after a couple of days. Another said that he was
going to call a taxi and let the cabbie listen to Kathi's tape....I then
gave out the maps [of the area where Kathi lives] and several of
them were able to trace the route from their notes. When I played
the second half of the tape, with the more complicated directions,
almost everyone was able to get it right. Even though Kathi wasn't
there today, having her input for the planning stage was very helpful, and I didn't feel like I was teaching alone. This feeling was of
course intensified by the fact that she did more talking (on the
tape) during the hour than I did (ibid., 170–171).

(David and Andy find it very amusing that Kathi could do the majority of the
talking during class even when she was absent!)

For some lessons, Benjamin and Kathi devised parallel lesson plans designed
for different learning styles, and allowed the students their choice of which to
participate in. For example, in a unit on learning styles, after the students had
examined their own learning style preferences, one teacher continued the lesson
with those students who wanted a more grammar-oriented approach with
explicit instruction. The other taught the same lesson content but with a more
interactive conversational approach, for the students who preferred that choice
on that day. Benjamin's journal entry states:

I really enjoy the fact that, being two teachers, we are able to act
on the idea of giving our students options when we do different
activities. The times we've done that, I really think that it's worked
out very well, both from our point of view and that of the students
(ibid., 171–172).

So Benjamin and Kathi's team teaching experience was positive. However, there can be drawbacks to team teaching, as we saw from Ruth Johnson's experience. In the following Frameworks section we will see what some other teachers think, based on two different research projects.

WHAT TEACHERS BELIEVE

Nora Shannon and Bonnie Meath-Lang, whose work we have referred to above, conducted research with 25 teachers at the National Technical Institute for the Deaf in the United States. They interviewed each teacher in depth and found that "a successful team teaching experience would appear to require factors beyond interest in the other teacher's area of expertise" (1992, 126). The themes that emerged in the interview data were (1) the need for team members to share a common philosophy and values; (2) the fact that successful team teaching is, of necessity, reflective work and must include opportunities for reflection; (3) that team teaching partners must have ego strength and that there was a balance between "having confidence in oneself and recognizing the gifts the other member brings to the team" (ibid., 132); and (4) the use of relational metaphors to describe team teaching. In fact, "every respondent resorted to describing team teaching in terms of other relationships" (ibid., 134). These included references to chemistry, to friendships, to parenting, and to marriage. (At a workshop that Andy and Kathi conducted, the group discussed the fact that sometimes team teaching works well even if the partners don't know one another prior to their assignment. One of the workshop participants likened this event to a successful "arranged marriage.")

The research by Shannon and Meath-Lang used in-depth interviews to elicit ideas from successful team teaching partners. In a different approach to research, Bailey et al. (1992) surveyed 60 language teachers who had had experience with team teaching. The full results are displayed in Appendix B (reprinted from Bailey et al., 1992, 175–176). Here we will simply note that the respondents strongly agreed with the statement, "It is only in an atmosphere of trust and mutual respect that teacher partnerships can achieve their full potential" (item 23). This item received the highest mean score (4.6 on the five-point scale) and the lowest standard deviation (0.7)—indicating the least variability in the answers. Item 20 received scores indicating general agreement (with a mean of 4.3 and a standard deviation of 0.9). It stated, "Serious problems could arise in situations where the collaborating teachers have different goals"—a remark that is reminiscent of Ruth Johnson's experience.

Another item that received strong agreement ratings (with a mean of 4.2 and a standard deviation of 1.0) is related to the theme of this book. It said, "Having a partner helped to give me a new perspective on my teaching." This is one of the key advantages of team teaching.

Appendix B starts on p. 262.

10.5 *WHICH SURVEY ITEMS RELATE MOST CLOSELY?*

Please refer to Appendix B as you complete these tasks. Look back at the Teachers' Voices section that reports on Ruth Johnson's team teaching experience (pp. 183–185). Choose the three survey items reported in Appendix B that relate most closely to Ruth's experience. Do you think she would agree or disagree with the respondents whose ratings are reported in Appendix B?

Appendix B starts on p. 262.

Now look back at the Teachers' Voices section that reports on Benjamin Squire's team teaching journal (pp. 189–192). Choose the three survey items reported in Appendix B that relate most closely to Benjamin's experience. Do you think he would agree or disagree with the respondents whose ratings are reported in Appendix B?

LEARNING TO TEACH TOGETHER

We wanted to represent some novice teachers' ideas in this chapter, so Kathi "interviewed" Komal Deshpande and Fukuko Mukai by e-mail. Komal and Fukuko chose to split a job by team teaching a Japanese course at a community college in California as they completed the practicum for their master's degrees in teaching foreign languages at the Monterey Institute of International Studies, which Fukuko refers to below as "MIIS." In the following conversation we gain their perspectives on the advantages and disadvantages of team teaching.

Teachers' Voices

Komal Deshpande
Fukuko Mukai

Kathi: First, I know that you team taught Japanese, but I have some questions about the class. To start, what were the students like?

Fukuko: There were eight students who registered and one student who didn't register but just came because her daughter was taking this class. They ranged in age from fourteen years old to the mid-sixties.

Kathi: What level was the class?

Fukuko: This was the second semester of elementary Japanese, but the students' levels were varied. Probably the highest one would be near intermediate and the lowest one would be lower beginner. Not all of the students took last semester's Japanese 1A class.

Kathi: Why did you decide to team teach, and why did you decide to team teach with each other?

Fukuko: The main reason for me is that I am a full-time graduate student at MIIS, therefore teaching by myself would be very hard. Besides, I had never taken a Japanese pedagogy class before and was afraid of teaching without anyone's help. The reason I decided to team teach with Komal is that we were both offered this job but, as I said above, neither of us wanted to be occupied by too much preparation. We are also roommates, so we could meet any time we wanted and be flexible. I particularly liked the fact that Komal is a nonnative and I am a native speaker of Japanese. I thought we could help each other. She has experience in learning Japanese as a foreign language and I can offer my language knowledge as a native.

Komal: We also decided to team teach because we did not hear about this job until our pedagogy professor called us over the winter break and asked us if we would like to teach at the community college for the spring semester. We were both hired for this job a week before the course started, so we only had one week to plan for it. Until that time, I had not planned on teaching at all except to fulfill my practicum hours since I was going to be so busy with my coursework. From Fukuko I learned that an e-mail was sent to both of us about the Japanese teaching position, so we both thought about what to do.

Since I had team taught in Japan, I asked Fukuko about team teaching. I thought that we could benefit from a team teaching experience since we had never taught Japanese before in the classroom and would not have a cooperating teacher helping us. I thought that the amount of work would be cut in half.

I also felt that I could benefit from Fukuko's Japanese tutoring experience since this would be my first time to teach Japanese. I already had classroom experience from teaching English in Japan for three years, but I thought that we could balance each other out in this way and I hoped the native speaker and nonnative speaker aspect of our teaching would also benefit our students, and that we could help the students more if there were two teachers in the classroom.

Kathi: What do you think the advantages of team teaching turned out to be in your case?

Komal: For me, the advantage was that I was able to learn a lot from observing Fukuko. We have different teaching styles and I was able to get inspired by her. We were able to observe each other and talk about the observations after class.

Fukuko: We could also give individual attention to the students. Especially when one of us was teaching and doing some activity, having another teacher to go around to the students is really helpful. For instance, one of our students did not participate in repeating something with the whole class, and I was wondering if he was not motivated. One day, Komal sat among the students and realized that this man was always quietly repeating whatever I said. He was actually motivated. If I hadn't had Komal as a partner, I would not have noticed this kind of situation.

We could also share the lesson planning. Sometimes I got stuck and couldn't think of any plan, and then I talked to Komal. She sometimes gave me some ideas which I would never have thought of. It's exciting.

Komal: I always appreciated the chance to be able to talk about my lesson with Fukuko and get her feedback. Practically speaking, we were able to split the amount of time spent on lesson planning and teaching. During a particularly busy week for me, Fukuko taught by herself and I taught alone when Fukuko went away. Also, we were able to share materials and lesson plans, discuss ideas for activities, split the amount of work that needed to be done outside the classroom. For example, we split the homework that needed to be checked and even the grading of tests and quizzes.

It is also nice to have Fukuko talk about her perspective when I talk about culture. I always like to have Fukuko participate during my lesson by asking her questions.

Kathi: What do you think the disadvantages of team teaching were in your case?

Fukuko: Time management was the biggest problem. Our class ran for four months, two nights a week, for two hours each night, on Tuesdays and Thursdays. We started teaching one hour each every night. However, I accidentally used Komal's time whenever I taught first and I always felt rushed. In the middle of the semester, we finally decided to teach two hours for one night (so I would teach on Tuesday and Komal would teach on Thursday). When I didn't finish, I felt very bad. At the beginning, I couldn't help comparing her teaching with mine and lost my confidence sometimes.

Komal: Yes, it was difficult to decide how to split the work in the beginning. Once we started teaching it was hard to plan the lessons to fit into a one-hour slot, especially if we wanted to try something new. There were times when my lesson would take about 10 minutes or so of Fukuko's lesson and vice versa, so we really had to figure how to make it fair for both of us. It was hard when I had planned a 50-minute lesson and then would only have 35 minutes to teach it.

Soon we decided to just take one day and teach for a full two hours, so Fukuko would teach on Tuesday and I would teach on Thursdays. This seemed to work for the first week, but then it was difficult for me to know what to teach on Thursday until after Fukuko had taught on Tuesday. I really couldn't do any lesson planning until Tuesday night. Recently, this has been very tough for me to do because I am usually too tired to think of a plan just the night before. I realized that lesson planning takes a lot of time for me to do and having a few extra days would be better.

Another point to mention is about teaching kanji [traditional Japanese writing]. I have been teaching kanji this semester because Fukuko felt she did not know the best way to teach kanji to non-native speakers. Again, it has been interesting to know that I can share the way I learned Japanese with Fukuko when we talk about our lessons. I can learn about teaching Japanese from her perspective as a native speaker.

10.6 ADVANTAGES AND DISADVANTAGES OF TEAM TEACHING

Skim through Fukuko's and Komal's comments and highlight any references to advantages and disadvantages of team teaching in language classrooms. Have they identified any factors that you did not identify in the first Investigation in this chapter? If so, what accounts for the difference(s) between your list and theirs?

Paul Kei Matsuda's ideas are found on pp. 113–114.

In Chapter 6 you read about Paul Kei Matsuda's experience as a nonnative teacher of English composition. What are the parallels between his situation and that of Fukuko and Komal? What are the differences?

In the Teachers' Voices section featuring Komal's and Fukuko's experience of team teaching, we were hearing from two relatively inexperienced language teachers. In the following Teachers' Voices section, we will get the perspectives of two veteran teachers—Andy and Kathi—who were undertaking a new course together. How do you expect their experiences will differ from those of Komal and Fukuko?

TEACHING TOGETHER AGAIN

Andy Curtis
Kathi Bailey

After teaching different courses in the same EFL program for two semesters, we decided to try team teaching together again. (We had done so briefly at the end of our first semester as colleagues.) This time the course was "Organizational Communication" and the participants were 43 businesspersons in Hong Kong working toward a postgraduate diploma in management communication. This module of the diploma course met on Saturday afternoons for four hours, on five consecutive weekends.

We chose to teach, and specifically to team teach, this course in spite of the following facts: (1) we knew very little about the topic; (2) making this commitment meant giving up five Saturdays in a row; (3) the course entailed a great deal of preparation and follow-up; (4) the course was reviewed by the university's personnel office as extraneous to our teaching; and (5) we had to split one salary in order to teach the course together. Why would anyone choose this course of action?

The following are excerpts from journal entries we wrote about the five team-taught sessions of the course, including the planning and follow-up. (Our original journals covered everything and anything we wanted to write about, but here we have included only those excerpts related to team teaching. The full journal entries were much longer and dealt with a wide variety of issues.) As you read these journal entries, you may find it useful to contrast the two sets of comments about the same session.

The First Saturday: Kathi's Entry

I'm really glad we talked ourselves into teaching this course. But I'm REALLY glad we're team teaching it. I would have been a basket case Saturday afternoon without Andy. We were pretty well prepared (a lot of Andy's stuff from the earlier MBA course works well with this class plus we had done a thorough and professional-looking job on the syllabus), but I still would not have felt as confident if I'd been running the session alone, even if I'd had exactly the same materials.

Andy is as picky as I am about getting stuff sorted out properly, but somehow he seems to notice things that I let slip. So we had our first class meeting with no hassles (other than the work) and in complete harmony. Plus he was really funny, so I think we set a great tone and the participants must have gotten the impression that we were organized and that we enjoyed working together.

Andy had a great idea for finding out what they already knew, and it worked well. We had prepared a list of five key topics from [the previous teacher's] syllabus and divided the participants into ten groups. Each group made a poster representing what they'd studied about one of those topics, so we ended up with two posters per topic….When they'd finished reading [the posters], we asked them in their groups to compare their poster with that of the other group that had treated the same theme.

Andy's transparencies worked nicely with what I had to say about equal power and unequal power discourse.…I am enjoying team teaching with Andy and I think I'll learn a lot by doing this class with him.

The First Saturday: Andy's Entry

Kathi and I spent quite a while laying out our papers, overhead transparencies, poster paper and pens, lesson plans, notes, etc.—not so much marking our territory as trying to reassure ourselves that it was going to be okay, we did know what we were doing and, if not, we could at least *look* like we did!

The small group poster activity went well and most of the participants seemed to remember quite a lot of stuff from the previous module.

I led a teacher-centered lecture style session, which, as Kathi pointed out, they might see as "the meat and potatoes" of the afternoon. I also led an activity on barriers to successful communication, which involved individual work and then pair exchanges with Kathi writing their ideas on the board as they shouted them out [after the pair work].… Some questions also gave me a chance to do a little stand-up comedy, and for Kathi and me to confirm the group's suspicions, if they were still in any doubt, that we liked to enjoy ourselves when teaching and especially when we were teaching together.

Kathi did an amazing job, pulling rabbits out of hats, with the session she led on equal and unequal power discourse. Luckily we were able to cut my not-very-well-thought-out bit on nonverbal communication and use Kathi's communication inventory for the final part. They all paid careful attention, even after their morning at work and four hours with us, partly as Kathi was showing an example of what they could do for their first assignment [their own communication inventories].

The Second Saturday: Kathi's Entry

We had our second meeting of the Organizational Communication course and it went quite well, in spite of the fact that I was pretty sick with a cold, cough, and sore throat. Thank heavens for team teaching. I would have been miserable without Andy. He carried a great deal of the load today—both in planning and in presenting.

We started our unit on running effective meetings with the transparencies we used last fall in the MBA course and a handout that Andy had produced. It got the students to think about the duration, frequency, and types of meetings they must attend. This was a good way of getting them focused on their own experiences as they relate to the material we are studying. For instance, Andy's handout asked them to list six things that annoy them about meetings and then the characteristics of effective meetings. I elicited their ideas while Andy made notes on the board.

That particular routine—focusing the students' attention on their own experience, eliciting their ideas, and comparing them with a model or with the experts' ideas—is an instructional procedure we use often. It seems to work quite well, especially as these people have lots of experience in business settings.

The Second Saturday: Andy's Entry

Kathi thanked me for carrying some of the session, as she wasn't well, but I don't think it was like that. We're agreed that it would have been very difficult, at times we think it would've been impossible, to do this module without each other's help. The other teachers on the course take the group solo, but as we're both new to this field, it certainly makes a huge difference having someone there whom I know I can rely on professionally, someone I can bounce comments off and have her do the same.

Planning and Reflection: Kathi's Entry

On Thursday Andy and I met from about 2:30 to nearly 6 PM, with some interruptions. We got all the grades resolved. Our grading was remarkably similar and we were able to compromise easily on all the papers where our marks differed. Also I really appreciated that Andy was willing to do the more time-consuming but pedagogically sound process of both of us reading all the papers independently and then averaging our scores (rather than simply splitting the pile of assignments between us). The papers were quite interesting, and we found a great follow-up activity using the data in the students' papers to apply the speech acts framework I'll be presenting tomorrow.

One of the things I like about working with Andy is that the work seems to get divided evenly—I never feel like I have to do more than my fair share. Also, the work gets done. He hasn't let me down yet with materials, arrangements, communicating with [the administration], etc. And besides—he volunteers to do these things so I don't have to do any persuading. For instance, he came up with two great transparencies for the review process that we are building into the beginning of each lesson.

Another funny thing about working with Andy is that we have different but remarkably compatible stuff. Today he showed me some ideas about team-building and leadership, and I showed him my ideas about innovation and change, and all of a sudden we went from not knowing what we'd be able to do next weekend to realizing that we had tons of material—probably even too much to cover in four hours!

Also, we seem to get ideas from working with each other. Today we got a great idea about how to utilize the "Learning From Effective Communicators" assignment that the students will submit next Saturday. The activities of the week have made me realize how much of successful team teaching is not in the teaching—it's in everything that goes on before and after the teaching as well.

The Third Saturday: Kathi's Entry

Andy used some transparencies from the MBA course we did last fall. He talked about the importance of effective meeting skills. While he was talking I had a flash (in fact, in my notes it says "FLASH") that the old transparencies had lots of connections to the speech act information I had introduced before the break. I hadn't seen that possibility before, and it didn't come up when we were doing our planning. But because Andy is so flexible and the teamwork between us is pretty fluid, I felt free to point this out. So Andy's stuff about meetings set the stage for the next step.

The Third Saturday: Andy's Entry

I started with a review of last week's work and some feedback on their first assignment. I wonder how it would have looked on videotape, as I felt I was stumbling and faltering quite a bit.... I looked over to Kathi a couple of times to see her reaction. She didn't look bored or confused, so I carried on!

The jigsaw readings went better than we expected. At one point I said to Kathi that these kinds of classes were great because they ran themselves. Later I changed my comment to one about the fact that these classes were great to teach because of the participants' interest and motivation, but that the activities went well because of all the time we put into setting them up so as to channel the group's enthusiasm.

The Big Finale of our MBA course on meetings last year was the role-play activity, which we revised for re-use today. The groups took different amounts of time to warm up, but once they were warm, they all seemed to get into it. Kathi and I circulated, congratulating ourselves for another job well done! We learned a lot from doing this module a second time, and would, of course, like all good reflective practitioners, change a number of things next time, but it was definitely a good show....

The Fourth Saturday: Kathi's Entry

Yesterday's class meeting was good, even though I had been gone for the entire week preceding the class. I made all my transparencies before I left and gave Andy copies so he could see what I planned to do. We discussed it a bit, and he roughed out a lesson plan that worked well....Then we met for an hour before class to finish our final assignment for the students. We got inspired (or at least he liked my ideas and found ways to improve them) and wrote a three-option assignment that should provide enough choices for everyone.

We started out with Andy's quick review of the last class (a great idea—especially for a class that meets only once a week). Then we had the students sit in groups of three...and read their colleagues' assignments about interviewing or shadowing an effective communicator....This was a great way to (1) show them that the assignments are due at the beginning of class, (2) show them we value their ideas and will build lessons around those ideas, and (3) get them settled down and quiet at the very beginning of class.

After the break I started on the transparencies about innovation. We gave as an extended example Andy being asked to start the medical English curriculum, which worked quite well. I got confused about the time because I was supposed to have done the innovations material before break but we didn't get to it until after the break. Once I started on the sequence of the transparencies I didn't think to check the lesson plan, and I just kept going until I'd finished —but then it turned out that I'd used up a huge chunk of the time Andy was planning to spend on team building, etc. He seemed to be okay with that though, because it means he's better prepared already for next week.

When we finished we offered the participants more opportunities to ask questions about the final assignment, but there were none. So I said good-bye to them and explained I couldn't be here next week but that Andy and I had planned the lesson together, that I would read the next set of their papers before I left, and I'd be back to read their final papers. I really have enjoyed teaching this course. The students were so eager and it's very easy to work with Andy. Our teaching and planning styles are compatible, our senses of humor are similar, and we get ideas from one another.

The Fourth Saturday: Andy's Entry

I started with a one-transparency review of last week's work, which we feel should be a regular thing, as it refreshes both their memories and ours. It also looks organized and professional, which may be especially important with participants like this. Perhaps we're also "playing to our strengths," in the sense that we do know about teaching, so whatever we lack in our knowledge of organizational communication we can make up for with our knowledge of teaching, and it may be that combining our knowledge as we have been doing makes that teaching knowledge base even stronger—the whole being more than the sum of the parts.

Something interesting happened after the break. Kathi was introducing the interactive show-and-tell about change and innovation. She led and I chipped in from time to time, sometimes invited by Kathi, at other times "uninvited." But the interesting thing was the timing. We thought it would take about 30 minutes, but somehow, it was an hour before Kathi finished! By that time, she and I had noticed the group's restlessness but I was surprised and Kathi shocked [that she had run over the allotted time]. It happened because the group asked a number of good clarification questions and partly because Kathi was keen to give lots of examples, from my medical English course and from her experiences, to illustrate the points she was making.…We then realized that this group activity would take us to the end of the session, leaving up to one hour's worth of material yet to be covered. This was good for me, since Kathi will not be here for the final session next week, so it's great to have less to prepare!

The Last Saturday: Andy Teaches Alone

Kathi could not be here for the last class—a fact we have both understood since the beginning of the course. What a difference a teaching partner makes! There were four "incidents" today that I don't think would have happened if Kathi'd been here. Or perhaps if they had happened, they would have been dealt with in a very different way.

At the break, one group… insisted I go with them for tea, which I did. During the break I asked them whether it was just my imagination or whether the class really was behaving differently this week, without Kathi around. They said that it wasn't my imagination, because when Kathi was there, the two of us were sort of able to limit the interruptions of the kind that had occurred in the first part of today's session.

Thinking back on the session…I realized that one of the reasons why this kind of stuff hadn't happened before was partly because between us we were effectively able to control the few "disruptive elements" in the group. Another reason for the with/without Kathi difference is that I wouldn't like to show her that side of my teaching nature, even though we both know that we have the ability to be defensive, authoritarian, or just downright nasty with the students when we feel pushed to do so. A third reason is that I was more insecure without Kathi, knowing that [with her gone] we wouldn't be able to collectively compensate for any holes in our content knowledge with our combined teaching knowledge. This insecurity led me to become defensive.

Sorting Out the Aftermath: Andy's Later Entry

...I can't remember if I've made any reference in previous entries to the importance (and the amount) of work that goes on before and after the actual teaching—I know that's true of most teaching, but I think it's especially true of team teaching. It may even be one of its defining characteristics.

Trying to keep a balanced reflection—and this is where it really does help to have a team teaching partner whom I trust—I think we worked as hard as we could've and came up with a lot of good ideas and activities.... We helped each other out, in many ways (giving the other confidence, and time to think, helping with reacting to tricky or unexpected stuff, and many other things), which I don't think I saw really clearly until I solo'd on the last day....How would I evaluate our teaching in the course? Good, at times very good, and without a doubt my teaching—especially with respect to the performance element so important with a group like that—was very much better than if I'd been on my own for all five weeks!

Investigations

10.7 TASKS FOR DEVELOPMENT

In this chapter we have considered the advantages and disadvantages of team teaching. It is not ideal for everyone, and the collaborative skills it demands are not necessarily innate; they too must be developed. As Kathi described it when watching a video of Andy and herself team teaching, "It's funny: it's so much like learning to dance" (Bailey et al., 1998, 553). We feel, however, that with the right partner, team teaching can provide valuable opportunities for professional development. The following tasks and suggested readings are intended to help you pursue this line of inquiry.

Appendix B starts on p. 262.

1. In Andy's and Kathi's journal entries, we have the reflections of two teachers who worked together but wrote separate journal entries, which they later shared. Look back at the Teachers' Voices section and choose three of the survey items in Appendix B that relate closely to points Andy raised in his journal entries. Next choose three items that relate to issues Kathi wrote about in her journal entries. Based on your reading of their journal excerpts, how do you think Andy and Kathi would respond to the items you selected (on a scale of "5 = strongly agree" to "1 = strongly disagree")?

This framework appears on p. 56.

2. Andy's and Kathi's journal entries are examples of *immediate retrospection*, in terms of the frameworks introduced in Chapter 4. The data from Komal and Fukuko are based on *delayed retrospection*. Do you find either set of data more compelling or revealing than the other? What are the advantages and disadvantages of immediate versus delayed retrospection?

3. Imagine yourself in a situation in which you were assigned to team teach a course with someone you didn't know. (This situation is not

unusual, as illustrated by Kathi and David's conversation about Andy at the beginning of Chapter 1, as well as Ruth Johnson's experience in one Teachers' Voices section of this chapter.) Write a list of questions you would like to ask your newly assigned teaching partner, as well as a list of things you would like to tell him or her about you and your teaching style and experience. (If you are working with a group, we suggest you compare your lists with those of your classmates or colleagues.)

This conversation appears on pp. 1–2.

4. Role-play the experience of meeting a team teacher to plan a course you will be teaching together. How does the role-play evolve under the following circumstances?

   A. You are colleagues who have chosen to work together.

   B. You are colleagues who have been assigned to work together.

   C. You are strangers who have been assigned to work together.

5. You can see that the factors that vary in task 4 above are [± choice] and [± known partner]. The teachers surveyed by Bailey et al. (1992, 175) generally agreed that "only teachers themselves should decide whether or not to enter into a team teaching arrangement." The average rating given to this statement was 3.8 on a scale of 5 (where 5 means "strongly agree," 4 means "agree," and so on). Where do you stand on this issue?

The following grid lays out the possible arrangements:

	Known Teaching Partner	Unknown Teaching Partner
Self-Selected Choice to Team Teach	1	3
Assigned to Team Teach	2	4

Looking at these four quadrants, which one represents Ruth Johnson's experience? Which represents Andy and Kathi's experience in the Organizational Communication course? Which represents Komal and Fukuko's team taught Japanese class?

We believe that team teaching is most likely to be successful if the teaching partners know and value one another, and if they choose to team teach together (Quadrant 1). We further believe that numbering in the four quadrants predicts the likelihood of a successful team teaching experience. In other words, the situation in Quadrant 4 (being forced to teach with an unknown partner) is the least likely to be successful (the "arranged marriage" situation).

And yet, if we return to David and Kathi's conversation in Chapter 1, we see that Andy and Kathi first team taught as total strangers. Thus their first team teaching experience on the MBA course is an example of Quadrant 3. The question is, *why* was this a successful experience, at least in the minds of the two teachers? (We have no achievement data from the students to determine the impact on their learning.) List the three most important traits that you think would lead to a successful team teaching experience. Compare your list with those of your colleagues or classmates.

6. Think of a person with whom you would be interested in setting up a team teaching arrangement. What are the qualities of this person that made you choose him or her as a potential team teaching partner?

Now think of a person with whom you would definitely NOT want to team teach. What are the characteristics of this person that influenced your choice?

Finally, think about your own characteristics as a potential team teaching partner. Do you think you would be the kind of team teacher that others would choose to work with? Why or why not?

7. We have used many "two-by-two" grids in the Investigations sections of this book (like the one in Task 5 above). Yet we know full well that life doesn't happen in neat little boxes. Particularly in teaching, shades of gray are much more prevalent than crisp black and white delineations. So in terms of our category labels, is it [± known] that matters, or is the really crucial variable whether or not you trust and respect your team teaching partner? What other team teaching factors can you diagram?

8. If you are currently teaching, make arrangements for someone to share at least one lesson's teaching responsibilities with you (including planning and follow-up). If you are a novice teacher who is not currently teaching, try to find someone who would be willing to team teach with you for at least one class period.

Before you teach together, we suggest that you plan to collect some data about the experience. What would you like to learn about your own team teaching experience, or about yourself as a team teacher? What kind(s) of data would be most useful? How might you collect the data, and how could you analyze them later?

Suggested Readings

Peter Sturman (1992) provides an interesting account of Japanese secondary school EFL teachers team teaching with experienced ESOL teachers in Tokyo. We recommend this article for anyone interested in team teaching in general, for those interested in the issues faced by cross-cultural team teaching, and for anyone interested in team teaching in Japan.

Gillian Giles, Susan Koenig, and Fredricka Stoller (1997) have written a brief but helpful article that highlights some of the advantages and disadvantages of team teaching, particularly in the context of Intensive English Programs (IEPs).

We recommend the report by Shannon and Meath-Lang (1992) on their interview research. It contains useful information that we have not reproduced here. This article and others on collaborative language learning and teaching appear in Nunan (1992c).

The article written by Bailey, Dale, and Squire (1992) was the source of the questionnaire reprinted in this chapter, as well as Benjamin Squire's journal entries. It also reports on some other team teaching experiences of the *associate type* and the *master teacher-beginner teacher type* (Cunningham, 1960).

Anné Knezevic and Mary Scholl (1996) wrote a candid report of their differences in a team taught practicum experience and what they learned. Peter Medgyes and Emese Nyilasi (1997) provide a different treatment of the same topic in their paper entitled "Pair Teaching in Preservice Teacher Education."

11

MENTORING AND COACHING: HELPING HANDS

New teachers need support. They need ongoing professional development. They need a sense of belonging, of common cause, and the knowledge that over time they will make a difference not only in the lives of individual children they teach, but in their profession (Eisenman and Thornton, 1999, 80).

Novice teachers leave teacher preparation programs with numerous skills, a current knowledge base, and high hopes of becoming effective professionals in their new positions. Yet many leave teaching within a few years of taking up their jobs, some of them overwhelmed by the workload, low pay, and other associated problems. And, as discussed in Chapter 1, experienced teachers sometimes face burnout and other negative aspects of the profession that lead to discouragement and a lack of motivation to improve.

For information about burnout, see pp. 8–9.

This chapter discusses two approaches to professional development—mentoring and coaching. Mentoring is typically used with novice teachers, but it can also be helpful to experienced teachers. Coaching has been used in first language education by teachers at all stages of their careers. Both of these approaches are designed to provide nonevaluative, nonthreatening sources of support and development options to practicing teachers. Although mentoring and coaching started as models of professional development in general education, they are both applicable to language teaching as well.

11.1   *A MATTER OF DEFINITIONS*

Before reading further, assess your current understanding of the dual themes of this chapter. What is mentoring? What is coaching? How are these two approaches similar, and how do they differ?

DEFINING MENTORING

Walking into a bookshop these days, we can see a bewildering array of books on the development of "leadership skills," most written by successful corporate managers. These books can be useful, but what they lack is any kind of ongoing reciprocal relationship between the reader and the author. This ongoing relationship is, in our opinion, part of what makes mentoring special. It can provide a degree of insight and understanding that even the very best books may not deliver.

What is mentoring? According to Eisenman and Thornton (1999, 80–81), the concept has ancient origins: "Mentoring goes back thousands of years to Homer's epic poem, the *Odyssey*. Homer tells of a wise old sea captain named Mentor who gives Odysseus's son, Telemachus, guidance in coping with his father's long absence." They add that nowadays the term *mentor* is applied to a "situation in which a knowledgeable person aids a less knowledgeable person" (ibid.).

In language teacher development, a mentoring relationship can develop naturally between two people with an affinity and shared professional interests. Or it can be structured between a cooperating teacher and a teacher-in-training during a practicum. Schools and programs have also established formal mentoring programs for novice teachers in the induction years, who are assigned to work with more experienced teachers.

Although formal mentoring might be thought to be a relatively new approach to professional development for language teachers, it is, in fact, a long-established way of imparting knowledge, skills, and understanding, going back to the origins of the apprenticeship system in crafts and trades. This one-to-one teaching and learning relationship would often last for many years, until the apprentice was ready to take up his or her role. The long-term nature of the relationship allows both the mentor and the person being mentored to see the growth that takes place.

As the term is used in this chapter, *mentoring* is an interpersonal, ongoing, situated, supportive, and informative professional relationship between two (or more) individuals, one of whom (the mentor) has more experience in the profession, craft, or skill in question. In language teaching, a mentor is typically a more experienced teacher working with a novice or a teacher new to a particular program. Although it is an unequal power relationship of sorts, mentoring is not supervisorial in nature. That is, in the professional development of teachers, mentors should not serve the supervisorial function of evaluation on behalf of the management of a school or program.

11.2 CHARACTERISTICS OF A MENTOR

If you hear someone say, "He's my mentor" or "She's my mentor," what does it mean to you? Think of someone who has served the role of mentor in your own professional development. Write down at least three characteristics or actions of this person that seem to characterize his/her role as your mentor.

If you are working with a group of colleagues or classmates, we suggest that you share your ideas with them. From your combined lists it should be possible to come up with a description of an effective mentor.

THE "CRAFT MODEL"

Michael Wallace has described the craft model of teacher education. This metaphor applies to the typical student teacher and master teacher relationship, as well as to other mentoring relationships described here. In this model, Wallace notes, an experienced professional practitioner, an expert in the particular craft, serves as a model, a guide, and a source of feedback: "The young trainee learns by imitating the expert's techniques, and by following the expert's instructions and advice. (Hopefully, what the expert *says* and *does* will not be in conflict.) By this process, expertise in the craft is passed on from generation to generation" (Wallace, 1991, 6).

However, there are some potential problems with the craft model. If the expert is not truly capable, or is capable at the craft but not capable of teaching it, the novice will have few resources for alternative input. Also, depending on the context, the novice can end up feeling isolated, with just one person to turn to for guidance, feedback, and support. In addition, as Wallace notes (ibid., 6–7), the craft model is basically conservative. It presumes that the craft is performed in a largely static society:

> [T]he one thing we can be sure of is that in ten years' time things will be very different from what they are now. Schools today exist in a dynamic society, geared to change. The concept of the venerable old master teacher is difficult to sustain in an educational context of new methodologies and new syllabuses, where the raw recruit from a College of Education may be, *in some ways,* better informed than the practising teacher.

For this reason, in order for a mentoring relationship to be successful, those teachers chosen to mentor novices must themselves have continued their own professional development, so as not to present an outdated model of teaching.

Some mentoring relationships simply evolve, rather than being formally established. In this Teachers' Voices section Kathi describes a person whom she considers to be her mentor, and addresses the task posed in the Investigations section above.

An Informal Mentoring Relationship

Teachers' Voices

Kathi Bailey

My mentor is Russ Campbell, a man whom many readers of this book may know. I met him when he was my professor for an introductory linguistics course at the University of California, Los Angeles (UCLA). I think of him as my mentor primarily in administration rather than in teaching, but I believe the key features of the mentoring relationship cut across different professional responsibilities.

What were the things Russ did over 25 years ago that still make me think of him as my mentor?

1. He trusted me with responsibilities that I myself did not know I was ready for, and then provided guidance as needed in carrying out those responsibilities.

2. He opened doors for me, in terms of creating or leveraging professional opportunities I would not otherwise have had.

3. He showed me how he gets things done, instead of just telling me, as we worked on projects together.

4. He promoted my career, by telling other people about my work and abilities.

5. He treated me as an intellectual equal from the very beginning of the relationship, even though I lacked his experience and training.

He has continued to take an interest in my career to this day, even though I left UCLA over 20 years ago.

Situational Leadership

Andrea Osburne has written an interesting article entitled "Situational Leadership and Teacher Education" (1989). In it she draws on her experience as an EFL teacher educator in China as well as on a model of situational leadership that originated in management (see Hersey, 1984, and Hersey and Blanchard, 1982). Osburne reviews the literature on two components of leadership behavior: *task behavior* and *relationship behavior*. These terms are defined as follows:

> *Task behavior* is "the extent to which leaders are likely to organize and define the roles of the members of their group (followers); to explain what activities each is to do, and when, where and how tasks are to be accomplished;" [and] *Relationship behavior* is "the extent to which leaders are likely to maintain personal relationships between themselves and members of their group (followers) by opening up channels of communication [and] providing socioemotional support" (Hersey and Blanchard, 1982, p. 96)

Osburne also quotes Hersey and Blanchard's definition of *leadership style* as "the behavior…[a] person exhibits when attempting to influence the activities of others as perceived by those others" (ibid., 95–96). According to the situational leadership model, effective leaders are flexible in their use of relationship behaviors and task behaviors. These two constructs can be depicted as overlapping continua, as in Figure 11.1 below.

Figure 11.1: Continua of Relationship and Task Behaviors in Situational Leadership

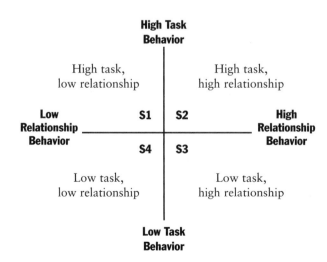

The four quadrants of Figure 11.1 are labeled S1, S2, and so on to identify four potential leadership styles: "high task/low relationship (S1), high task/high relationship (S2), low task/high relationship (S3), and low task/low relationship (S4)" (Osburne, 1989, 411).

The situational leadership model can be helpful in thinking about mentoring and language teaching. While we certainly wouldn't want to characterize all the novice teachers in mentoring relationships as followers, Hersey and Blanchard's work on readiness is pertinent in this context. They define *readiness level* as the followers' "ability and willingness...to take responsibility for their own behavior" (Hersey and Blanchard, 1982, 151). They state that there are two components of readiness: *job readiness*, which is the "knowledge, ability and experience to perform certain tasks without direction from others" (ibid.), and *psychological readiness*, which is the "confidence and commitment, or...willingness to do something" (ibid.). These two constructs can also be depicted as two overlapping continua, as in Figure 11.2:

Figure 11.2: Continua of Job and Psychological Readiness in Situational Leadership

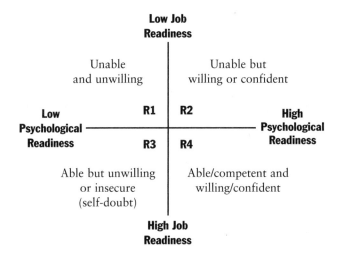

Effective mentors (and effective teacher educators, for that matter) are able to interpret the readiness of the teachers with whom they work and to provide appropriate support. Such support might be primarily related to the job or task at hand, or to building the novice's confidence, or both. For instance, according to Osburne, in Figure 11.1, S1 is best for people at R1 and S4 is best for people at R4.

The professional literature supports claims that mentoring programs provide professional models, opportunities for skills development, and affective support for new teachers (see, e.g., Eisenman and Thornton, 1999). But what do such teachers think? We asked Suzanne Laurens, who holds a master's degree in TESOL, to tell us about the mentoring program in place at her school. Here is Suzanne's reply.

A PSYCHOLOGICAL SAFETY NET

I am currently teaching second grade for Salinas City Elementary School District in California. This is my second year teaching for this district, but my first year both for teaching second grade and for working at my current school. In August of last year, I began teaching a bilingual fourth and fifth grade combination class at one school, and by October I'd been moved to another site and spent the rest of the year teaching an English-only combination kindergarten and first grade class. Out of twenty students fifteen are Latino, one is African-American-Latino, one is Vietnamese-Latino, and three are Anglo. All of the fifteen Latino students have parents who speak Spanish, and seven of these have Spanish as the home language. The children (ten girls and ten boys) are seven and eight years old.

Suzanne Laurens

This experience of having to switch horses in midstream and hit the ground sprinting was horrendous. I was not prepared for the task at hand other than having the will to survive and succeed.

This time marked the beginning of my association with BTSA— Beginning Teacher Support and Assessment. The State of California in conjunction with Educational Testing Service, WestEd, and the University of California at Santa Cruz, is responsible for BTSA, which is a support system for new teachers. A critical component of the BTSA program is reflection. The process encourages reflection through personal writing and discussion with a mentor, as well as peers. The foundation for the BTSA process is the California Standards for the Teaching Profession. The Standards document offers an itemized model of teaching for the inexperienced professional to strive for. These standards define what a mature and effective teacher does.

For me personally, the BTSA process has provided a framework within which to work, with clear performance objectives. There are specific and detailed instructional and assessment activities that I've followed that have been quite helpful. On any day I might choose to look at my teaching of reading, let's say, and have a systematic method of doing so. All such practices involve a discussion and/or personal reflection at the end.

BTSA has been a psychological safety net for me. I've had the confidence to take risks in my classroom, knowing that I have a structure to follow, a target, and an accomplished mentor with whom to analyze my lesson plans, materials, my students' work — all the after-the-fact evidence, in order to evaluate my effectiveness as a teacher. The Standards are used as a rubric for my mentor and me to follow in our evaluation of my professional development.

The mentor with whom I've worked for the past two years is Joyce Edwards. She happens to be a second grade teacher at another school in our district. Joyce and I have met regularly after school in either my classroom or hers. She's very generous with her time, materials, and ideas. Joyce has been teaching for about 10 years and is a classic primary teacher—patient and gentle in her manner. She is open-minded and as eager to learn from me and our exchanges as she is to provide support. There is no problem with her ego trying to dictate how things go. I've been honest with Joyce about my self-doubt and feelings of failure or inadequacy as I struggle to understand what it is I need to do in order to improve. On the flip side too, I've had many successes that I was able to recognize as such because I had the voice of experience giving me honest feedback.

DIFFERENT EXPERIENCE LEVELS

As Suzanne's situation illustrates, mentoring is not restricted to the situation of total novices, though that is the context in which many formal mentoring arrangements are established. Mentoring is also useful in situations in which a teacher has experience but is teaching a new level or a new type of student, either within the same program or in a totally new environment.

Figure 11.3 is reprinted from an article by Seaman, Sweeny, Meadows, and Sweeny (1997). It provides contrasting entry points for teachers with varying levels of experience. The last column on the right indicates the possibility of the teacher transitioning from a mentoring relationship to a peer coaching relationship.

Figure 11.3: Mentoring Strategies for Differing Experience Levels

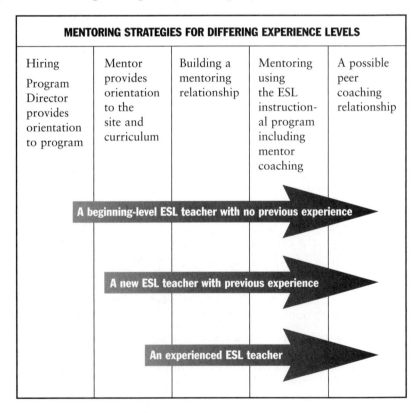

11.3 *A Mentoring Process of Your Own*

If you are an experienced teacher working in an established language program, imagine yourself being tasked with setting up a mentoring program for the three types of teachers depicted in Figure 11.3:

1. beginning level language teachers with no previous teaching experience;

2. experienced teachers new to language teaching; and

3. experienced language teachers new to your program.

In the context of your particular program, how can you use the model proposed by Seaman et al. (1997, 32)? What specific activities could be employed in each of the columns of Figure 11.3? Are additional category headings needed? Are some of the headings irrelevant in your situation?

What we are suggesting is that you use the Seaman et al. model as a springboard for developing a mentoring program of your own.

MENTORING ROLES

Angi Malderez and Caroline Bodóczky have written a book entitled *Mentor Courses: A Resource Book for Teacher-Trainers*, based on their experiences in an innovative, intensive three-year training program for English language teachers at Eötvös Lörand University in Budapest, Hungary. Malderez and Bodóczky explain that their approach was based on the literature on mentoring as well as their own personal histories, "perhaps most notably, experiences in motherhood, psychiatric nursing, counseling training, drama teaching as well as EFL teaching and teacher education" (1999, 2).

These authors note that *mentoring* means many different things. To help clarify what they refer to as "the bewildering range of interpretations" (ibid., 4) of the term, they describe five different roles that mentors take. The five roles are (1) *models*, who inspire and demonstrate; (2) *acculturators*, who show mentees the ropes; (3) *sponsors*, who introduce mentees to the "right people"; (4) *supporters*, who are there to act as sounding boards for cathartic reasons if mentees need to let off steam; and (5) *educators*, who act as sounding boards for the articulation of ideas, to help new teachers achieve professional learning objectives. Although each role has different functions, Malderez and Bodóczky point out that "most mentors will be involved to a greater or lesser degree in all five roles" (ibid., 4).

11.4 *Mentor Roles*

If someone has been a mentor to you, which of the five roles described by Malderez and Bodóczky (1998) did that person play?

Think of yourself as a potential mentor to a novice teacher. Which of these five roles are you best equipped to enact? Which might require some development on your part, in order for you to be an effective mentor?

DEFINING COACHING

While mentoring is definitely a collaborative endeavor, it does involve teachers whose status is unequal. By definition, a more experienced teacher mentors a newer colleague. In this part of the chapter we will consider a different sort of helping relationship—one that is commonly called *coaching* in first language education.

Glatthorn (1987) used the phrase *collaborative professional development* as a cover term to refer to situations in which teachers work together as peers. *Peer coaching* is one such type of developmental collaboration. It is a developmental process in which teachers meet regularly to focus on a particular skill (Joyce and Showers, 1982).

Coaching as an approach to staff development began at the University of Oregon. During the 1980s, teacher educators there conducted research on a model of peer work that would promote the transfer of skills from training programs to classroom application. (See, e.g., Joyce, 1990; Joyce and Showers, 1982, 1987; Showers, 1985; Showers and Joyce, 1996; Showers, Joyce, and Bennett, 1987). According to Showers (1985, 43–44), coaching serves three main purposes:

1. to build communities of teachers who continuously engage in the study of their craft;

2. to develop the shared language and set of common understandings necessary for the collegial study of new knowledge and skills; and

3. to provide a structure for the follow-up to training that is essential for acquiring new teaching skills and strategies.

Coaching is a cyclical process in which teams of peers "study the rationale of the new skills, see them demonstrated, practice them, and learn to provide feedback to one another as they experiment with the skills" (ibid., 44). One element that is repeatedly stressed in the coaching literature is that the "feedback must be accurate, specific, and nonevaluative" (ibid.). The equal power basis of the coaching partners is significant because when "peers engage in such technical, objective discussion, they can begin to discover how they can best represent subject matter in suitable and captivating ways and think about content from the learner's perspective" (Benedetti, 1997, 41).

Benedetti defines three different types of peer coaching:

1. *Technical coaching* asks peers to focus on helping each other transfer a new skill to their teaching.

2. *Collegial coaching* focuses on the refinement of teaching practices. Peers work on skills already present in their teaching repertoire with which they believe they may need help and feedback. For example, peers may focus on assessment practices and help each other ensure a match between these and their instructional practices.

3. *Challenge coaching* resolves a problematic situation in instruction and begins with the identification of a persistent problem. For instance, a teacher may find it difficult to devise her own information gap activities or be unable to elicit second language output from her students. Peers work together to discuss the content and procedural knowledge needed in order to make these activities work in their classrooms (ibid.).

Lorraine Valdez Pierce adds that *technical coaching* is often used in connection with inservice training, in that it facilitates the transfer of material covered "from inservice training to classroom practice" (1988, 1). It also promotes dialogues among teachers and the development of a shared professional vocabulary (ibid.).

Valdez also adds a fourth type which she refers to as *team coaching*. She states that it is a combination of team teaching and peer coaching:

> Visiting mentors or resource teachers, instead of observing class-room teachers, teach right alongside them. These resource teachers should have considerable expertise in the teaching methodology used by the teachers they are coaching. Together the coach and the teacher plan, teach and evaluate the lesson as partners (ibid., 6).

Although there appears to be some overlap here in the notion of *team coaching* with what we have called *mentoring*, Pierce emphasizes the point that "the coach should always be someone who is a peer; otherwise teachers may perceive coaching as evaluation rather than collaboration" (ibid.). In the following conversation, we hear from Ellie Mason, who teaches adult learners in California, about what she gains from team coaching.

ELLIE'S COACHING EXPERIENCE

Kathi: Why did you decide to do peer coaching? Isn't it time-consuming?

Ellie: Peer coaching for me is the best form of professional develop-ment because I learn so much from others. To have a colleague with me in the classroom is great because we can bounce ideas off each other. I rarely find it time-consuming at all. On the contrary, when I'm teaching alone, I spend much more time planning. With my peer coach, I can just turn to him or her for questions and ideas.

Kathi: What did you expect to learn by coaching?

Ellie: I've always expected to gain new insight into teaching. More than that, however, I hope to offer my students two unique instruc-tors who complement each other. At the community college, for example, Eve and I brought our two personalities to the classroom, and the students really benefited from that. I spoke Spanish often and the students knew they could turn to me with problems that they could not articulate in English. Eve was really focused on skills practice, and so they learned a great deal from her in terms of English. We played two complementary roles.

Kathi: Now that you have actually started your peer coaching prac-tice, what sorts of things do you focus on? How do you work together as you carry out your peer coaching?

Ellie: We strive to meet once a week, but it does not always work out. However, we spend a lot of time before the course actually starts to sort things out and to determine who does what. Once the course

Ellie Mason

takes off, a lot of what goes on is really just filling each other in. We usually talk at the beginning of the week to map things out. However, there are times when things come up and we hold more meetings.

Kathi: Are you learning anything about your teaching so far?

Ellie: Yes! I'm learning to let go. So much of what goes on in the classroom is focused on teacher control. For me, peer coaching is liberating because I do not have complete control of the classroom. I'm just one part of the whole learning process that includes what the students bring. As a student, I never liked instructors who "knew it all" and had nothing to learn from me, so I'm glad that I can relinquish a bit of control too!

When I worked as a Bilingual Coordinator, I tried to participate in peer coaching situations two separate times with veteran teachers who had more experience than I. However, I became more of a teacher's assistant than a coach because they were in control and I was sort of tagging along. I either had to do what they wanted in terms of curriculum, materials development, and so on, or we wouldn't team teach.

Kathi: Do you have any advice for teachers who are considering trying peer coaching to promote their own professional development?

Ellie: Be aware of your colleague's teaching style. If one prefers center stage, that can cause problems. Also, be sure to pull your own weight! There's nothing worse than being in a coaching or team teaching situation when you feel as if you're doing all the work. However, when problems come up, as they inevitably will, the best bet is communication and clarification. Communication is essential.

NEEDS FOR PEER COACHING

A key characteristic of all types of coaching is that coaching is not supervisorial in nature. Coaching partners can work candidly on developing their teaching skills and not feel awkward or threatened by revealing their weaknesses to someone who conducts their official evaluations. According to Benedetti, peer coaching arose out of teachers' needs for the following:

- companionship, reducing the sense of isolation that teachers tend to feel;

- objective, technical, nonevaluative feedback as the new teaching skill is practiced;

- continual emphasis on the application of the teaching skill that keeps the peers focused;

- analysis of students' responses to the teachers' implementation;

- adaptation of the new skill to the needs of particular groups of students; and

- support during early attempts to use the new skill (Benedetti, 1997, 41).

She goes on to suggest clear procedures that can be used to set up a coaching program.

11.5 *WHAT ARE YOUR NEEDS?*

Look at the bulleted list of six needs identified by Benedetti. Skim Ellie Mason's comments in the Teachers' Voices section above. Which of the six needs identified by Benedetti are mentioned in Ellie's discussion of peer coaching?

In terms of your own current career stage as a language teacher, rank these needs from one to six (with one being the most important and six being the least important for you at the present time). Now think about your life as a language teacher five or even ten years from now. How does your ordering change if you consider your likely future needs? Are there other needs not listed above that you have encountered (or anticipate that you might encounter) in your life as a language teacher?

A CONVERSATION WITH EVE AND PETER

The following conversation took place when Kathi interviewed Eve Connell and Peter Shaw, two experienced teachers and teacher educators. They had entered into a coaching relationship as they team taught a practicum for language teachers.

Eve Connell
Peter Shaw

Kathi: Eve and Peter, you are both really experienced teachers, but you've entered into a peer coaching agreement. Why did you decide to do this?

Eve: Coaching is a natural part of team teaching—planning, creating, teaching, evaluating, and coaching together are one process. Plus we like each other, so it's fun!

Peter: I think the key word in what Eve said is "natural." The question is not really why did we decide to do this, but why wouldn't we? Any team teaching format is an opportunity for professional development. And in the practicum it's even more significant and upfront. In fact, one of the first things we did in the class was to model the peer coaching process. Eve did a preobservation session with me, I then immediately did a short piece of instruction, and then we did the postobservation session. This was not only a useful thing for the class, it set the tone for our own collaboration.

Kathi: What did you expect to learn by coaching one another?

Eve: More insights into our teaching strengths and weaknesses, as well as how to collaborate effectively with another colleague.

Peter: Yes, to both points. Specifically, we had a class that was large (25 or 26 students) and quite varied, so at both the planning and execution stage, we had to think about providing for the varying needs of our population—and, certainly, the specific difficulties raised by certain individuals. So "effective collaboration" took on a lot of shades of meaning in this context.

Kathi: Now that you have actually started your peer coaching practice, what sorts of things do you focus on? How do you work together as you carry out your peer coaching?

Eve: We meet once a week to plan the course activities. We meet before each class to touch base and have a reality check. Also we meet during class to make adjustments. We share the floor during class and are in constant discussion regarding how our students are "getting" our material and the activities.

Peter: I would emphasize the informality and flexibility of our arrangement. While we certainly planned together carefully, the constant adjustments during each class session (two-and-a-half hours, three times a week) were facilitated by the coaching relationship. Indeed, much of the feedback was delivered on the run and somewhat piecemeal, which is only a good idea when you have maximum trust and confidence in each other.

Kathi: Can you give me some examples about what you are learning?

Eve: YES! I'm not as compulsive about organization and planning as I thought. I don't mind ditching lesson plans or switching things around in midstream. I feel I have to uphold my credibility but at the same time, I know more than I give myself credit for.

Peter: I've learned that I am not as "laid-back" as I thought. Eve did a great job confirming the details of my planning and the validity of what I brought to the table, while holding up her own worthy contributions and being flexible as we changed and improvised on the run. It's the old principle of cooperative learning: The outcome is never exactly what you yourself had in mind, but it's always better. And when a lot of it is also being co-created with the students themselves, it's a strong confidence boost to be able to maintain one's professional identity and key messages amidst such ambiguity.

Kathi: Do you have any advice for teachers who are considering trying peer coaching to promote their own professional development?

Eve: Find a safe, fun, familiar colleague who is willing to really dig deep—preferably someone to team teach with or at least someone who has the same group of students or the same subject matter. There's so much to be learned and observed!

Peter: As usual, Eve has put her finger on the key: "safe." Making coaching work well is 90 percent in the affective domain. You have to both have good boundaries, not be prone to being upset or pouting in the face of frank feedback, and not prone to outbursts when under stress. It helps too to have some clearly articulated goals for your development and to have a track record of reflective teaching.

11.6 *TASKS FOR DEVELOPMENT*

This chapter has discussed two collaborative approaches to professional development: mentoring and coaching. Both involve teams of two or more teachers working together in a nonsupervisorial relationship to improve their teaching effectiveness. The main difference is that mentoring, by definition, is somewhat of an unequal power relationship between an able and experienced teacher and a less experienced and/or less able teacher. Coaching, on the other hand, is a reciprocal arrangement in which peers work together for mutual improvement. The following tasks and suggestions for further reading are intended to help you develop a personal understanding of the material covered in this chapter.

1. Based on your reading and your prior knowledge, which would you prefer to engage in—mentoring or coaching? Why? Does your answer change if you imagine yourself as a novice language teacher or a very experienced language teacher? Think of the advantages and disadvantages of each.

2. Think of a person whom you would like to have as a mentor. What are the personal and professional qualities of this person that made you choose him or her?

   Now think of a person whom you would definitely NOT want as your mentor. What characteristics of this person influenced your choice?

   Finally, return to the list of your own characteristics as a potential mentor that emerged from the second Investigation in this chapter. Would you be the kind of mentor that others would choose to work with? Why or why not?

3. Think of a past context in which you were new at a particular job—in a teaching position if possible. Which of the following combinations of factors (based on Figure 11.2 on page 210) best characterizes your situation at that time? Were you (A) unable and unwilling to perform the job (R1); (B) unable but willing to perform the job (R2); (C) able but insecure or unwilling to perform the job (R3); or (D) competent

and also willing and confident about performing the job (R4)? If you had a mentor in the context you identified, what did that person do to help you develop your skills and/or your confidence level? If you did not have a mentor in that context, what steps were you able to take yourself in order to enhance your skills and/or confidence? Again, thinking of that same context, if you *had* had a mentor, what would you have wanted that person to do for you or with you?

4. If someone has served as your mentor or your peer coach, how did that person influence you in terms of the four components of teacher development identified by Freeman (1989a, 36)? Write one statement for each category in Figure 2.1 on page 23 (attitude, awareness, knowledge, and skills).

   If you have already served as a mentor to a novice teacher, how do you think your work together influenced that teacher in terms of Freeman's four components listed above? Give a specific example in each category.

5. If you could design the perfect mentor for you, what would that person be like? Try to do this task even if you are an experienced teacher. (You can recall your own earlier situation as a novice, or you can imagine yourself as an experienced teacher working in a new position.) List three to five characteristics of your ideal mentor.

   Compare this list with the one you made in response to investigation 11.2 in which you described a real mentor. Do your answers change if you are thinking about the role of a peer coach, rather than that of a mentor?

6. Think of yourself as a potential peer coach, whether you are a preservice teacher, a novice teacher, or an experienced teacher. What are your own personal qualities that would make you a good peer coach? List three to five of your own characteristics that would serve you well in this role.

7. If you were to enter into a mentoring relationship (either as a mentor or as a new teacher), you might simply talk with your mentoring partner about teaching. As an alternative, you could engage in any number of professional development activities together, including some of those discussed in this book (e.g., videotaping, journaling together, peer observation, and so on).

   Choose any three professional development activities and list the possible outcomes of engaging in those activities, for both the mentor and the novice teacher. Use a grid like the one that follows to record your ideas:

Development Activity	Outcomes for the Mentor	Outcomes for the Novice Teacher
1. _____		
2. _____		
3. _____		

Do your choices of collaborative professional development activities change if you think about a coaching situation rather than a mentoring context? If so, why? How might the outcomes change for the peer coaching partners?

Now think about areas for potential growth on your part. What are two or three of your own characteristics that might be detrimental if you were to serve as a peer coach? How could you change those characteristics (or work within the constraints they impose) if you were to become a coaching partner?

Suggested Readings

Jodi Crandall (1993) has written an article about professionalism and the professionalization of adult ESL literacy instruction. The paper includes a discussion of mentoring and coaching in the adult school context.

Ingrid Wisniewska's (1998) article, "What's Your Mentoring Style?," depicts a conversation between a student teacher and her mentor teacher. The possible comments of the mentor are listed in a multiple-choice format. By checking the options you can get a rough estimate of your mentoring style.

Gordon Eisenman and Holly Thornton (1999) have written about the evolution of a mentoring program (for non-language teachers) that relies largely on electronic communication systems to sustain the mentoring relationship in a convenient way. For other information on electronic mentoring, see Haworth (1998), Mather (1997), and O'Neil, Wagner, and Gomez (1996).

Andrea Osburne's (1989) paper is related to her work as a teacher educator, and draws on ideas from Hersey (1984), and Hersey and Blanchard's (1982) book, *Management of Organizational Behavior: Utilizing Human Resources*.

We recommend the article by Seaman, Sweeny, Meadows, and Sweeny (1997), which describes the mentoring program in use at the World Relief Refugee Services. These colleagues have also written a training manual for mentors, *Mentoring for ESL Teachers* (Lewis, Meadows, Seaman, Sweeny, and Sweeny, 1996). It uses the Hersey and Blanchard (1982) model of situational leadership to suggest varying combinations of mentoring styles and protégé needs. For more information on mentor development, see Malderez and Bodóczky (1998).

For an update on coaching as it has developed over two decades, see Beverly Showers and Bruce Joyce's (1996) article, "The Evolution of Peer Coaching." Although it focuses on general education, it is relevant in language teaching contexts too.

Paul F. Caccia (1996) has written an article entitled "Linguistic Coaching: Helping Beginning Teachers Defeat Discouragement." His ideas are based on speech act theory and focus on the value of improved communication skills in professional development.

Judith Shulman and Joel Colbert (1987) edited *The Mentor Teacher Casebook*, which includes a helpful annotated bibliography. It is geared for first language educators, but could be valuable to language teachers, too.

12
TEACHING PORTFOLIOS: COGENT COLLAGES

The teaching portfolio as a strategy for professional development is based on the premise that the best assessment is self-assessment. Teachers are more likely to act on what they find out about themselves (Green and Smyser, 1996, x).

For many years, portfolios have been used by architects, designers, and artists to show the range and quality of their work. Recently, accompanying the product-process shift in the teaching of writing, authors have used portfolios to demonstrate how they arrived at their final texts by presenting the various drafts they produced leading up to the last one. Portfolios have been used in math and music instruction as well. The portfolio concept has also become increasingly popular as a means of monitoring and assessing students' work in first and second or foreign language classrooms.

A more recent use of portfolios has been in teacher education and development. This trend has prompted a number of authors to describe teaching portfolios. In the Frameworks section below we will review some of the available literature.

BACKGROUND INFORMATION

In this Frameworks section, the literature review is structured around a series of questions that teachers may ask about teaching portfolios. The purpose of this review is to raise some of the issues to consider if you wish to compile your own teaching portfolio.

WHAT IS A PORTFOLIO?

Carol Porter and Janell Cleland define a portfolio as "a collection of artifacts accompanied by a reflective narrative that not only helps the learner to understand and extend learning, but invites the reader of the portfolio to gain insight about learning and the learner" (1995, 154). Porter and Cleland's emphasis on the learners can be applied to teachers learning about teaching as well.

According to James Stronge (1997, 194), "In its most basic form, a teaching portfolio is a collection of information about a teacher's practice." Stronge adds that portfolios should be "*structured* around sound professional content standards and individual schools' goals" and should contain "commentaries and explanations of... carefully selected examples of both student and teacher work" (ibid., 195).

James Dean Brown and Kate Wolfe-Quintero (1997, 28) highlight the narrative aspect of teaching portfolios. They say a portfolio is "a purposeful collection of any aspect of a teacher's work that tells the story of a teacher's efforts, skills, abilities, achievements, and contributions to his/her colleagues, institution, academic discipline or community." These authors see the portfolio creation process as enabling teachers to

> present a rich array of the information that best represents their professional personas. The very process of compiling a portfolio can help them to gather together their thoughts about their professional strengths and synthesize them into a cogent collage (ibid., 29).

They add that "Because of the reflective nature of portfolios, developing one inevitably enlarges one's view of what teaching is" (ibid.).

Brown and Wolfe-Quintero's metaphor is useful here. A collage is a single, unified piece of art that consists of several different components—sometimes drawn from many different media. In the process of selecting and arranging the components of a collage, a unity of purpose emerges. The result of a successful portfolio process—the crafting of coherence—is a "cogent collage."

WHY COMPILE OR CREATE A PORTFOLIO?

You may want to look back at Chapter 3 in this book for a closer look at reflection in professional development.

At the heart of most current approaches to teacher development is the notion of reflection. Like Brown and Wolfe-Quintero (1997), Porter and Cleland (1995, 37–48) highlight the relationship between the compiler's portfolio and reflective learning. In the case of teaching portfolios, reflection enables us as teachers to:

1. examine our teaching process,
2. take responsibility for our own teaching,
3. see gaps in our teaching,
4. determine strategies that support our teaching,
5. celebrate risk-taking and inquiry,
6. set goals for future experiences, and
7. see changes and development over time.

Robert Yagleski (1997, 250) also identifies reflection as a key characteristic of portfolios. He notes that portfolios "encourage on-going reflection and [do] not simply document the students' work; grow out of and reflect a range of experiences and competencies related to teaching and learning; and include a variety of student-selected materials related to those experiences and competencies." Yagleski's comments about students' portfolios apply to teaching portfolios as well.

James Green and Sheryl Smyser emphasize that portfolios are *not* just products. As they put it, "a portfolio must be viewed as an on-going process" (1996, 25). They provide seven answers to the question, "What makes a teaching portfolio a different kind of evaluation?" (ibid., 4–8). They say that portfolios:

1. give teaching a context,
2. accommodate diversity,
3. encourage teachers to capitalize on strengths,

4. allow teachers to self-identify areas for improvement,

5. empower teachers by making them reflective,

6. encourage professional dialogue, and

7. integrate all aspects of teaching.

Other reasons for compiling teaching portfolios come from studies such as those reported by Maureen McLaughlin and MaryEllen Vogt (1996). One reason is that teachers and teachers-in-training apparently find the portfolio process to be beneficial. For example, one study of 156 preservice teachers found that the majority of the student teachers (98 percent elementary; 89 percent secondary) expressed positive feelings about portfolios (Vogt, McLaughlin, and Ruddell, 1993, 76). McLaughlin and Vogt (1996, 99) provide an additional answer to the question, "Why compile a portfolio?"

> Portfolio assessment for preservice and inservice teachers is being endorsed at state and national levels in the United States… and accreditation associations are including portfolios in their call for diverse assessments.

In fact, an increasing number of states in the United States are requiring teaching portfolios, and many educational agencies have undertaken work in this area. (See our Suggested Readings at the end of this chapter.) Although these comments refer specifically to the United States, in other regions (Hong Kong and Uruguay, for example) teaching portfolios are also being tested.

A recurring theme in discussions of portfolios relates to the "big picture" they present, in contrast with the "snapshot" that can be gained from a single peer observation or video recording, for example. Even the most detailed portfolio will not represent every facet of a teacher's life; however, the more complete the picture that emerges, the more likely that it will be seen by the compiler (and by the administration when used for evaluation) as an accurate representation of the teacher's professional persona.

Another theme relates to the difficulty of trying to explain to a nonteacher or a preservice teacher what it means to be a teacher, beyond planning and presenting lessons, or marking, grading, and assessing students' work. Here, the portfolio comes into its own, as a record of the many different roles and responsibilities teachers have.

As we were writing this book, David had just finished compiling a teaching portfolio, and Andy was assigned to do one for evaluation purposes. Later, Kathi learned that she would need to compile a teaching portfolio as well. The comments below present David's response to this challenge. (Andy's and Kathi's follow later in the chapter.)

DAVID'S FIRST PORTFOLIO

> As Director of the English Centre at the University of Hong Kong, as well as a practicing teacher, my motivation in developing a portfolio was somewhat different from most teachers'. While I was keen to develop a portfolio for my own professional purposes, I also wanted to encourage the teachers in my program to develop

David Nunan

their portfolios as part of our ongoing professional development. So it was important for me to show my colleagues the value I placed on portfolio development.

My major concern in sharing my portfolio with the rest of the staff was that it might be taken as a blueprint for others to follow. I didn't want this to happen because a portfolio should represent the professional persona of the teacher, and each should be unique, not only in terms of its structure and content, but also in terms of the process through which it is created. I was also a little concerned at the reaction of my colleagues to negative comments and feedback from my students, but these had to be a part of the portfolio. If they were to be omitted, if I presented a cleaned-up version of my professional self, the value of the process, as well as the document itself, would be greatly diminished.

As I began developing the portfolio, numerous questions and doubts came to mind. I have been teaching for around 27 years, and had kept student evaluations and other documentary evidence for most of those years. How far should I reach into my professional past in order to provide an account of myself? In the end I decided to restrict the portfolio largely to my current teaching post, with some selective extracts from my former position to provide some points of comparison.

The next issue concerned content. What should the portfolio look like? What should it contain? I chose a large loose-leaf binder so I could "grow" the portfolio over time. The first things that went into the binder were an outline of my teaching duties and a statement of philosophy. I felt that the statement of philosophy was central to the portfolio creation process because it provided a reference point for what was to come.

In terms of evidence, I wanted to include material from as many different sources as possible. As a large part of my work is concerned with curriculum and materials development, I included samples of these kinds of products. Since it is crucial to present evidence from external sources, I also compiled data provided by students and colleagues. Student data included the formal end-of-course evaluations that are conducted by an independent unit within the university, the Centre for the Advancement of University Teaching. I also included extracts from my students' journals. In addition, I asked my research students to do written evaluations of my style as a research supervisor.

As soon as I had begun to assemble the various bits of evidence of myself as a teacher, I was confronted with another imperative: What was I to do with the stuff that was negative, or, if not negative, that showed a person I barely recognized, and, in some cases, didn't particularly like? Data from several of my classes showed that I needed to pay closer attention to the area of evaluation, particularly when it came to making the grading criteria explicit. Point taken. I'll work on this aspect of my teaching next semester. In another instance, the graduate students taking my course in curriculum design said they want more input from me. In other words, they want to be lectured at. This suggestion I plan to resist. With these students, the most effective learning takes place when they're productively engaged in small-group tasks. I decided to add commentary on the student evaluations in which I present my interpretation of the data along with my response to it. I work hard (although not always entirely successfully) at avoiding self-justification. Ideally, I should show the students my commentary and get their reaction to it. Unfortunately, they are now beyond my grasp.

Creating a portfolio is an enormous undertaking. I do a little each day, and by the end of the term I have a substantial document. My professional self! Or is it just one of the many professional personas that I draw on each day? My sense of satisfaction evaporates as I realize that the portfolio is never complete, that, although it is the end of semester and I can pause to draw breath professionally, this thing will grow beside me as long as I teach.

WHAT TO INCLUDE?

What can be included in a teaching portfolio? In terms of the portfolio's contents, we see three main thematic categories: documents related to our actual teaching duties, to our professional development, and to our administrative responsibilities. The question "What does this document tell me and other readers about my teaching and learning?" can be helpful in deciding what to include in a teaching portfolio.

Maureen McLaughlin and MaryEllen Vogt (1996) describe five sorts of content that could be included in teaching portfolios: educational philosophy, professional development, curriculum and instruction, student growth, and contributions to school and community.

In terms of what a preservice teacher's portfolio might contain, Karen Johnson (1996a, 12) has identified four types of documentation:

1. **artifacts**, which are produced during the normal course work of the teacher education program;

2. **reproductions**, which relate to typical events in the work of preservice teachers that are not captured in artifacts;

3. **attestations** about the work of the novice teacher prepared by someone else; and

4. **productions**, which are prepared especially for the portfolio.

Although Johnson's list was prepared with preservice teachers in mind, these categories can certainly be used by inservice teachers as well.

In cases in which teaching portfolios are institutionalized as part of the evaluation process, teachers may not have sufficient input into decisions taken regarding the contents of their portfolios. This situation can lead to teachers being presented with a shopping list of items that they are expected to compile, often in an insufficient period of time. (Andy's commentary in the Teachers'

Voices section below deals with this issue.) The suggestions we present here are not, therefore, meant to be an example of an externally imposed list. Rather, they are meant to give teachers some ideas about the breadth of items to consider including. The list of examples is certainly not definitive and would need to be adapted and modified to suit particular contexts, including the intended use and audience for the portfolio. With these caveats in mind, here is our list:

Your teaching philosophy: What you believe teaching and learning are, how they are best achieved, and what factors enhance or inhibit these processes.

Details of courses taught: General course descriptions, week-by-week syllabi, reading lists, assignments, documentation of your assessment procedures.

Peer observation notes: Pre-, during, and postobservation notes, in both roles (as the observer and the teacher being observed).

Journal entries: Accounts both of lessons that went well and "as expected" and those lessons in which unexpected events occurred.

Video recordings: Of your teaching, possibly accompanied by your own observational notes made while viewing the tape(s).

Feedback from learners: Mid-course and end-of-course (institution-required and self-designed) evaluation instruments and results.

Examples of learners' work: From courses you've taught, with your comments and responses on the work.

Teaching materials produced: Handouts, worksheets, outlines, and tests, as well as commercially produced materials that you have adapted.

Any professional items you have written: A range of documents from published journal articles to training manuals to pieces written for in-house newsletters.

Teaching/learning presentations: Records of workshops or conference presentations you have given, from major international events to in-house sessions.

Conferences attended: Summaries of what you learned as a participant at professional conferences and workshops.

Committee work: Aims of (selected) committees, with a description of your particular roles and responsibilities.

Additional support: The "above and beyond the call of duty" section, documenting the main additional support you've provided to students, parents, clubs, colleagues, novice teachers, etc.

Teaching portfolios usually begin with a statement of the compiler's teaching philosophy. This section is an account of what you believe teaching and learning are, how they are best achieved, and what factors enhance or inhibit these processes. It is also a record of thoughts and feelings as well as an account of specific approaches, methods, and techniques. The teaching philosophy is usually the first part of the portfolio, since everything else that follows is shaped by these beliefs.

The section on courses taught can include general course descriptions, more detailed week-by-week syllabi, reading lists, assignments, and assessment procedures. Changes made to the contents and structure of courses can serve as signs of professional development. Even small changes are an indication that the teacher is putting into effect new ideas or feedback received from learners and colleagues. Any changes made can be accompanied by a brief account of the reasons for those changes. Similarly, if no changes have been made, include an account of why that is so.

As with all the approaches to professional development, one key purpose of compiling a portfolio is to facilitate our development and lifelong learning as teachers. For a portfolio to show this growth, most of the items included will need to be accompanied by a descriptive, narrative, or explanatory account, in the form of a cover note or introduction to each section. Such accounts will be particularly useful in highlighting any changes in the approaches, methods, or techniques we use, as well as any changes in materials, activities, and tasks, because they provide evidence of both our recollections and our interpretations. Since such changes occur at the levels of attitude and awareness, as well as at the knowledge and skills level, these commentaries can make explicit those changes that are not so visible to the reader.

Some teachers may adopt an "If it ain't broke, don't fix it" approach to teaching, perhaps based on knowledge and experience that have led them to believe that they have tried and tested most of the teaching options available and do not wish to make any changes at this time. In this case, the commentaries can present reasons for a conscious, informed choice not to change in one or more areas.

12.1 *YOUR OWN PORTFOLIO*

What would you put in your own teaching portfolio for each of the following: artifacts, reproductions, attestations, and productions (Johnson, 1996a)? Consider Johnson's four categories along with the three macro-categories of content suggested here. What materials would you want to include in your portfolio materials to represent each of these cells?

	Teaching Duties	Professional Development	Administrative Responsibilities
Artifacts			
Reproductions			
Attestations			
Productions			

If you have a file cabinet or a box of materials related to your recent teaching and/or administrative responsibilities, it may be useful for you to look at those materials in terms of what items you already have that would be suitable to include in your teaching portfolio. The grid provided above may help you identify possible items for inclusion.

PROBLEMS WITH TEACHING PORTFOLIOS

As with all approaches to professional development, there are limitations and potential problems to be overcome in creating a teaching portfolio. Vogt, McLaughlin, and Ruddell (1993, 76) found that a small proportion of secondary school student teachers expressed negative feelings about compiling portfolios. For example, one teacher complained that it was "annoying that I had to prove my knowledge and come up with a way of proving it" (ibid.). Others reported a balanced view of the problems and benefits, for example, "Portfolio goals were difficult to conceptualize and complete. Yet completion definitely brought me positive, even cathartic, insights" (ibid.).

This negativity relates to the point above about the developmental versus judgmental difference, which may lead to teachers feeling that they have not had enough opportunity to shape the evaluative process of which their portfolios are an essential part. They might then feel understandable resistance, and even resentment, at the way they view the process as being "done to them" rather than "done with them." This is why teachers' input is so important, in avoiding such negative reactions.

One of the biggest problems in developing a teaching portfolio is time. It should be clear by now that compiling a portfolio is not quick or easy. In fact, Green and Smyser (1996, 114) recommend that "a timeline of *at least three years* [emphasis added] should be allowed for complete implementation" of teaching portfolios within an organization, and one year for developing an individual teacher's portfolio.

Concerns about time requirements generally go hand-in-hand with the use of resources, and teaching portfolios are no exception. Some teachers may, understandably, feel that there is already too much paperwork, and may be reluctant to add to the volumes of already growing documentation.

Finally, some teachers feel that paper is flat, but teaching and learning are three-dimensional events, and therefore a portfolio can do little more than present an edited view of teaching rather than the complete picture. This objection also raises the issue of selection. The portfolio cannot, of course, contain every shred of documentation from all our teaching activities, so it must be a collection of selected examples. But some questions remain: Who will choose these examples, and who will decide, using what criteria, whether and how typical these examples are?

What can be done to minimize the problems? Many potential reservations about teaching portfolios can be addressed by ensuring that we as teachers have ample opportunities for input, so that the portfolio's purpose and contents are negotiated and agreed upon with the administration in advance. If portfolios are to be used as part of an evaluation system, such input should occur in at least two key stages: (1) determining the content and evaluative criteria, and (2) selecting and compiling the materials to be included. Our position is that teachers should have a major say in the former and total control over the latter.

Trying out the portfolio process on a small scale may be helpful. If students' portfolios are already being used in an institution, these could be viewed as a basis for discussion, as well as motivation for us as teachers and administrators to "practice what we preach." Or teachers who work with various courses could develop a first portfolio related to a particular class, level, or course.

Portfolio compilation can be carried out collaboratively, as advocated by Green and Smyser (1996, 20), who state that "the entire process of preparing a teaching portfolio should be undertaken with a peer mentor." The main role of the peer mentor in this approach is to talk with and offer advice to the teacher compiling the portfolio.

ANDY'S FIRST PORTFOLIO

Andy Curtis

Great. Just what we need. More paperwork. It is possible that the greatest challenge to the Modern Academic is finding the time to teach. Teach well. Not just that stuff that comes in between research papers and the fight for tenure. The Real Thing. So I really did not welcome the announcement that we all had to compile portfolios, because they were good for us. No explanation of why or how. "You will compile a portfolio," said our Personnel Department. "Great idea," said our Head of Department. "Do you people have any idea of the amount of work something like this involves?" I thought. I guess that's what happens when a basically good idea gets hijacked by the Powers That Be. Cue the Institutionalized Portfolio.

Growth and development driven by administrative imperative. Interpreted for us. Arranged for us. How many sections. The contents of each section. How much, how many items to include per section, what to include. Notice anything missing? The Why. How come they create a 10-section portfolio, the rationale for which is given (endlessly) as being the importance of Good Teaching, then forget to ask us to include a section on our Teaching Philosophy?

That's why I now do workshops on teaching portfolios. Because it gives me the chance to say to the teachers in the audience, "Look, if you don't get together and tell them what you feel, think, and believe should go into this thing—so that this will actually be of some real use to you—then they'll tell you." The "them" and "they" being all those people who haven't been near a classroom since I was learning to walk, telling me what would be good for me as a developing teacher. Yeah, right.

Empowerment had already become one of those cliché, buzz-words-for-today, especially when applied to teaching and learning. Portfolios as Empowerment. Catchy but not true, unless the teacher-compiler shapes the what and how of the portfolio. Contract-renewal, possibility of tenure, instruments of evaluation and assessment. That's what it feels like the Powers That Be were thinking of when they made us do this.

No consultation. No explanation. That's the big problem with the hijack. "Please go shopping. Select the following items from your professional persona and present them as soon as possible." We can then end up with portfolios as manufactured and misleading (mis)representations of our professional selves. How not to help teachers to learn.

I am the one there in the classroom every day. Who are they to tell me what is representative of who I am as a teacher?

You know the way we learn to turn disadvantageous situations to our benefit? Well, that's how I approached the institutionalized portfolio. For example, all those times my EFL students turned up at 5 PM on a Friday evening wanting someone to read and give feedback by the following Monday on a 20-page report written in English. So finally there is somewhere for me to officially record all that stuff. Service Above and Beyond the Call of Duty. Recorded. Which means, for one, that the administration cannot ignore it quite so easily.

Such a damning indictment of the institutionalized portfolio. Anything to recommend it? Yes. Surprisingly, yes. I've got the first portfolio I compiled—was made to compile—here in front of me, as I write this. It's a beauty. There's all this good stuff in there—for example, heartfelt thank-you notes, letters and cards from students and colleagues. My whole professional self, laid out, page by page, section by section. Even without the Powers That Be rating and ranking my portfolio, it's still scary.

All that resentment about not having been consulted on yet another thing that was supposedly good for us. I would never have imagined that something I felt so negative about being made to do could in any way be of some use to me.

In spite of all the annoyances, putting it all together made me ask a lot of questions. What do *teaching* and *learning* mean for me? I look at the page, thinking, "Is that really an accurate portrayal of me? And if it isn't, why do I want to include it? How much is my portfolio a representation of my professional self as I would like to be, rather than as I actually am?" Documentation legitimizing Idealization. Even more catchy.

My years as a hospital biochemist taught me that medical doctors can sometimes make the worst patients. So has my time teaching and learning in schools, colleges, and universities shown me that teachers can sometimes make the worst learners. But, in spite of the way in which it was done *to* us rather than *with* us, I did learn a lot from putting my first portfolio together. All kinds of things about myself as a person, as well as myself as a teacher. Lots of big questions raised that I'm not sure I'm willing or able to fully address and confront yet. But I'll get there. In time.

12.2 *More About Your Own Portfolio*

Imagine that you are a new teacher just completing your first two years of service in a particular program. Or perhaps you are a more experienced teacher who has recently begun teaching in a new program. Please imagine further that you are now about to be evaluated to determine whether you are to be retained and promoted. How would you react to the following?

Memo to: Teachers in line for retention/ promotion decisions
From: Your headmaster/dean/coordinator/department chair
Re: The promotion process

Based on the outcomes of the recent discussions between the Faculty Evaluation Committee and the administration, it has been determined that retention and promotion decisions for faculty members will be based on the model of portfolio assessment.

It is your responsibility, as a teacher scheduled for review, to produce such a portfolio and submit it to me within one month of receipt of this memo. If you have any questions about what should be included in the portfolio or how it will be evaluated, please feel free to contact me.

---

1. What questions would you have for this administrator about the expected contents of your portfolio?

2. What questions would you have for this administrator about the process of compiling your portfolio (e.g., the time constraints)?

3. What questions would you have about the criteria that would be used to evaluate your portfolio?

Or, taking a more proactive stance, you could address these issues this way instead:

4. Given your experience as a teacher, what items (both in terms of categories of submission and particular examples) would you want to include in your portfolio?

5. Given your experiences as a teacher and as a learner, what processes would you want to incorporate in compiling your portfolio?

6. Given your experiences as both a teacher and a learner, by what criteria would you want your portfolio to be evaluated?

(This task is based on Bailey, 1998a, 223–224.)

KATHI'S RESPONSE

Kathi Bailey

Okay, David and Andy. As it turns out, I too must compile a teaching portfolio. Mine is a case of what Andy is calling "The Institutionalized Portfolio," but I seem to have more of the freedom and self-determination that David described as part of his experience. And fortunately, I have some lead time, since my portfolio doesn't need to be submitted for about a year. So I'm trying to begin now to decide what it will contain, to choose the items that will create my collage. There are some things I already have (drafts of my written work in progress, some testimonials from students and colleagues, programs of conferences at which I have given talks, and so on), and there are other things that I must produce.

So I am trying to use your experiences and the literature review in this chapter to guide me in beginning to create my own teaching portfolio. Since I will be creating this portfolio as part of an evaluation process, I especially liked one suggestion, the idea from James Stronge (1997, 195) that portfolios "should be structured around sound professional content standards and individual schools' goals." Here at the Monterey Institute of International Studies, teachers are evaluated on the basis of four criteria: (1) effectiveness as a teacher, (2) research and scholarship, (3) professional stature, and (4) service to the institute and the community.

Now I am thinking about having one subsection of my teaching portfolio devoted to each of these categories. I do not know yet whether using these categories, and therefore trying to align my teaching portfolio to the administration's assessment goals, will bastardize the process. But I feel that these evaluative categories give some shape to the kinds of things I will want to include. (I will create categories for my teaching philosophy and my own professional development as well.)

Your advice has already begun to influence me, in terms of what documentation (especially *artifacts* and *attestations*, in Karen Johnson's terms) I am saving. Andy, I no longer routinely toss out thank-you notes or acknowledgments, in case I want to include them in my portfolio. And David, what you wrote has made me think more closely about how I will respond to negative input from my students.

I cannot honestly say that I am looking forward to compiling my teaching portfolio. It sounds like a lot of work, and I am worried about where I'll find the time. On the other hand, I do think that my portfolio will show the administration more of what I really do than the previously required evaluation documents (a "Faculty Activities Report" with preset categories to fill out) ever did. I wonder what I will learn about my own teaching in the process.

This chapter is near the end of this book because portfolios can include so many different sorts of evidence about teachers' professional development. We hope that the material covered in earlier chapters has given you both ideas and experiences that will sustain the compilation of your own teaching portfolio. We also hope the following tasks and reading ideas will promote your thinking on this topic.

1. Some of the ideas in this chapter may be appropriate for your situation, and some may not be. Skim through the chapter again, noting your reactions to our suggestions. You may find it helpful to record those reactions, for instance by drawing a smiling face or a frowning face in the margin, or by putting a plus "+," minus "–," or question mark "?" next to the text.

   Look at the instances where you have recorded a frowning face or a "?" or a minus "–" as a response. What common patterns, if any, cut across those suggestions that you found questionable? If you compare your reactions with those of a classmate or colleague who is also reading this book, what similarities and/or differences do you find?

2. Having found some existing items you can use in your teaching portfolio, you can now see what elements are missing. For example, Kathi realized from reading David's and Andy's accounts that she needed to write her teaching philosophy (a *production*, in Johnson's [1996a] terms). List three or more items that you do not currently have but would like to include in your portfolio. Here is Kathi's list:

   A. I need to write my teaching philosophy. Just realizing that I need to do so has made me think about my philosophy quite a bit.

   B. Both this semester and last semester, I participated in one-hour conference calls with a colleague and his students. They are using a book I co-edited in a class he's teaching. Why did he ask me to do this? What did the students gain from it? Should I do it again? I will ask him to talk with me about these questions.

   C. Since I am working with graduate students, a fair amount of my teaching (and perhaps some of my most effective teaching) happens in one-on-one office hour discussions. To me it feels as if these meetings are half my life, but they never figure in the evaluation of me-the-teacher. I'd like to examine and document this one-on-one teaching in my portfolio.

3. Do you know of a teacher who has already compiled a teaching portfolio? If so, ask that person if you can read the portfolio and then discuss its development with him or her. If you do have this opportunity, it may be informative to compare that person's perspectives with those recorded in this chapter.

4. If you work in or have access to a context in which students produce portfolios, ask the students for their advice about compiling your teaching portfolio. Try to get them to comment on both the process

and the product. Again, it may be helpful to compare the students' ideas with those presented in this chapter.

5. Imagine you are asked to be a mentor for two younger colleagues who are preparing their first teaching portfolios. How would you help them? What would you look for in their portfolio drafts? What personal and professional qualities would you bring to the task? What would you expect to learn about teaching and learning in the process?

Suggested Readings

We recommend the brief article by James Dean Brown and Kate Wolfe-Quintero (1997) entitled "Teacher Portfolios in Evaluation: A Great Idea or a Waste of Time?" It contains many practical suggestions for teachers developing portfolios.

Karen E. Johnson's (1996a) article about portfolios in preservice teacher education, discussed in a Frameworks section above, is very accessible and interesting. Her ideas are applicable to professional development purposes of experienced teachers as well. See also Curtis (2000).

We recommend *The Teacher Portfolio: A Strategy for Professional Development and Evaluation* by James E. Green and Sheryl O'Sullivan Smyser (1996). This book is aimed at teachers working in elementary and secondary schools, but most of the ideas are applicable in many teaching contexts. The book is based on the following themes: introduction, influences, instruction, individualization, and integration. The chapters use case studies of three teachers' portfolios.

A similar (though briefer) treatment can be found in Linda Van Wagenen and K. Michael Hibbard's (1998) article entitled "Building Teacher Portfolios." See also Kenneth Wolf's (1996) article, "Developing an Effective Teaching Portfolio."

Lía Kamhi-Stein and José Galvan (1997) have described a teacher education program in Los Angeles that used a reflective teaching model in working with Egyptian EFL teachers and local teachers. They discuss four principles for teacher development, one of which focuses on the group portfolio.

Books on teaching portfolios are now available in general education. One that you may find useful is *How To Develop a Professional Portfolio: A Manual for Teachers* by Dorothy Campbell, Pamela Bondi Cignetti, Beverly J. Melenyzer, Diane Hood Nettles, and Richard M. Wyman (1997).

There are also a number of websites that provide helpful input about teaching portfolios. These are a few of the websites you may find to be useful:

1. **WestEd**: http://www.wested.org

2. **National Board for Professional Teaching Standards:** http://www.nbpt.org

3. **Association for Supervision and Curriculum Development:** http://www.ascd.org

4. **Interstate New Teacher Assessment and Support Consortium:** http://www.ccsso.org

13

CONCLUSION: THE HEART OF THE PARADOX

I intend to go on teaching as long as I feel I can learn from my students and those around me. If I feel too self-confident...that there is nothing for me to learn, this will be my last moment as a teacher. In other words, as long as I feel that there is so much for me to learn, and I am so uncertain of myself, and I always have more...and I always have to...do things differently...and be frustrated and uncertain, I will continue (R., an expert teacher, translated from Hebrew and quoted in Olshtain and Kupferberg, 1998, 198).

In this book, we have argued the case for professional development as a career-long endeavor. We have described several procedures through which teachers can take direct control of their own professional development. We have also tried to illustrate ways in which the various approaches we've described can connect theory, research, and practice. We hope the Frameworks, Investigations, and Teachers' Voices sections have shown that professional development opportunities do not have to be externally structured. While we value traditional venues for professional development, such as conferences, workshops, and formal courses of study, we have chosen to present a view of professional development that is embedded in our own practice as language teachers.

In Chapter 1, Andy spoke of the importance of choice, trust, and honesty, mutuality and reciprocity, and a developmental rather than judgmental attitude toward practice. Underlying each of these concepts is the notion of autonomy. "Two features," van Lier claims (1996, 12), "are central to autonomy: choice and responsibility." In this book we have extended the concepts of autonomy and control to the area of professional development. People who have no autonomy or control over what they do and are not responsible for how they do it can hardly claim to be professionals. As we indicated earlier in this volume, no one else can make a teacher develop. Just as, ultimately, language students must do the learning for themselves, so too, if we are to develop professionally, we teachers have to do the developing for ourselves. We hope the ideas, perspectives, and procedures presented in this book will facilitate that process for you.

13.1 *WHERE DO YOU STAND?*

In Chapter 3, we cite Zeichner and Liston, who argue that a reflective teacher "questions the assumptions and values that he or she brings to teaching"

(1993, 11). One of the assumptions underpinning this book is that career-long development is a good thing. What do you think? Jot down three reasons for embracing and affirming this assumption. Next write down three possible reasons for rejecting this assumption. How would you respond to a teacher who questioned the assumption that lifelong professional development is a good thing?

We also believe that ongoing professional development is our own responsibility. As teachers, we cannot always rely on our school districts or our departments to provide professional development opportunities for us, though we certainly feel that appropriate avenues for growth should be available in our work contexts. Where do you stand on this issue after reading this book? It may be valuable, if you are working with a group of classmates or colleagues, to stage a small debate based on the following assumption:

BE IT RESOLVED:

Ongoing professional development is the responsibility of individual language teachers, rather than the schools, programs, or universities for which they work.

For Lange see p. 4 and for Freeman see pp. 23–24.

In Chapter 1, we cited Dale Lange (1990), who defined professional development in terms of intellectual, experiential, and attitudinal growth. In Chapter 2 we saw Freeman (1989a) use the construct of *attitude* to connect the other three key constituents of teaching: *awareness, knowledge,* and *skills* (see Figure 2.1, p. 23). What are the connection(s) between Lange's ideas and Freeman's?

DAVID'S REFLECTIONS

In the following Teachers' Voices section, David uses Freeman's and Lange's concepts to reflect on the professional growth that he experienced when he moved from Australia and took up a new teaching position in Hong Kong.

David Nunan

As we were working on the draft of this book, I was struck by similarities in the ways that Dale Lange and Donald Freeman write about teaching and professional development. It seemed to me that Freeman's *knowledge* constituent equated to Lange's intellectual dimension, his *skills* component parallels Lange's experiential dimension, and the *attitude* constituent was basically the same as Lange's attitudinal dimension.

I got to thinking about the opportunities for professional growth that we encounter when we move into a new job, and reflected on the ways in which I changed when I took up my teaching position in Hong Kong. It was relatively easy for me to list the new knowledge and the skills I had gained. For example, in terms of knowledge, I learned about the common phonological problems of Cantonese L1 learners speaking English. I also learned about the sociocultural and educational backgrounds of my students, and the ways in which their backgrounds influenced their approach to learning English. In the experiential/skills domain, I developed new techniques for encouraging oral interaction.

But when it came to identifying aspects of attitudinal change, I really struggled. This partly had to do with the fact that I was reluctant to reveal, even to myself, attitudes that I was uncomfortable with. (In terms of the Johari Window referred to in Chapter 2, I was struggling to move from the "hidden self" to the "secret self" quadrant, and, ultimately, to the "open self" quadrant.) Those attitudes that I did identify were largely negative. For example, in my academic essay writing course, I disliked giving feedback on students' drafts, because my feedback appeared to make very little difference to subsequent drafts. I began to work on this problem, and ultimately came up with a checklist of 10 key aspects of essay writing that caused problems for my students. These ranged from global concerns (e.g., "inappropriate academic style") to local or mechanical problems (such as "failure to follow referencing conventions"). Basing feedback on the checklist and training students to apply the checklist to their own writing led to a substantial improvement in most students' final drafts.

This experience caused me to see that in practice the intellectual/knowledge, experiential/skills, and attitudinal dimensions are not separate, but rather they interact with one another. In my case, the attitudinal change—my dislike of giving feedback—led to an opportunity for growth in the experiential domain. That is, I became more skilled at giving meaningful feedback on my students' written work.

13.2 *IDEAL, ACCEPTABLE, OR NOT APPROPRIATE*

The main professional development procedures discussed in this book are listed again below. Next to each item, put a plus "+," a check "✓," or a minus "−" to indicate whether you think that particular procedure would be ideal, acceptable, or not appropriate for you to use in pursuing your own professional development.

_____ Peer Observation   _____ Reflective Teaching

_____ Action Research   _____ Team Teaching

_____ Teaching Portfolios   _____ Self-awareness and Self-observation

_____ Teaching Journals   _____ Video for Professional Development

_____ Case Studies   _____ Language Learning Experiences

_____ Coaching   _____ Mentoring

Think about your likely role as a teacher five or ten years from now. How do you think the preferences you indicated above will change in that time period? (If you are an experienced teacher, you could also reflect on how your preferences have changed over the past decade.)

Now think about the three or four procedures above that are best suited for you in your current situation. List them in the blanks of a grid like the one below. Then in each cell of the grid, put a "+," a "✓," or a "–" to indicate how valuable you think that particular procedure would be for you in developing your awareness, your attitudes, your knowledge, and your skills.

Procedure	Awareness	Attitudes	Knowledge	Skills
1. _____				
2. _____				
3. _____				
4. _____				

We suggest that you share your ideas with your colleagues or classmates since it is possible that different teachers will choose various procedures, and also that they will judge those procedures as offering different benefits.

DIMENSIONS OF ACTIVITY AND COLLABORATION

The procedures described in this book can be classified in various ways. Here, they are conceptualized in terms of two dimensions: individual/collaborative, and observing/doing. The combinations of these constructs represent continua, rather than discrete categories. As we noted in Chapter 1, almost any professional *development* technique can have a collaborative dimension. Let us return to a point from Julian Edge (1992, 4), which we quoted in Chapter 1:

> I want to investigate and assess my own teaching. I can't do that without understanding it better, and I can't understand it on my own. Here, we are close to the heart of the paradox. When I use the word development, I always mean self-development. But that can't be done in isolation. Self-development needs other people: colleagues and students. By cooperating with others, we can come to understand better our own experiences and opinions.

So, for example, teaching journals, which are near the individual end of the individual/collaborative continuum, can be made more collaborative. For instance, we can get colleagues to read and comment on our journals (Brock et al., 1992), or journals can even be collaboratively written (Cole et al., 1998).

The other continuum we have identified is that of observing/doing. Thus, self- and peer-observation can involve some forms of action, although they may be less action-oriented than, say, writing case studies or conducting action research. Which of these techniques, or combinations of techniques, you choose to work with will depend on your own teaching context and the substantive areas you wish to develop, as well as on your teaching style and personality. Although we have argued the benefits of collaboration, we realize that some people prefer to work alone. Similarly, some teachers are more action-oriented while others prefer to adopt a watching role.

Figure 13.1 presents the individual/collaborative continuum and the observing/doing continuum in an overlapping arrangement, with the various professional development procedures we've discussed arrayed on the resulting display. For example, teaching journals are typically more individual than collaborative, while peer observation is clearly collaborative and closer to observing than doing.

Figure 13.1: Professional Development Activities (Relative to Individual Versus Collaborative Efforts and Observing Versus Doing)

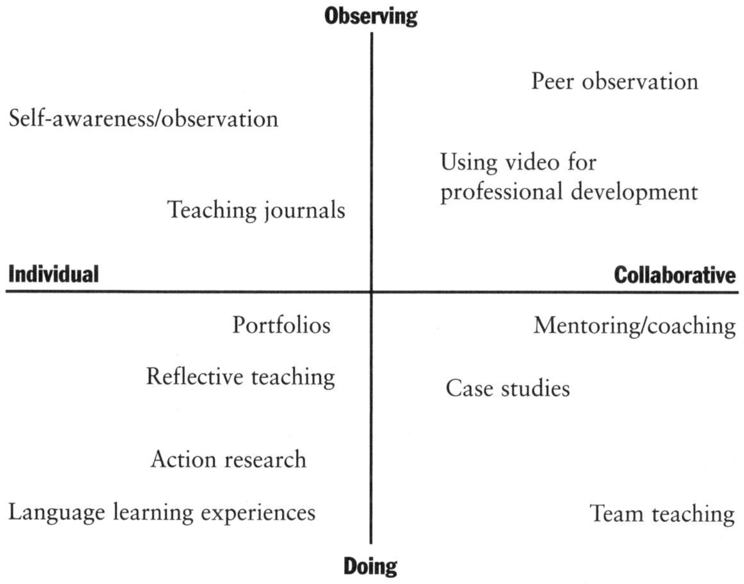

Observing

Self-awareness/observation

Peer observation

Using video for professional development

Teaching journals

Individual   **Collaborative**

Portfolios   Mentoring/coaching

Reflective teaching

Case studies

Action research

Language learning experiences   Team teaching

Doing

Of course, these four categories are not as tight as they appear. Many of these approaches can be made more or less collaborative, and more or less active, depending on your particular situation and your preferences.

While it could be argued that development entails action, we do not necessarily go along with this view. Changes in attitude and awareness (which may lead to increased understanding) can result from observation and reflection. It is also possible, as Donald Freeman (1989a, 38) notes, that reflection and introspection can result in an affirmation of current practice, that "change does not necessarily mean doing something differently...." For example, in Chapter 4, we presented an instance of affirmation on the part of Deborah, a novice teacher, who said, "I was still a beginner but for that class, I felt like a tennis player" (Numrich, 1986, 149).

In Chapter 1 we stated that the changes that surround us are a good reason to engage in professional development activities. In the following Teachers' Voices section, Andy talks about his ideas regarding change.

ANDY TALKS ABOUT CHANGE

Andy Curtis

Change is constant. Not only that, it's often difficult and can be very hard to predict, both its coming and its aftermath. Resorting to models and metaphors from my previous professional incarnation as a clinical biochemist, change is not only constant and difficult, but also essential. No living system, no organic entity can exist without it. In the absence of any change, there is no growth. Without growth, there is, at best, stagnation, and at worst, death. Change and growth in our professional lives, as in life itself, are, for better and for worse, intimately and inextricably intertwined (Curtis, 1999c).

One thing that makes change so difficult, apart from its very constancy, is that it involves uncertainty and risk. As human beings, we would not have been able to populate this entire planet if we had not learned to avoid risk as much as possible. If the first cave dwellers who discovered fire had not also very quickly learned that this stuff will burn your skin off if you're not careful, then that particular discovery, far from being the beginning of a new age in mankind's development, could have been the end of our particular species. So avoidance of risk makes good biological sense.

On the walk to school, we tend to step out into a familiar road, when crossing it, at the same point every day, sometimes for years. Next time you're there, consider moving a few meters to the right or left of your usual spot. You may well get a bit of a buzz as you step off the curb this time. Stepping into the unknown, even in the smallest way, is not generally how humans have been programmed to behave. Changing the way we have gotten used to teaching and learning involves unknowns, and is therefore risky. But in one of Nature's many ironies, living systems cannot grow, develop, and adapt to their changing environments without themselves changing.

At the risk of beating the biological metaphor to death, I do see classrooms as living entities, as they involve the same kind of almost incalculable, impossible-to-predict-with-certainty interactions that characterize not only living organisms, but also communities of living entities. So for us as language teachers, bringing about planned change in our professional environments is difficult but necessary. And if classrooms can be seen as organic environments, then so too can the whole school.

13.3 *YOUR ACTION PLAN*

The following list, which has been adapted from Richards (1990, 129–130), was first mentioned in Chapter 2. It is included here as an Investigation to encourage you to synthesize the material presented in this book as well as to develop an action plan to apply the ideas to your own practice. If possible, you should carry out the procedure collaboratively with your colleagues or fellow students.

1. Brainstorm aspects of your teaching that you would be interested in learning more about.

2. Narrow your choices to those that seem most important to you.

3. Develop an action plan to address an issue that is important to you.

4. Try to incorporate several of the procedures described in this book.

5. List the resources you will need to enact your plan.

6. Decide upon a time frame for carrying out your goals.

For example, your issue might be how to encourage greater participation by the more passive members of your class. You could begin by observing and documenting instances of participation on an observation sheet, supplemented perhaps by a teaching journal. Alternatively, you could tape-record your lesson, and count the students' verbal turns. This step could provide the basis for writing a number of brief case studies focused on reluctant participants which, in turn, could lead to an action research project designed to test strategies for encouraging greater participation. You might then decide you will need to get a copy of *The Action Research Planner* (Kemmis and McTaggart, 1988) and to enlist the help of a colleague to do some peer observations of your teaching. The time frame might be based upon the particular units of your textbook or the weeks of the semester—whatever fits with your particular situation.

INTER-RELATING SUBSYSTEMS

Change can be either "top-down" or "bottom-up" in terms of its origin. *Top-down changes* are initiated by those at the top of the organizational chart. These are typically administrators rather than teachers (the people Andy has called "the Powers That Be" in previous chapters). *Bottom-up changes* are those initiated at the "grassroots" level (e.g., by teachers or students in language programs). Our contention throughout this book has been that professional development entails change. Bottom-up changes may occur at the level of awareness, attitude, skills, or knowledge (or any combination of these). But professional development can also occur as a result of top-down changes (e.g., all three of us authors were required to compile portfolios, by administrative decree).

Throughout this book, we have been discussing professional development activities which we as teachers can do on our own—hence the subtitle, *The Self as Source*. Yet we have also tried to acknowledge that professional development is influenced by situational variables, because language teaching and learning occur in social contexts, and factors inherent in those contexts impinge upon teachers' work. The influence of contextual variables has been discussed by Chris Kennedy (1988, 332), who offers the following diagram:

Figure 13.2 The Hierarchy of Inter-Relating Subsystems in Which an Innovation Has to Operate

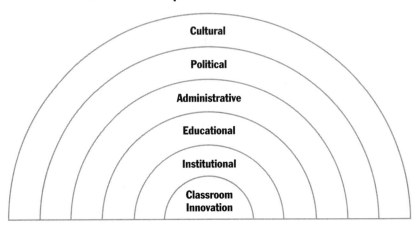

This figure portrays the idea that classroom innovations are surrounded by institutional, educational, administrative, political, and cultural variables that influence teachers' abilities to bring about positive and lasting changes in their classrooms. Kennedy explains his diagram as follows (ibid.):

> The influence and impact and the relative weighting of the circles will no doubt vary from situation to situation but their order of influence should be generalizable. Thus the cultural system is assumed to be the most powerful as it will influence both political and administrative structures and behavior.

> These in turn will produce a particular educational system reflecting the values and beliefs of the society in question, a system which must be taken into account when innovating within an institution and ultimately in the classroom.

While Kennedy was writing primarily about curricular innovations in programs and schools, his model is applicable to individual teacher development too.

13.4 *Factors Promoting or Hindering Change*

If you are teaching now (or have had teaching experience), think about a change you tried to make in your own classroom (whether you were successful or unsuccessful). What were the factors (institutional, educational, administrative, political, and/or cultural) that promoted or hindered the change you wanted to make? Use Kennedy's model, reprinted as Figure 13.2, to help you structure your analysis.

What does Kennedy's model remind you of? Various teachers have described it as a rainbow, an igloo, half a target, an onion, or part of the image of ripples on a pond. (In fact, when we asked Chris Kennedy, he said that the model started out as concentric circles, like a target or successive ripples, but that he'd been forced to cut it in half due to space constraints in the journal where he published his article.) Does your thinking about the model change if you call it a rainbow, an onion, an igloo, or a target?

METAPHORS WE TEACH BY

In an insightful and entertaining book, Lakoff and Johnson (1980) explore the metaphors we live by. We have adapted their phrase to refer to the metaphoric uses of language that have cropped up as we have written about professional development.

A metaphor is a figure of speech in which an entity, experience, or state of affairs is described in terms of something else. In other words, a metaphor is a parallel or an analogy. Why is it that metaphors are so pervasive in our lives? Is it that some aspects of experience are so complex and abstract that we need to fall back on metaphors as a shorthand way of conveying our experiences to others? (Note the metaphoric use of language in the preceding sentence—"fall back on" and "shorthand".)

As we reviewed the manuscript of this book as a dress rehearsal for preparing this final chapter, we were struck by the fact that it is infused with metaphors, similes, and figurative language to describe the teaching experience. Teaching is referred to as an "egg carton profession" and team teachers are "learning to dance." Teachers doing diary studies "triangulate" their data and their journals are "tools." Reflective practitioners "open closed doors," while case studies are likened to "stories in the air."

As we asked ourselves why such metaphors are so pervasive, we brainstormed several possibilities. Maybe we're lazy—just as formulaic utterances provide communicative shortcuts for language learners, so do metaphors for us. Or we're not lazy, but metaphors are efficient in terms of their evocative nature. (If we share a common understanding of "dress rehearsal," then in using the phrase, we have communicated a great deal.) And because these labels are so rich, they add visual and dramatic dimensions to what might otherwise be abstract concepts and ideas. As a result, metaphoric uses of language make ideas more concrete and therefore more memorable.

13.5 *THE POWER OF METAPHORS*

Think about the metaphors we've used in this book (without looking back through the pages). Write down three or four such images (other than those printed above) that you can recall from memory.

> Now turn back, skimming through the pages, and select your five favorite metaphors. Think about why they are powerful for you, and how they illuminate the teaching and learning process for you. Do the ones you selected as your favorites include those that you recalled without looking back?

CLOSING COMMENTS

The subtitle for this book, *Self as Source,* has both a literal and a metaphorical meaning. In literal terms, the expression refers to the fact that we discover opportunities for professional development and renewal in our own experiences and working contexts. Metaphorically, the word *source* evokes for us powerful images of fountains, springs, and streams that nourish and sustain growth and development.

Professional development is not something that just happens: It must be actively pursued. We also believe that, while taking courses and attending workshops are great ways to promote professional development, ultimately we as teachers must be our own sources of renewal and continuance. We hope that this book has provided you with many ideas for generating your own professional development opportunities and has also encouraged you to take active steps in that direction.

Investigations

13.6 *TASKS FOR DEVELOPMENT*

This last set of tasks is designed to help you move forward with whatever program of professional development you feel is appropriate for you. We believe that there are numerous useful approaches to professional development, many of which have been described in the foregoing chapters. We also believe that teachers should exercise choice and responsibility in pursuing professional development, and that many options can be used in combination.

1. Skim through the reference list for this book and pick three to five references that you could read as likely resources for your own program of professional development. You might choose to diversify your reading across several topics, or to focus on one particular approach to professional development (e.g., portfolios or teachers' journals). If you are working with a group, please share your selections and your reasons for them with your classmates or colleagues. You may find others who wish to pool resources with you.

2. Think about the various Frameworks, including the visual models, presented in this book. Choose two or three that seem to be particularly relevant to your situation. Explain to a colleague or a classmate (or articulate to yourself) why you felt they were relevant.

3. Next, choose a Framework (whether it is a model, a list, or a theoretical explanation) that you feel you could explain well to other teachers, using your own experiences as the source of illustrative data. Try to sketch an outline of a 20- to 30-minute presentation you could make to other teachers (or parents or administrators or future teachers), based on the received knowledge of the field (as represented in the Framework) and your own experiential knowledge.

4. We do not mean to suggest that published works by experts are the only viable source of frameworks and principles to guide our professional lives. Look back through your own professional development journal, or though the various responses you have made to the Investigations in this book. What are the principles you have articulated? What are the frameworks you have generated through your own reflection? These ideas can also be the basis for presentations you could give.

5. Complete the prompt below by putting a noun phrase in the first blank and completing the "because" clause in the second:

Professional development is like _____ **because**

_____

_____

Here are three examples:

Kathi: Professional development is like living in a never-ending story because the chapters blend into one another. As you are working on one area for improvement, other opportunities and areas open up for new exploration, like the old story of Scheherezade and the *Thousand and One Arabian Nights.*

David: Professional development is like detective work because it gives you tools to make sense of the mysteries of classroom life.

Andy: Professional development is like a journey, a long voyage, at the end of which we find ourselves back at the beginning, but with much more knowledge of the route and having had the trip of a lifetime, because professional development is about moving forward through a greater understanding of where we are now by reflecting on how we got to be here.

6. Here is the "final exam" for you based on all you've read about in this book and thought about as you did so. The "test" consists of two short answer essay questions, as well as one true/false statement (quoted again from Joachim Appel [1995, 134]):

FINAL EXAMINATION

1. What is professional development?

2. Why should language teachers bother with it?

3. True or False: "School is over, yet it is never over."

Figures and Tables

Appendix A
TRANSCRIPT OF A LESSON
(Reprinted from Nunan and Lamb, 1996, 254–276)

T: Well, good morning. Because this is the very first class that we're having, um, we're going to be doing some things this morning that involve exchanging personal information and talking about ourselves and describing ourselves. OK. And the first thing I'd like you to do—if you open your book on page 2. Open up to page 2, you'll see in the warm up section, the very first task asks you to think about the language you already know, and to think about how well you can do the things we're going to practice this morning. So what I'd like you to do is to take your pen or your pencil and look at each of these things that we're going to be practicing, and put a circle around the words "yes," or "a little," or "not yet. " Think about how well you can do these things. "Exchange personal information". OK? So, "My name is Derek. What's your name?" Can you do this very well, or a little bit, or not at all? Put a circle around the words that describe how well you can do these things. So one of the things we're going to practice this morning is "Exchange personal information." "My name is Derek. What's your name? Where are you from? I'm from Boston. You're from…?"

S: From Tokyo.

T: From Tokyo. Um. What about the next thing we're going to practice? To describe yourself and others? "I'm 23." Well, I'm not….

Ss: [Laughter.]

T: ….I'm 24.

Ss: [Laughter.]

T: Um, "I'm 23, I have dark hair." How well can you do that?   "Yes," "a little," or "no."

[Ss complete task, talking quietly among themselves.]

T: How well can you describe yourself?…OK? And, the third thing we're going to practice is "Introducing people." "This is Yoko."

Ss: [Laughter.]

S: That her name.

T: OK, just compare what you've written with the person you're working with. OK? With your partner. Just check what you've circled and compare. You all done the same thing or something different?

[T circulates and checks Ss' responses.]

T: So some people feel that they can exchange personal information, but they're not very sure about describing themselves and others. All right, before, before we actually, before I ask you to do some talking, I'm going to ask you to listen to somebody else talking. And you're going to hear a number of people talking, and something happens in the conversation. And the conversation takes place [points to book]… somewhere. Look at the pictures in task # 2. Can you see those pictures? What do you think is happening in those pictures? Can anybody guess what's happening? In those pictures? Where do you think those pictures are taking place?

S: At airport.

T: At an airport? OK. How do you know it's an airport? You're right, but how do you know? Because of the big, because of the big airplane in the background?

Ss: [Laughter.]

S: The sign of "arrival."

T: Arrivals. Yes. Arrivals. That gives us the clue. We can see some bags there as well. OK. Now I'm going to play this tape and you'll hear three short conversations, and after I've played the tape I'm going to ask you to give me some information. I want to know who's talking, and I want to know what's happened. OK?

TAPE:

A: Can I help you, Sir?
B: Yes. I lost my bag.
A: Where?
B: I don't know!
A: What was in it?
B: My passport, money, ticket, credit cards, driver's license—everything.

A: All right, now I'd just like to ask you some questions.
B: Certainly officer.
A: Last name?
B: Frota.
A: How do you spell that?
B: F-R-O-T-A

A: Are you Mike Frota?
B: That's right.
A: Good news, Mr. Frota. We've got your bag back for you.
B: Great! Where did you find it?
A: You left it in the men's restroom.

T: OK. How many people did you hear talking? How many different people?

S: Three

S: Four

T: Four different people. OK. Um, the conversation took place in an airport. What happened? What happened?

S: Lost bag.

T: The man lost his bag. Do you know the man's name?

Ss: Roul, Froul...?

T: Frota. That's his, that's his last name, that's his last name. Yes. Did you hear what his first name was? [Pause.] Never mind. OK. So he lost his bag. Why was he worried? What was in the bag?

Ss: Passport, passport, credit card.

T: OK. Passport, credit card, everything. And...did he get his bag back?

Ss: Yes. Yes.

T: Yes, he did. Yes, he did. Where did he leave it?

Ss: Men's room. Men's restroom. [Laughter.]

T: In the men's room. OK. One of the other things...in a minute we'll hear, we'll hear some more conversation from Mr. Frota, but before that we'll also in this unit we'll look at we'll listen to how people describe themselves—words for describing themselves. In the United States, when people describe themselves they talk about things like how big they are, the size, color of hair, color of eyes, but in different cultures, different culture use have different ways to describe themselves. What about in Japan? How do you describe yourself? How do people describe each other in Japan? Color of hair? [Laughter.] Color of eyes. [Laughter.]

Ss: No.

S: Hair style.

T: Hair style? Yeah? If you were describing a friend, or an interesting person you met, to your friends, how would you describe her? [er] Or him?

S: Tall.

T: So.

S: Tall.

T: OK.

S: How tall she is.

T: OK. Somebody told me Japanese people also describe each other by the shape of the nose. Is this true?

Ss: [Laughter.] No. No.

T: No? [laughs.]

S: Never do that.

T: You never do that? OK. Have a look at task 4 on page 3. You'll see some words. Two lists of words that're used for describing people. Just look through them, and just put a check mark next to the words you know as I read them through. [T reads list as Ss check words they know.] OK, just, just compare with your partner to see if there are any words that you didn't know there.

Ss: [Inaudible.]

T: Very difficult, eh? [Laughter.] OK, the next task, the next task is slightly more difficult. One of the things, er, we practice in this course … is … or some of the things we practice are learning strategies. And one of the learning strategies that will help you learn new words is the learning strategy of "classifying." Do you know what "classifying" means?

Ss: No, no.

T: Have you heard this word before?

Ss: No.

T: Classifying means putting things that are similar together in groups. OK? So if I said, er, I want all the girls to go down to that corner of the room, and all the boys to go into this corner of the room, I would be classifying the class according to their sex or their gender. What I'd like you to do now in task 5 is to classify some of the words from the list in task 4. OK? [Ss carry out task as T writes headings on board.]

T: Finished.

Ss: Yes.

T: OK. Someone like to call out the color words for me please.

S: Dark.

T: Yeah, interesting. Is "dark" a color?

Ss: [Inaudible.]

T: Is dark a color?

S: [Inaudible.]

T: Let's put it in anyway. [Writes on board.] OK. Next one?

Ss: White, white.

T: [Writes on board.] Next one?

Ss: Blue.

T: [Writes on board.] And?

Ss: Blond.

T: Blond. [Writes on board.] What about the "age" words?

S: Eld….

T: How do you say that word? How do you pronounce that word?

Ss: Elderly.

T: Next one?

Ss: [Inaudible.]

T: [Writes on board.] Next one?

Ss: Old.

T: [Writes on board] Next one?

Ss: Middle-aged.

T: [Writes on board.] And the last one?

Ss: Teenage.

T: [Writes on board.] OK. And the last list? Size. Big?

Ss: Short.

T: h-huh.

Ss: Tall.

T: Uh-huh.

Ss: Small.

T: Right. What's the difference between this word [points to "elderly"] and this word [points to "old"]? Elderly and old? Does anybody know the difference?

S: I know in Japanese.

T: You can't explain in Japanese, because I wouldn't understand.

Ss: [Laughter.]

T: If I said that, um, that Mr. Smith was elderly, but Mr. Jones was old, I think that probably I would imagine that old, someone who's old, is slightly older than someone who is elderly. Elderly also is slightly more polite. To say that someone is elderly it doesn't sound quite as, quite as very direct as if you say that somebody is old.... Although I'm not sure. I'd have to check with some other native speakers [Laughter]. How would you describe yourself? How would you describe yourself? I would say that I'm, well in my culture, I guess I'm short. I'm fairly short. I used to like living in Asia because I was very big there. I was tall 'cause most people in [Asia] are about that tall. [Gestures.]

Ss: [Laughter.]

T: I wouldn't say I was elderly. I guess I'm middle-aged. I used to have blond hair, but now it's gone a kind of dirty brown, and is going gray. OK. Over the page then. These are some of the things we're going to be practicing this morning. I'm going to ask you to listen to another conversation now. And I'm going to play the conversation three or four times. The first time, I just want you to listen and to check off the words in task 1 when you hear them. OK? Just listen for these words and I'm going to ask you if you actually hear these words, 'cause they may not all be on the tape. So the first time you listen I just want you to check off these words. Do you know the meaning of all these words? "last name," "first name," "address," "telephone number," "date of birth," "occupation," and "marital status." Do you know the meaning of all of those words?

S: What word is "occupation"?

T: Sorry?

S: What is "occupation"?

T: Occupation. Can anybody tell, explain what "occupation" is?

S: Work.

S: [Inaudible.]

T: Sorry?

Ss: [Inaudible.] Work.

T: Yes. What sort of job that someone does. What sort of job. Or what work that somebody does. What about "marital status"? Do you know that word? That phrase?

Ss: No, no.

T: That simply means are you married or single or divorced or widowed. OK. Do you have a husband or wife? Or are you single? Or are you divorced? So if somebody asks you your marital status. So if somebody asks you "What's your marital status?" You would say "I'm…? …single. I'm single." OK, let's listen to the next conversation.

TAPE:

A: All right, now I'd just like to get some information.

B: Certainly officer.

A: What's the date today? March, fifth, isn't it?

B: That's right.

A: OK, then, last name?

B: Frota.

A: How do you spell that?

B: F-R-O-T-A.

A: First name?

B: Mike.

A: What's your address, Mr. Frota?

B: I'm staying at the Settler's Guest House, 24 Smith Street, North Beach.

A: Telephone?

B: Let's see—712-3847.

A: Thanks. And what's your date of birth.

B: November eleventh, 1975.

A: OK. And what's your occupation?

B: I'm a student.

A: A student. Right. Now, you lost a bag.

B: Yes, a black travel bag.

T: Did you hear all the words on the list, or not?

Ss: No, no.

T: Did you hear "last name"?

Ss: Yes, yes.

T: Check off "last name"? "First name"?

Ss: Yes, yes.

T: "Address"?

Ss: Yes, yes.

T: "Telephone number"?

Ss: Yes, yes.

T: Did you? I didn't hear "telephone number." I didn't hear "telephone number."

S: Mmm?

T: Mmm.

S: Just "telephone."

T: Just "telephone." Very good. Yes. He doesn't say "telephone number," he says "telephone"?

Ss: Ahh.

T: Did you hear "date of birth"?

Ss: Yes, yes.

T: Did you hear "occupation"?

Ss: Yes, yes.

T: Did you hear "marital status"?

Ss: No, no.

T: No. Neither did I. OK. I'm going to play the conversation again, this time I want you to fill in the form in task 2. I want you to fill in the information as you hear it. [Plays the conversation again, pausing the tape at certain points, and replaying as students fill in the form.] Do you want me to, do you want me to play that again? Can you see where you put that information? The date. Can you see "date" on the form? It's in a strange place. Just listen again. [Replays tape.] OK. Did you hear that?

Ss: [Inaudible.]

T: Well, we'll check in a minute. Let's just listen, listen for the rest of the information. [Ss complete rest of task.]

T: Now, I want you to work with another student and compare your responses. [Students spend five minutes checking each other's work as the teacher circulates and checks.]

T: Now, someone who doesn't know Mike is meeting him, and she sent a postcard to Mike before she left, and she put in the postcard a description of herself, and also of him. If you look at task 3 you'll see the postcard and the message to Mike. Look through and with the person... with your partner,

I want you to put a circle around all of the words that describe the woman who's coming to meet him, and also the words that describe Mike. OK? [Students read postcard and identify description words.]

T: OK. Have you found any, any... [pauses and writes the following on the board].

Marcia: _____

Mike: _____

T: Finished.

Ss: Yes, yes.

T: OK. What words describe Marcia?

Ss: Twenty years old.

T: OK. [Writes on board.] What else?

Ss: Short, short.

T: Short.

S: Red hair.

T: [Writes on board.] Do any people in Japan have red hair?

S: [Inaudible.]

T: Sorry? In Japan, do people have red hair?

S: [Laughter.] No, no.

T: I saw somebody. I've seen some people with red hair, but I don't know if they, maybe they have it dyed red, to look different.

S: Yeah.

T: When I was in Tokyo, when I was in Tokyo last month, I saw some young people with red hair....

Ss: [Laughter.]

T: ...and I thought [pulls face].

Ss: [Laughter.]

T: How do you, how, how is how is Mike described?

Ss: Tall.

T: Tall. [Writes on board.]

Ss: Dark hair, dark hair, blue eyes, blue eyes. [T writes on board.]

T: OK. Turn over to page six. Mike has finally managed to leave the airport, he has his bag, and he goes to a party for new students.

TAPE:

A: Hello. Are you Mike?
B: Yes, I am. Sorry I'm late.
A: That's OK. I'm John.

B: Nice to meet you, John.

A: And this is Anna.

B: Hello, Anna—good to meet you.

C: Hi!

A: And this is Maggie.

B: Pleased to meet you, Maggie.

D: Hi, Mike—come and have a drink and tell us what happened to you.

B: Well, I lost my bag at the airport....

T: OK. What does John, how does John introduce Anna?

Ss: This is Anna.

T: This is Anna. This is Anna. And, what does Mike say to Anna?

S: [Inaudible.]

T: What does he say?

Ss: Good to meet you.

T: Good to meet you. Good to meet you. And then John says?

Ss: This is Maggie.

T: This is Maggie. This is Maggie. OK. So these are some of the ways that we can introduce ourselves and other people and what we say when we greet people. Have a look on page seven at task 4.

Extract from Students' Book Task 4: a) Groupwork. Read/discuss the following box.

HOW DO SINGLE MEN AND WOMEN MEET EACH OTHER?		
	% of men	% of women
Through friends	30%	36%
At parties	22%	18%
At bars, discos	24%	18%
At singles parties/dances	14%	18%
At work	10%	9%
Through newspaper ads	1%	1%
Don't remember	1%	2%

These are some of the ways single people meet each other in the United States. Do you understand all of the words here? [Ss spend several minutes studying the table.]

S: What is "singles parties"?

T: Singles parties are special parties for people who are single, they can go to meet. At work. Through newspaper ads. And don't remember. [Laughter.] OK, that's what I'm going to ask you to do now. I want you to work with your partner and to er to look through the information in part b, and to do the task.

Extract from Students' Book: b) Groupwork. Where can you meet new people?

	YES	NO
At school	_____	_____
At a party	_____	_____
At the movies	_____	_____
At a shopping center	_____	_____
At a sports event	_____	_____
At a concert	_____	_____
At a friend's home	_____	_____
_____	_____	_____
_____	_____	_____

Add to the list and ask some other students. [Ss in pairs begin to do the task. The teacher circulates, answering queries such as the following:]

S: What is sports event?

T: Maybe at a tennis match, or at football or hockey.

S: Playing or watching.

T: Yeah, just watching. Um. Oh, it could be either. Could be either. [T circulates and stops by one pair.]

T: What kind of sports do you have, do you play? Do you play sports?

S: [Inaudible.]

T: What else did you come up with?

S: Part-time job.

T: Oh, that's a good one, yeah. [T reproduces table on whiteboard.]

T: That's interesting—everybody's put part-time job. Do you have a part-time job?

S: Yes. I was kindergarten teacher when I was in Japan.

T: Oh, really?

T: Most people have managed to find extra things…

T: OK, let's check your responses. At school?

Ss: Yes, yes.

T: At a party.

Ss: Yes.

S: No.

T: Never been to a party? Oh you poor thing. [Laughter.] At the movies?

Ss: No, no.

T: No. Why not?

Ss: [Inaudible laughter.]

T: What about at a shopping center?

Ss: No.

T: Sports event?

Ss: Yes. No.

S: Why?

S: Not at sports event. [Discussion ensues between students.]

S: What sports event?

S: Baseball game. Stadium.

S: Stadium, stadium, yes.

S: You mean watching.

S: Watching, yeah.

S: Or playing tennis.

Ss: [Confusion.]

T: OK, difference of opinion there. What about at a concert?

Ss: No.

T: No?

Ss: [Inaudible laughter.]

T: What about at a friend's home?

S: Yes, yes.

S: No. [Laughter.]

T: No as well. You don't have any friends either. [Laughter.]

S: I didn't meet new people.

T: New people. OK. What other, what other places can you meet?

S: Part-time job.

T: Part-time job.

Ss: Oh! oh!

T: Yeah! Good one. Yeah. Any more?

S: Church.

T: Church.

S: [Inaudible; laughter.]

S: Travel, travel, traveling.

T: Traveling.

S: Some people meet new people at beach or er swimming pool.

T OK.

Ss: [Laughter and teasing of S making last remark.]

T: Is this where you meet new people? [Laughter.]

S: Huh?

T: Is this where you meet new people?

S: Yeah. [Laughter.]

T: Any others?

S: At, er organizations.

T: Organizations. What kind?

S: Oh, like er environment group or…

T: Environmental groups—that's good. OK. I think I'll have to put some of these on my list because they're very interesting.…What, what sort of language do you use if you're meeting people in an English speaking er place such as you are now. What kind of language do you use. Let's just listen to the next conversation. And I'm going to ask you to listen to the conversation and then practice it, but I want you to use, I want you to use language that is true for you. So use your own name, where you're from, and so on.

TAPE:

A: Hi! I'm Yongsue. What's your name?

B: Vera.

A: Where are you from?

B: Chicago. What about you?

A: I'm from Seoul, Korea. What do you do?

B: I'm a student. What do you do?

A: I'm a student, too.

T: OK, I want you to practice that conversation with your partner. But, use your own name, use where you're from and say what you do. OK?

Ss: Mm.

T Off you go. [Ss mill around practicing the conversation for several minutes. T circulates and monitors.]

T: When you've finished I want to you to practice the questions in #3, the questions and answers. And you'll get the answers from the box. OK. Practice with your partner. "What's Mike's last name?" "His last name is Frota." OK? Off you go. [Ss practice in pairs. T circulates and monitors.]

T: [Leans over one student and points to an error.] OK, look you've left out ... I want you to see what you've left out here. OK? Just check in the [grammar] box to see which words you've left out here.

T: OK, then where is Mike from?

Ss: From Chicago.

T: He's from Chicago. And where is he now? Is he in Chicago now? Where is he now?

S: San Francisco.

T: San Francisco.

T: Now I want you to practice all the language we learned in this unit. Work in pairs, say who you are, where you're from, what you do, then introduce your partner to another pair. [Ss complete task. T circulates and monitors.]

Appendix B

STATEMENTS ABOUT TEAM TEACHING

(from Bailey, Dale, and Squire, 1992, 175–176)

In this table the *mean* represents the mathematical average and *S* represents the standard deviation—a measure of the average distance of the ratings from the mean rating on each item. (So, for instance, there was more disagreement among the respondents about a statement where *S* = 2.5 than there was where *S* = 1.) In the final column, *N* indicates the number of teachers who responded to that particular item. A rating of 5 means the respondent strongly agreed with the statement, while a rating of 1 indicates strong disagreement.

Teachers' Reactions to Statements About Team Teaching

	Mean	S	N
1. Only teachers themselves should decide whether or not to enter into a team teaching arrangement.	3.8	1.2	60
2. Planning together is the most valuable part of team teaching.	4.2	0.9	58
3. Team teaching works best if the partners' teaching styles match.	3.5	1.2	59
4. Working in class together is the most valuable part of team teaching.	3.4	1.1	59
5. My students seem to appreciate team teaching.	3.9	0.9	59
6. Team teaching is an effective way to teach languages.	3.9	0.9	60
7. Sometimes situations of shared responsibility result in no one taking full responsibility.	3.3	1.3	59
8. Serious problems could arise in situations where the collaborating teachers have widely divergent teaching styles.	3.8	1.1	60
9. It is helpful to agree to disagree in advance of entering a team teaching arrangement.	4.1	0.9	57
10. Having a partner helped to give me a new perspective on my teaching.	4.2	1.0	59
11. Having a partner was helpful in evaluating students.	4.0	1.1	59

12. Team teaching didn't seem to work for my students.	1.9	1.0	58
13. Having a partner gives me someone to appeal to for examples or clarification of explanations in class.	3.9	1.1	54
14. Our students seem to like having a choice of which teacher to seek out for help.	3.6	1.0	57
15. Working collaboratively provides two perspectives for self-evaluation of our team teaching.	3.9	1.0	56
16. Working collaboratively provides two perspectives for evaluation of my individual work.	3.7	1.1	58
17. I have learned things about myself from working with a partner.	4.1	0.9	60
18. The amount of time necessary to collaborate on goal setting, syllabus design, and lesson planning is more trouble than it's worth.	2.2	1.1	58
19. Team teaching is an effective means for teacher development.	4.0	0.9	60
20. Serious problems could arise in situations where the collaborating teachers have different goals.	4.3	0.9	59
21. Team teaching is more trouble than it's worth.	2.1	1.0	58
22. Only teachers themselves should decide who their teaching partners will be.	3.7	1.2	60
23. It is only in an atmosphere of trust and mutual respect that teacher partnerships can achieve their full potential.	4.6	0.7	59
24. In team teaching it is useful to focus on goals rather than personalities in order to lessen power struggles.	4.1	0.8	57
25. My partner's feedback after our lessons was not helpful.	2.2	1.2	55
26. Recognizing that alternative solutions exist makes planning and follow-up easier and smoother.	4.1	0.8	57
27. The benefits of team teaching far outweigh the effort involved.	3.8	1.0	59

References

Ackerman, Richard, Patricia Maslin-Ostrowski, and Chuck Christensen. 1996. Case stories: Telling tales about school. *Educational Leadership* 53 (6): 21–23.

Allen, Patrick, Maria Fröhlich, and Nina Spada. 1984. The communicative orientation of language teaching: An observation scheme. In Jean Handscombe, Richard A. Orem, and Barry P. Taylor (eds.), *On TESOL '83: The question of control*. Washington, DC: TESOL. 231–252.

Allwright, Dick. 1988. *Observation in the language classroom*. New York: Longman.

Allwright, Dick, and Kathleen M. Bailey. 1991. *Focus on the language classroom: An introduction to classroom research for language teachers*. Cambridge: Cambridge University Press.

Allwright, Dick, and Rosa Lenzuen. 1997. Exploratory practice: Work at the Cultura Iglesa, Rio de Janeiro, Brazil. *Language Teaching Research* 1 (1): 73–79.

Appel, Joachim. 1995. *Diary of a language teacher*. Oxford: Heinemann English Language Teaching.

Apple, Michael. 1985. *Education and Power*. New York: Routledge.

Apple, Michael, and S. Jungck. 1990. You don't have to be a teacher to teach this unit: Teaching technology and gender in the classroom. *American Educational Research Journal* 27:227–254.

Armstrong, David G. 1977. Team teaching and academic achievement. *Review of Educational Research* 47 (1): 65–86.

Bailey, Kathleen M. 1981. An introspective analysis of an individual's language learning experience. In Stephen Krashen and Robin Scarcella (eds.), *Issues in second language acquisition: Selected papers of the Los Angeles Second Language Research Forum*. Boston, MA: Heinle & Heinle/Newbury House. 58–65.

Bailey, Kathleen M. 1983. Competitiveness and anxiety in adult second language learning: Looking at and through the diary studies. In Herbert W. Seliger and Michael H. Long (eds.), *Classroom oriented research in second language acquisition*. Boston, MA: Heinle & Heinle/Newbury House. 67–103.

Bailey, Kathleen M. 1990. The use of diary studies in teacher education programs. In Jack C. Richards and David Nunan (eds.), *Second language teacher education*. New York: Cambridge University Press. 215–226.

Bailey, Kathleen M. 1991. Diary studies of classroom language learning: The doubting game and the believing game. In Eugenius Sadtono (ed.), *Language acquisition and the second/foreign language classroom*. Singapore: SEAMEO Regional Language Centre (Anthology Series 28). 60–102.

Bailey, Kathleen M. 1992. The processes of innovation in language teacher development: What, why and how teachers change. In John Flowerdew, Mark N. Brock, and Sophie Hsia (eds.), *Perspectives on second language teacher development*. Hong Kong: City Polytechnic of Hong Kong. 253–282.

Bailey, Kathleen M. 1996. The best laid plans: Teachers' in-class decisions to depart from their lesson plans. In Kathleen M. Bailey and David Nunan (eds.), *Voices from the language classroom: Qualitative research in language education.* Cambridge: Cambridge University Press. 15–40.

Bailey, Kathleen M. 1997. Reflective teaching: Situating our stories. *Asian Journal of English Language Teaching* 7 (1): 1–19.

Bailey, Kathleen M. 1998a. *Learning about language assessment: Dilemmas, decisions, and directions.* Boston: Heinle & Heinle.

Bailey, Kathleen M. 1998b. First impressions: Beginning new EFL classes. In Willy A. Renandya and George M. Jacobs (eds.). *Learners and language learning* (Anthology Series 39). Singapore: SEAMEO Regional Language Centre. 89–114.

Bailey, Kathleen M., Bret Bergthold, Belinda Braunstein, Natascha J. Fleischman, Matthew P. Holbrook, Jennifer Tuman, Ximena Waissbluth, and Leslie J. Zambo. 1996. The language teacher's autobiography: Examining "the apprenticeship of observation." In Donald Freeman and Jack C. Richards (eds.), *Teacher learning in language teaching.* Cambridge: Cambridge University Press. 11–29.

Bailey, Kathleen M., Andy Curtis, and David Nunan. 1998. Undeniable insights: The collaborative use of three professional development practices. *TESOL Quarterly* 32 (3): 546–556.

Bailey, Kathleen M., Ted Dale, and Benjamin Squire. 1992. Some reflections on collaborative language teaching. In David Nunan (ed.), *Collaborative language learning and teaching.* Cambridge: Cambridge University Press. 162–178.

Bailey, Kathleen M., and Robert Ochsner. 1983. A methodological review of the diary studies: Windmill tilting or social science? In Kathleen M. Bailey, Michael H. Long, and Sabrina Peck (eds.), *Second language acquisition studies.* Boston, MA: Heinle & Heinle/Newbury House. 188–198.

Bartlett, Leo. 1990. Teacher development through reflective teaching. In Jack C. Richards and David Nunan (eds.), *Second language teacher education.* New York: Cambridge University Press. 202–214.

Bateson, Gregory. 1972. *Steps to an ecology of mind.* New York: Ballantine.

Batey, John, and David Westgate. 1994. Video action replay. In Antony Peck and David Westgate (eds.), *Language teaching in the mirror.* London: Centre for Information on Language Teaching and Research. 37–41.

Bellack, Arno, Herbert Kliebard, Ronald T. Hyman, and Frank L. Smith. 1966. *The language classroom.* New York: Teachers College Press.

Benedetti, Teresa. 1997. Enhancing teaching and teacher education with peer coaching. *TESOL Journal* 7 (1): 41–42.

Birch, Gary J. 1992. Language learning case study approach to second language teacher education. In John Flowerdew, Mark N. Brock, and Sophie Hsia (eds.), *Perspectives on second language teacher education.* Hong Kong: City Polytechnic of Hong Kong. 283–294.

Bond, Michael. 1991. *Beyond the Chinese face: Insights from psychology.* New York: Oxford University Press.

Borg, Walter, M.L. Kelley, Philip Langer, and Meredith Damien Gall. 1970. *The mini-course: A micro teaching approach to teacher education.* London: Collier-Macmillan.

Braine, George. 1998. Nonnative speakers and ELT. *TESOL Matters* 8 (1):14.

Braine, George (ed.) 1999. *Non-native educators in English language teaching.* Mahwah, NJ: Lawrence Erlbaum.

Braine, George, Jun Liu, and Lía Kamhi-Stein. 1988. Statement of purpose: Nonnative English Speaking Teachers Caucus. Unpublished manuscript, Alexandria, VA: TESOL.

Brindley, Geoff. 1991. Becoming a researcher: Teacher-conducted research and professional growth. In Eugenius Sadtono (ed.), *Issues in language teacher education.* Singapore: SEAMEO Regional Language Centre (Anthology Series 30). 89–105.

Brock, Mark N., Bartholomew Yu, and Matilda Wong. 1992. 'Journalling' together: Collaborative diary-keeping and teacher development. In John Flowerdew, Mark N. Brock, and Sophie Hsia (eds.), *Perspectives on second language teacher development.* Hong Kong: City University of Hong Kong. 295–307.

Brown, Cheryl. 1985. Two windows on the classroom world: Diary studies and participant observation differences. In Penny Larsen, Elliott E. Judd, and Dorothy Messerschmitt (eds.), *On TESOL'84: A brave new world for TESOL.* Washington, DC: TESOL. 121–134.

Brown, James Dean, and Kate Wolfe-Quintero. 1997. Teacher portfolios for evaluation: A great idea or a waste of time? *Language Teacher* 21 (1): 28–30.

Burns, Anne. 1997. Valuing diversity: Action researching disparate learner groups. *TESOL Journal* 7 (1): 6–9.

Burns, Anne. 1998. *Collaborative action research for English language teachers.* Cambridge: Cambridge University Press.

Burton, Jill. 1987. The powers of observation: An investigation of current practice and issues in teacher education. In Bikram K. Das (ed.), *Patterns of classroom interaction in Southeast Asia.* Singapore: SEAMEO Regional Language Centre (Anthology Series 17). 153–166.

Butler-Wall, Brita. 1979. Diary studies. In Engie Arafa, Cheryl Brown, Brita Butler-Wall, and Margaret Early. *Classroom analysis.* Unpublished manuscript, Applied Linguistics Ph.D. Program, University of California, Los Angeles.

Caccia, Paul F. 1996. Linguistic coaching: Helping beginning teachers defeat discouragement. *Educational Leadership* 53 (6): 17–20.

Campbell, Cherry C. 1996. Socializing with the teachers and prior language learning experience: A diary study. In Kathleen M. Bailey and David Nunan (eds.), *Voices from the language classroom: Qualitative research in second language education.* Cambridge: Cambridge University Press. 201–223.

Campbell, Dorothy M., Pamela Bondi Cignetti, Beverly J. Melenyzer, Diane Hood Nettles, and Richard M. Wyman, Jr. 1997. *How to develop a professional portfolio: A manual for teachers.* Boston: Allyn and Bacon.

Carlson, Anne. 1992. The card game. *TESOL Journal* 2 (1): 8.

Carter, Kathy. 1993. The place of story in the study of teaching and teacher education. *Educational Researcher* 22 (1): 5–12, 18.

Casanave, Christine Pearson, and Sandra R. Schecter (eds.). 1997. *On becoming a language educator: Personal essays on professional development.* Mahwah, NJ: Lawrence Erlbaum.

Chamot, Anna Uhl. 1995. The teacher's voice: Action research in your classroom. *ERIC/CLL News Bulletin* 19 (2): 1, 5–8.

Chapple, Lynda, and Andy Curtis. 2000. Content-based instruction in Hong Kong: Student responses to film. *System* 28 (3): 419–433.

Christison, Mary Ann, and Sharon K. Bassano. 1995. Action research: Techniques for collecting data through surveys and interviews. *CATESOL Journal* 8 (1): 89–103.

Clandinin, D. Jean, and F. Michael Connelly. 1991. Narrative and story in practice and research. In Donald A. Schön (ed.), *The reflective turn: Case studies in and on educational practice*. New York: Teachers College Press. 258–281.

Clarke, Mark A. 1982. On bandwagons, tyranny, and common sense. *TESOL Quarterly* 16 (4): 437–448.

Cohen, Andrew D., and Carol Hosenfeld. 1981. Some uses of mentalistic data in second language research. *Language Learning* 31 (2): 285–313.

Cohen, L., and L. Manion. 1980. *Research methods in education*. London: Croom Helm.

Cole, Robert, Linda McCarthy Raffier, Peter Rogan, and Leigh Schleicher. 1998. Interactive group journals: Learning as a dialogue among learners. *TESOL Quarterly* 32 (3): 556–568.

Collins Cobuild English Dictionary. 1995. London: William Collins and Sons.

Cooper, James M. 1995. *Teachers' problem solving: A casebook of award-winning teaching cases*. Boston: Allyn and Bacon.

Crandall, Joann (Jodi). 1993. Professionalism and professionalization of adult ESL literacy. *TESOL Quarterly* 27 (3): 497–515.

Cruickshank, Donald R., and Jane H. Applegate. 1981. Reflective teaching as a strategy for teacher growth. *Educational Leadership* 38 (7): 553–554.

Cullen, Richard. 1991. Video in teacher training: The use of local materials. *English Language Teaching Journal* 45 (1): 33–42.

Cummings, Martha Clark. 1996. Sardo revisited: Voice, faith and multiple repeaters. In Kathleen M. Bailey and David Nunan (eds.), *Voices from the language classroom: Qualitative research in second language education*. Cambridge: Cambridge University Press. 224–235.

Cunningham, Luvern L. 1960. Team teaching: Where do we stand? *Administrator's Notebook* 8: 1–4.

Curtis, Andy. 1997. Teacher development: Why bother? Plenary Address. Lembaga-Bahasa Indonesia Language Association (LB-LIA) Conference: Teacher development: Becoming aware of our development as language teachers. Yayasan, LIA. Jakarta, Indonesia.

Curtis, Andy. 1998. Action research: What, how and why? *The English Connection* 3 (1): 12–14.

Curtis, Andy. 1999a. Re-visioning our roles: Teachers as experts, researchers, and reflective practitioners. *ThaiTESOL Bulletin*. 12 (2): 24–32.

Curtis, Andy. 1999b. Use of of action research in exploring the use of spoken English in Hong Kong classrooms. In Cheah Yin Mee and Ng Seok Moi (eds.), *IDAC Monograph: Language instructional issues in the Asian classroom*. Newark, DE: International Reading Association. 75–88.

Curtis, Andy. 1999c. Changing the management of change in language education: Learning from the past, lessons for the future. *PASSA, A Journal of ThaiTESOL*. 29: 92–100.

Curtis, Andy, and Liying Cheng. 1998. Video as a source of data in classroom observation. *ThaiTESOL Bulletin* 11 (2): 31–38.

Day, Richard R. 1990. Teacher observation in second language teacher education. In Jack C. Richards and David Nunan (eds.), *Second language teacher education*. New York: Cambridge University Press. 43–61.

Denny, Terry. 1978. Story-telling and educational understanding. *Occasional paper Series*, No. 12. Kalamazoo: College of Education, Western Michigan University. Reprinted in Leo Bartlett, Stephen Kemmis, and G. Gillard (eds.) 1982, *Perspectives on case study*. Geelong, Australia: Deakin University Press. 1–24.

Denzin, Norman K. 1970. *Sociological methods: A source book*. Chicago: Aldine.

Dewey, John. 1933. *How we think*. Chicago: Henry Regnery.

Edge, Julian, and Keith Richards (eds.). 1993. *Teachers develop teachers research: Papers on classroom research and teacher development*. Oxford: Heinemann International.

Eisenman, Gordon, and Holly Thornton. 1999. Telementoring: Helping new teachers through the first year. *T.H.E. Journal* 26 (9): 79–82.

Elbaz, Freema. 1992. Hope, attentiveness, and caring for difference: The moral voice of teaching. *Teaching and Teacher Education* 8 (1): 5–6.

Enright, Lee. 1981. The diary of a classroom. In Jon Nixon (ed.), *A teacher's guide to action research: Evaluation, enquiry and development in the classroom*. London: Grant McIntyre Ltd. 37–51.

Fanselow, John. 1977. Beyond "Rashomon"—conceptualizing and describing the teaching act. *TESOL Quarterly* 11 (1): 17–39.

Fanselow, John. 1978. Breaking the rules of the classroom game through self-analysis. In *Teaching English as a second language: Themes, practices, viewpoints*. New York: New York State English to Speakers of Other Languages Bilingual Educator's Association. ERIC ED 145 720.

Fanselow, John. 1980. "It's too damn tight"—Media in ESOL classrooms: Structural features in technical/subtechnical English. *TESOL Quarterly* 14 (2): 141–155.

Fanselow, John. 1987. *Breaking the rules: Generating and exploring alternatives in language teaching*. New York: Longman.

Fanselow, John. 1988. "Let's see": Contrasting conversations about teaching. *TESOL Quarterly* 22 (1): 113–130.

Fanselow, John. 1997. Post card realities. In Christine Pearson Casanave and Sandra R. Schechter (eds.), *On becoming a language teacher*. Mahwah, NJ: Lawrence Erlbaum. 157–172.

Flowerdew, John. 1998. Language learning experience in L2 teacher education. *TESOL Quarterly* 32 (3): 529–536.

Freedman, S., J. Jackson, and K. Boles. 1983. Teaching: An imperiled "profession." In Lee Shulman and G. Sykes (eds.), *Handbook of teaching and policy*. New York: Longman. 261–299.

Freeman, Donald. 1982. Observing teachers: Three approaches to inservice training and development. *TESOL Quarterly* 16 (1): 21–28.

Freeman, Donald. 1989a. Teacher training, development and decision making: A model of teaching and related strategies for language teacher education. *TESOL Quarterly* 23 (1): 27–45.

Freeman, Donald. 1989b. Learning to teach: Four instructional patterns in language teacher education. *Prospect, A Journal of Australian TESOL* 4 (2): 31–47.

Freeman, Donald. 1992. Language teacher education, emerging discourse, and change in classroom practice. In John Flowerdew, Mark N. Brock, and Sophie Hsia (eds.), *Perspectives on second language teacher development.* Hong Kong: City Polytechnic of Hong Kong. 1–21.

Freeman, Donald. 1998a. *Doing teacher research: From inquiry to understanding.* Boston: Heinle & Heinle.

Freeman, Donald. 1998b. Workshop on observation presented at the National Security Agency, Baltimore, MD.

Freeman, Donald, and Jack C. Richards (eds.). 1996. *Teacher learning in language teaching.* Cambridge: Cambridge University Press.

Fry, John. 1988. Diary studies in classroom SLA research: Problems and prospects. *JALT Journal* 9 (2): 158–167.

Gebhard, Jerry G. 1996. *Teaching English as a foreign or second language: A self-development and methodology guide.* Ann Arbor: University of Michigan Press.

Gebhard, Jerry G., and Robert Oprandy. 1999. *Language teaching awareness: A guide to exploring beliefs and practices.* New York: Cambridge University Press.

Giles, Gillian, Susan Koenig, and Fredricka L. Stoller. 1997. Team teaching in intensive English programs. *TESOL Matters* 7 (6): 15.

Glatthorn, Allan A. 1987. Cooperative professional development: Peer centered options for teacher growth. *Educational Leadership* 45 (3): 31–35.

Goodson, I., and Rob Walker, 1982. Telling tales. In Leo Bartlett, Stephen Kemmis, and G. Gillard (eds.), *Perspectives on case study.* Geelong, Australia: Deakin University Press. 25–40.

Green, James E., and Sheryl O. Smyser. 1996. *The teacher portfolio: A strategy for professional development and evaluation.* Lancaster, PA: Technomic Publishing.

Grotjahn, Rüdiger. 1987. On the methodological basis of introspective methods. In Claus Færch and Gabriele Kasper (eds.), *Introspection in second language research.* Clevedon: Multilingual Matters. 54–81.

Harri-Augstein, E. Shiela, and Laurie F. Thomas. 1981. The self-organised learner and the relativity of personal learning: Constructing referents for the assessment of processes of achieving meaning. Uxbridge, Middlesex: Centre for the Study of Human Learning, Brunel University.

Haworth, K. 1998. Mentoring programs provide support via e-mail to women studying science. *Chronicle of Higher Education* 44 (32): A29–A30.

Hersey, Paul. 1984. *The situational leader.* New York: Warner Books.

Hersey, Paul, and Kenneth H. Blanchard. 1982. *Management of organizational behavior: Utilizing human resources* (4th ed.). Englewood Cliffs, NJ: Prentice Hall.

Ho, Belinda, and Jack C. Richards. 1993. Reflective thinking through teacher journal writing: Myths and realities. *Prospect, A Journal of Australian TESOL* 8 (3): 7–24.

Hutchinson, Barry, and Peter Bryson. 1997. Video, reflection and transformation: Action research in vocational education and training in a European context. *Educational Action Research* 5 (2): 283–303.

Jackson, Jane. 1997. Cases in TESOL teacher education: Creating a forum for reflection. *TESL Canada Journal* 14 (2): 1–16.

Jackson, Jane. 1998. Reality-based decision cases in ESP teacher education: Windows on practice. *English for Specific Purposes* 17 (2): 151–166.

Jarvis, Jennifer. 1992. Using diaries for teacher reflection on in-service courses. *English Language Teaching Journal* 46 (2): 133–143.

Johnson, Karen E. 1992a. The instructional decisions of pre-service English as a second language teachers: New directions for teacher preparation programs. In John Flowerdew, Mark N. Brock, and Sophie Hsia (eds.), *Perspectives on second language teacher development*. Hong Kong: City Polytechnic of Hong Kong. 115–134.

Johnson, Karen E. 1992b. Learning to teach: Instructional actions and decisions of pre-service ESL teachers. *TESOL Quarterly* 26 (3): 507–535

Johnson, Karen E. 1996a. Portfolio assessment in second language teacher education. *TESOL Journal* 6 (2): 11–14.

Johnson, Karen E. 1996b. Cognitive apprenticeship in second language teacher education. In Gertrude Tinker Sachs, Mark N. Brock, and Regina Lo (eds.), *Directions in second language teacher education*. Hong Kong: City University of Hong Kong. 23–36.

Johnson, Karen E. 1999. *Understanding language teaching: Reasoning in action*. Boston: Heinle & Heinle.

Johnson, Ray H., and M. Delbert Lobb. 1959. Jefferson County, Colorado completes three-year study of staffing, changing class size, programming and scheduling. *National Association of Secondary School Principals Bulletin* 43: 57–78.

Johnson, Ruth. 1999. Cross-cultural misunderstanding in a team teaching situation. *TESOL Matters* 9 (1): 16.

Joyce, Bruce (ed.). 1990. *Changing school culture through staff development: The 1990 ASCD yearbook of the Association for Supervision and Curriculum Development*. Alexandria, VA: Association for Supervision and Curriculum Development.

Joyce, Bruce, and Beverly Showers. 1982. The coaching of teaching. *Educational Leadership* 40 (1): 4–8, 10.

Joyce, Bruce, and Beverly Showers. 1987. Low-cost arrangements for peer-coaching. *Journal of Staff Development* 8 (1): 22–24.

Kamhi-Stein, Lía D., and José L. Galván. 1997. EFL teacher development through critical reflection. *TESOL Journal* 7 (1): 12–18.

Kemmis, Stephen. 1986. Critical reflection. Unpublished manuscript. Deakin University, Geelong, Australia.

Kemmis, Stephen, and Robin McTaggart. 1988. *The action research planner*. Geelong, Australia: Deakin University Press.

Kennedy, Chris. 1988. Evaluation of the management of change in ELT projects. *Applied Linguistics* 9 (4): 329–342.

Kennedy, Mary. 1990. *Policy issues in teacher education*. East Lansing, MI: National Center for Research on Language Teaching.

Knezevic, Anné, and Mary Scholl. 1996. Learning to teach together: Teaching to learn together. In Donald Freeman and Jack C. Richards (eds.), *Teacher learning in language teaching*. Cambridge: Cambridge University Press. 79–96.

Krashen, Stephen D. 1982. *Principles and practice in second language acquisition*. Oxford: Pergamon Press.

Labov, William. 1972. Some principles of linguistic methodology. *Language in Society* 1: 97–120.

Lakoff, George, and Mark Johnson. 1980. *Metaphors we live by*. Chicago: University of Chicago Press.

Lange, Dale E. 1990. A blueprint for teacher development. In Jack C. Richards and David Nunan (eds.), *Second language teacher education*. New York: Cambridge University Press. 245–268.

Larsen-Freeman, Diane. 1983. Training teachers or educating a teacher. In James E. Alatis, H.H. Stern, and Peter Strevens (eds.), *Georgetown University Round Table on language and linguistics: Applied linguistics and the preparation of second language teachers: Toward a rationale*. Washington, DC: Georgetown University Press. 264–274.

Larsen-Freeman, Diane. 1998. Expanding roles of learners and teachers in learner-centered instruction. In Willy A. Renandya and George M. Jacobs (eds.), *Learners and language learning* (Anthology Series 39). Singapore: SEAMEO Regional Language Centre, 207–226.

Latulippe, Laura. 1999. Lessons learned from being a student again (Part I). *TESOL Matters* 9 (1): 18.

Laycock, John, and Piranya Bunnag. 1991. Developing teacher self-awareness: Feedback and the use of video. *English Language Teaching Journal* 45 (1): 43–53.

Lewis, Marcella, Pamela Meadows, Alan Seaman, Barry Sweeny, and Marilyn Sweeny. 1996. *Mentoring for ESL teachers: A mentor training manual*. Wheaton, IL: World Relief DePage.

Lewis, Marilyn. 1998. A study of feedback to language teachers. *Prospect, A Journal of Australian TESOL* 13 (1): 68–83.

Levine, Linda New, and Nancy Cloud. 1997. Reaching all learners: Endless possibilities for teacher growth. *TESOL Journal* 7 (1): 5.

Lin, Yu-tang. 1935. *My country, and my people*. New York: John Day.

Long, Michael H., Leslie Adams, Marilyn McLean, and Fernando Castaños. 1976. Doing things with words: Verbal interaction in lockstep and small group classroom situations. In John F. Fanselow and Ruth Crymes (eds.), *On TESOL 1976*. Washington, DC: TESOL. 137–153.

Long, N., and R.G. Newman. 1961. The teacher and his mental health. In *The teacher's handling of children in conflict*. Bloomington: School of Education, Indiana University. 5–26.

Lortie, Dan. 1975. *Schoolteacher: A sociological study*. Chicago: University of Chicago Press.

Lowe, Tim. 1987. An experiment in role reversal: Teachers as language learners. *English Language Teaching Journal* 42 (2): 89–96.

Luft, Joseph, and Harry Ingram. 1969. *Of human interaction*. New York: National Press Books.

Lynch, Tony. 1989. Researching teachers: Behavior and belief. In Christopher Brumfit and Rosamond Mitchell (eds.), *ELT Documents 133—Research in the language classroom*. London: Modern English Publications in Association with the British Council. 117–127.

Malderez, Angi, and Caroline Bodóczky. 1999. *Mentor courses: A resource book for trainer-trainers*. Cambridge: Cambridge University Press.

Markee, Numa. 1996. Making second language classroom research work. In Jacquelyn Schachter and Susan Gass (eds.), *Second language classroom research: Issues and opportunities*. Mahwah, NJ: Lawrence Erlbaum. 117–155.

Maslach, Christina. 1982. *Burnout: The cost of caring.* Englewood Cliffs, NJ: Prentice Hall.

Maslach, C., and S. E. Jackson. 1986. *Maslach Burnout Inventory Manual.* (Second Edition.) Palo Alto, CA: Consulting Psychologists Press.

Masters, Peter. 1983. The etiquette of observing. *TESOL Quarterly* 17 (3): 497–501.

Mather, Mary Anne. 1997. Mentoring digital style. *Technology and Learning* 18 (4): 16–21.

Matsuda, Paul Kei. 1999. Teacher development through native speaker-nonnative speaker collaboration. *TESOL Matters* 9 (6): 1, 10.

Matsumoto, Kazuko. 1987. Diary studies of second language acquisition: A critical overview. *JALT Journal* 9 (1): 17–34.

Mattingly, Cheryl. 1991. Narrative reflections on practical actions: Two learning experiments in reflective storytelling. In Donald A. Schön (ed.), *The reflective turn: Case studies in and on educational practice.* New York: Teachers College Press. 235–257.

McDonough, Jo. 1994. A teacher looks at teachers' diaries. *English Language Teaching Journal* 48 (1): 57–65.

McLaughlin, Maureen, and MaryEllen Vogt. 1996. *Portfolios in teacher education.* Newark, DE: The International Reading Association.

Medgyes, Péter, and Emese Nyilasi. 1997. Pair teaching in preservice teacher education. *Foreign Language Annals* 30 (3): 352–368.

Michon'ska-Stadnik, Anna. 1997. Introduction. Action research in the Lower Silesia Cluster Colleges: A special edition of *Orbis Linguarum* 2: 7–9.

Mingucci, Monica. 1999. Action research in ESL staff development. *TESOL Matters* 9 (2): 16.

Mok, Angela. 1997. Student empowerment in an English language enrichment programme: An action research project in Hong Kong. *Educational Action Research* 5 (2): 305–320.

Morrison, Toni. 1994. *Nobel lecture on literature.* New York: Alfred Knopf.

Munby, Hugh, and Tom Russell. 1989. Educating the reflective teacher: An essay review of two books by Donald Schön. *Journal of Curriculum Studies* 21: 71–80.

Murphy, John M. 1992. An etiquette for the nonsupervisory observation of L2 classrooms. *Foreign Language Annals* 25 (3): 215–225.

Murphy-O'Dwyer, Lynette M. 1985. Diary studies as a method of evaluating teacher training. In J. Charles Alderson (ed.), *Evaluation: Practical papers in English language education.* Oxford: Pergamon Press. 97–128.

Newbury House Dictionary of American English. 1996. Boston: Heinle & Heinle.

Numrich, Carol. 1996. On becoming a language teacher: Insights from diary studies. *TESOL Quarterly* 30 (1): 131–151.

Nunan, David. 1989. *Understanding language classrooms: A guide for teacher-initiated action.* New York: Prentice Hall.

Nunan, David. 1990. Action research in the language classroom. In Jack C. Richards and David Nunan (eds.), *Second language teacher education.* New York: Cambridge University Press. 62–81.

Nunan, David. 1992a. The teacher as decision-maker. In John Flowerdew, Mark N. Brock, and Sophie Hsia (eds.), *Perspectives on second language teacher education.* Hong Kong: City Polytechnic of Hong Kong. 135–165.

Nunan, David. 1992b. *Research methods in language learning*. Cambridge: Cambridge University Press.

Nunan, David (ed.). 1992c. *Collaborative language learning and teaching*. Cambridge: Cambridge University Press.

Nunan, David. 1993. Action research in language education. In Julian Edge and Keith Richards (eds.), *Teachers develop teachers research: Papers on classroom research and teacher development*. Oxford: Heinemann International. 39–50.

Nunan, David. 1996. Hidden voices: Insiders' perspectives on classroom interaction. In Kathleen M. Bailey and David Nunan (eds.), *Voices from the language classroom: Qualitative research in language education*. Cambridge: Cambridge University Press. 41–56.

Nunan, David. 1999a. So you think that language teaching is a profession? (Part 1). *TESOL Matters* 9 (3): 3.

Nunan, David. 1999b. So you think that language teaching is a profession? (Part 2). *TESOL Matters* 9 (4): 3.

Nunan, David, and Clarice Lamb. 1996. *The self-directed teacher: Managing the learning process*. Cambridge: Cambridge University Press.

Olshtain, Elite, and Irit Kupferberg. 1998. Reflective-narrative discourse of FL teachers exhibits professional knowledge. *Language Teaching Research* 2 (3): 185–202.

O'Neil, D. Kevin, Rory Wagner, and Louis M. Gomez. 1996. Online mentoring: Experimenting in science class. *Educational Leadership* 54 (3): 39–42.

Osburne, Andrea G. 1989. Situational leadership and teacher education. *System* 17 (3): 409–420.

Oxford English Dictionary (New Edition). 1994. Oxford: Oxford University Press.

Paley, Vivian Gussin. 1997. Talking to myself in a daily journal: Reflections of a kindergarten teacher. In Christine Pearson Casanave and Sandra R. Schecter (eds.), *On becoming a language educator*. Mahwah, NJ: Lawrence Erlbaum. 115–122.

Palmer, Gillian. 1992. The practical feasibility of diary studies for INSET. *European Journal of Teacher Education* 15 (3): 239–254.

Paulston, Christina Bratt. 1974. Using videotape at Pittsburgh. *English Teaching Forum* 12 (4): 57–60.

Pennington, Martha, and Belinda Ho. 1995. Do ESL educators suffer from burnout? *Prospect, A Journal of Australian TESOL* 10 (1): 4–53.

Pierce, Lorraine Valdez. 1988. Peer coaching: An innovative approach to staff development. *NCBE Forum* 11 (3): 1, 6.

Plaister, Ted. 1993. *ESOL case studies: The real world of L2 teaching and administration*. Englewood Cliffs, NJ: Regents/Prentice Hall.

Porter, Carol, and Janell Cleland. 1995. *The portfolio as a learning strategy*. Portsmouth, NH: Boynton/Cook Publishers.

Porter, Patricia A., Lynn M. Goldstein, Judith Leatherman, and Susan Conrad. 1990. An ongoing dialogue: Learner logs for teacher preparation. In Jack C. Richards and David Nunan (eds.), *Second language teacher education*. Cambridge: Cambridge University Press. 227–240.

Powell, Garry. 1999. How to avoid being the fly on the wall. *The Teacher Trainer* 13 (1): 3–4.

Reason, Peter, and Peter Hawkins. 1988. Storytelling as inquiry. In Peter Reason (ed.), *Human inquiry in action: Developments in new paradigm research*. Beverly Hills: Sage. 79–101.

Richards, Jack C. 1990. The teacher as self-observer: Self-monitoring in teacher development. In Jack C. Richards, *The language teaching matrix*. Cambridge: Cambridge University Press. 118–143.

Richards, Jack C. (ed.). 1998. *Teaching in action: Case studies from second language classrooms*. Alexandria, VA: TESOL.

Richards, Jack C., and Charles Lockhart. 1991–92. Teacher development through peer observation. *TESOL Journal* 1 (2): 7–10.

Richards, Jack C., and Charles Lockhart. 1994. *Reflective teaching in second language classrooms*. Cambridge: Cambridge University Press.

Richards, Jack C., and David Nunan. 1990. *Second language teacher education*. New York: Cambridge University Press.

Rorschach, Elizabeth, and Robert Whitney. 1986. Relearning to teach: Peer observation as a means of professional development. *American Educator* 38 (1): 40–44.

Rowley, James B., and Patricia M. Hart. 1996. How video case studies can promote reflective dialogue. *Educational Leadership* 53 (6): 28–29.

Rubin, Joan, and Rosemary Henze. 1981. The foreign language requirement: A suggestion to enhance its educational role in teacher training. *TESOL Newsletter* 15 (1): 17, 19, and 24.

Ruiz de Gauna, Pilar, Capitolina Díaz, Valentín Gonzalez, and Isabel Garaizar. 1995. Teachers' professional development as a process of critical action research. *Educational Action Research* 3 (2): 183–194.

Russell, Tom, and Hugh Munby. 1991. Reframing: The role of experience in developing teachers' professional knowledge. In Donald A. Schön (ed.), *The reflective turn: Case studies in and on educational practice*. New York: Teachers College Press. 164–187.

Samway, Katharine Davis. 1994. But it's hard to keep fieldnotes while also teaching. *TESOL Journal* 4 (1): 47–48.

Schmidt, Richard W., and Sylvia Nagem Frota. 1986. Developing basic conversational ability in a second language: A case study of an adult learner of Portuguese. In Richard R. Day (ed.), *Talking to learn: Conversation in second language acquisition*. Boston, MA: Heinle & Heinle/Newbury House. 237–326.

Schön, Donald A. 1983. *The reflective practitioner: How professionals think in action*. New York: Basic Books.

Schön, Donald A. 1987. *Educating the reflective practitioner: Toward a new design for teaching and learning in the professions*. San Francisco: Jossey-Bass.

Schön, Donald A. (ed.). 1991. Introduction. In Donald A. Schön (ed.), *The reflective turn: Case studies in and on educational practice*. New York: Teachers College Press.

Seaman, Alan, Barry Sweeny, Pamela Meadows, and Marilyn Sweeny. 1997. Collaboration, reflection, and professional growth: A mentoring program for adult ESL teachers. *TESOL Journal* 7 (1): 31–34.

Shannon, Nora B., and Bonnie Meath-Lang. 1992. Collaborative language teaching: A co-investigation. In David Nunan (ed.), *Collaborative language learning and teaching*. Cambridge: Cambridge University Press. 120–140.

Shaw, Peter A. 1997. With one stone: Models of instruction and their curricular implications in an advanced content-based foreign language program. In Stephen B. Stryker and Betty Lou Leaver (eds.), *Content-based instruction in foreign language education: Models and methods*. Washington, DC: Georgetown University Press. 261–282.

Sheal, Peter. 1989. Classroom observation: Training the observers. *English Language Teaching Journal* 43 (2): 92–103.

Short, Deborah J. 1993. Assessing integrated language and content instruction. *TESOL Quarterly* 27 (4): 627–656.

Showers, Beverly. 1985. Teachers coaching teachers: Schools restructured to support the development of peer coaching teams create norms of collegiality and experimentation. *Educational Leadership* 47: 43–48.

Showers, Beverly, and Bruce Joyce. 1996. The evolution of peer coaching. *Educational Leadership*, 53 (6): 12–16.

Showers, Beverly, Bruce Joyce, and Barrie Bennett. 1987. Synthesis of research on staff development: A framework for future study and a state-of-the-art analysis. *Educational Leadership*. 45 (3): 77–87.

Shulman, Judith H., and Joel A. Colbert (eds.). 1987. *The mentor teacher casebook*. San Francisco: Far West Laboratory.

Shulman, Lee S. 1992. Toward a pedagogy of cases: Case methods in teacher education. In Judith H. Shulman (ed.), *Case methods in teacher education*. New York: Teachers College Press, Columbia University. 1–30.

Shulman, Lee S. 1998. The disciplines of inquiry in education. In Richard M. Jaeger (ed.), *Complementary methods of research in education*. Washington, DC: American Educational Research Association. 3–17.

Sinclair, John, and Malcolm Coulthard. 1975. *Towards an analysis of discourse*. Oxford: Oxford University Press.

Sizer, Theodore. 1983. *Horace's compromise: The dilemma of the American high school*. Boston: Houghton Mifflin.

Smith, Lou, and William Geoffrey. 1968. *The complexities of an urban classroom*. New York: Holt, Rinehart and Winston.

Snow, Marguerite Ann, and Donna Brinton (eds.). 1997. *The content-based classroom*. White Plains, NY: Longman. 187–200.

Snow, Marguerite Ann, John Hyland, Lía Kamhi-Stein, and Janet Harclerode Yu. 1996. U.S. language minority students: Voices from the junior high classroom. In Kathleen M. Bailey and David Nunan (eds.), *Voices from the language classroom: Qualitative research in language education*. Cambridge: Cambridge University Press. 304–317.

Spradley, James P. 1980. *Participant observation*. London: Longman.

Stanley, Claire. 1998. A framework for teacher reflectivity. *TESOL Quarterly* 32 (3): 584–591.

Stempleski, Susan, and Barry Tomalin. 1990. *Video in action: Recipes for using video in language teaching*. New York: Prentice Hall International.

Stenhouse, Lawrence. 1975. *An introduction to curriculum research and development*. London: Heinemann.

Stenson, Nancy, Jan Smith, and William Perry. 1979. Videotape and the training and evaluation of language teachers. Paper presented at the 1979 TESOL Convention, Boston, MA.

Stronge, James. H. (ed.). 1997. *Evaluating teaching: A guide to current thinking and best practice*. Thousand Oaks, CA: Corwin Press.

Sturman, Peter. 1992. Team teaching: A case study from Japan. In David Nunan (ed.), *Collaborative language learning and teaching*. Cambridge: Cambridge University Press. 141–161.

Telatnik, Mary Ann. 1978. The intensive journal as self-evaluative instrument. Paper presented at the 1978 Annual TESOL Convention, Mexico City.

Todd, Richard Watson. 1998. A teacher's essay on criticism. *The Teacher Trainer* 12 (1): 11.

Tsui, Amy B. M. 1996. Reticence and anxiety in second language learning. In Kathleen M. Bailey and David Nunan (eds.), *Voices from the language classroom: Qualitative research in second language education*. Cambridge: Cambridge University Press. 145–167.

Turner, Jean L. 1992. Creating content-based language tests: Guidelines for teachers. *The CATESOL Journal* 5 (1): 43–58. Reprinted in Marguerite Anne Snow and Donna Brinton (eds.), 1997, *The content-based classroom*. White Plains, NY: Longman. 187–200.

van Lier, Leo. 1988. *The classroom and the language learner: Ethnography and second language classroom research*. New York: Longman.

van Lier, Leo. 1992. Not the nine o'clock linguistics class: Investigating contingency grammar. *Language Awareness* 1 (2): 91–108.

van Lier, Leo. 1994. Action research. *Sintagma* 6: 31–37.

van Lier, Leo. 1995. *Introducing language awareness*. London: Penguin English.

van Lier, Leo. 1996. *Interaction in the language curriculum: Awareness, autonomy and authenticity*. New York: Longman.

van Lier, Leo. 1998. The relationship between consciousness, interaction and language awareness. *Language Awareness* 7 (2 & 3): 128–145.

Van Wagenen, Linda, and K. Michael Hibbard. 1998. Building teacher portfolios. *Educational Leadership* 55 (5): 26–29.

Vogt, MaryEllen, Maureen McLaughlin, and Martha Rapp Ruddell. 1993. *Do as I do: Using portfolios to evaluate students in reading methods courses*. Paper presented at the 43rd Annual Meeting of the National Reading Conference. Charleston, SC.

Wajnryb, Ruth. 1993. *Classroom observation tasks: A resource book for language teachers and trainers*. New York: Cambridge University Press.

Wajnryb, Ruth. 1994. Pragmatics and supervisory discourse: Matching method and purpose. *Prospect, A Journal of Australian TESOL* 9 (1): 29–38.

Walker, Rob. 1982. On the uses of fiction in educational research (and I don't mean Cyril Burt). *Case Study Methods* 4: 57–81.

Wallace, Michael J. 1979. *Microteaching and the teaching of English as a second or foreign language in teacher training institutions*. Edinburgh: Scottish Centre of Education Overseas, Moray House College of Education.

Wallace, Michael J. 1981. The use of video in EFL teacher training. *ELT Documents 110 —Focus on the teacher: Communicative approaches to teacher training*. London: The British Council. 7–21

Wallace, Michael J. 1991. *Training foreign language teachers: A reflective approach*. Cambridge: Cambridge University Press.

Wallace, Michael J. 1998. *Action research for language teachers*. Cambridge: Cambridge University Press.

Waters, Alan, Jane Sunderland, Terry Bray, and Joan Allwright. 1990. Getting the best out of the language-learning experience. *English Language Teaching Journal* 44 (4): 305–315.

Watson-Gegeo, Karen. 1988. Ethnography in ESL: Defining the essentials. *TESOL Quarterly* 22 (4): 575–592.

Webster's Collegiate Dictionary. 1990. Springfield, MA: Merriam-Webster, Inc.

Wells, Margaret. 1994. The loneliness of the long-distance reflector. In Anthony Peck and David Westgate (eds.), *Language teaching in the mirror*. London: Centre for Information on Language and Teaching Research. 11–14.

Williams, Marion. 1989. A developmental view of classroom observation. *English Language Teaching Journal* 43 (2): 85–91.

Wisniewska, Ingrid. 1998. What's your mentoring style? *The Teacher Trainer* 12 (1): 10–11.

Wolf, Kenneth. 1996. Developing an effective teaching portfolio. *Educational Leadership* 53 (6): 34–37.

Wong, Shelley. 1994. Dialogic approaches to teacher research: Lessening the tension. *TESOL Journal* 4 (1): 11–13.

Woods, Devon. 1996. *Teacher cognition in language teaching: Beliefs, decision-making, and classroom practice*. Cambridge: Cambridge University Press.

Yagleski, Robert P. 1997. Portfolios as a way to encourage reflective practice among pre-service English teachers. In Kathleen B. Yancey and Irwin Weisner (eds.), *Situating portfolios: Four perspectives*. Logan: Utah State University Press. 225–243.

Zeichner, Kenneth M., and Daniel P. Liston. 1987. Teaching student teachers to reflect. *Harvard Educational Review* 57 (1): 23–47.

Zeichner, Kenneth M., and Daniel P. Liston. 1996. *Reflective teaching: An introduction*. Mahwah, NJ: Lawrence Erlbaum.

Zuck, Joyce Gilmour. 1984. Comments on Peter Master's "the etiquette of observing." *TESOL Quarterly* 17 (4): 337–341.